MICROSOFT WORD 4.0

Second Edition

INCLUDING STYLE SHEETS & DESKTOP PUBLISHING

Timothy Perrin

MIS: PRESS

MANAGEMENT INFORMATION SOURCE, INC.

COPYRIGHT

DEDICATION

To Connie, who waited a long time for this one.

TABLE OF CONTENTS

INTRODUCTION

I first saw a word processing program demonstrated at a writer's conference in 1980. Toronto science writer Lydia Dotto was demonstrating a program on an Apple II. Considering today's packages, describing the system as "primitive" is an understatement; nonetheless, I was impressed. As I slaved away writing with a noisy IBM Selectric typewriter, I dreamed of joining the computer age.

Within two years I bought my first computer — an Osborne I — and learned to make WordStar jump through hoops. Since then, I have used and reviewed more than a dozen word processing programs including WRITE, Perfect Writer, Palantir, Super Writer, WordPerfect, and, finally, Microsoft Word.

Of all these programs, I choose to work with Word. Word is subtle, powerful, and friendly. If you have never used a word processor before, it is easy to learn. If you are experienced with word processing, you will be amazed at how quickly you can adapt to and take full advantage of Word's special features.

Word is a program worth getting to know, and I hope this book helps you do just that.

What this Book Covers

This is a book about the IBM-PC (and compatible) version of Microsoft Word. More specifically, the book covers versions 4.0, 3.1, and 3.0 of Word for the PC.

This book does not specifically cover earlier versions of Word, but much of the book's information applies to those earlier incarnations. Of course, sections on features such as the Outliner, which first appeared in version 3.0, or the Thesaurus, which debuted in version 3.1, will not apply to earlier versions of Word. Also, each version of Word has slightly different menus, but you can usually figure out earlier version menus from the explanations of comparable menus in later versions.

This book does *not* cover the Apple Macintosh version of Word, nor does it cover the version of Word found on some laptop computers, such as the Zenith ZP-150.

How this Book is Different

In two ways, this book is different from other Word books.

First, it shows how Word can do more than make your documents look pretty on the page; Word also can make you a better writer. This concept is supported by recent research into how successful writers write. Research has shown that no matter what kind of writing you do, by doing it a certain way, you can get better results. One characteristic of Word is that, by design or accident, it is well set up for this kind of systematic approach to writing.

When it does become time to make your documents look pretty on the page, Word is unequalled. You'll learn how Word, with its masterful control of printers, can often replace expensive desktop publishing software.

Form Vs. Content

To show you these other sides of Word, an explicit distinction must be made between content and form.

Most word processing books focus on how to improve your document's appearance or form. This book is different. Form is covered in detail, but fancy formatting and laser printer output cannot revive a dead piece of writing.

This book emphasizes content. Only when you have a document worth reading is it worth the time to make it appear attractive and easier to read.

How this Book is Organized

This book is organized a bit differently than other books on word processing. Instead of grouping commands together (as they are on Word's menus), commands and features have been grouped according to the logic of writing, which means that topics other books deal with entirely in one section may at first seem spread out in this book. They're not. They're right where they belong — where you will need them while learning how to become a better writer with Microsoft Word.

The book contains six parts. To get the most out of it, read the book from front to back. In this way, you will meet each concept and group of related Word commands in a logical sequence.

Headstart

Part I of the book is called "Fundamentals of Word." It is designed to get you immediately up and running with basic skills. After finishing this section, you will be able work on letters that must go out immediately, or you can get started on that major project – a report, article, or term paper – that's due in a few weeks. If you continue working with this book, by the time that major project is due, you will be ready to include features like an automatically generated index and table of contents, footnotes, and bonuses such as multiple fonts, varying type sizes, and other stylistic flourishes.

There are four chapters in Part I. Chapter 1 illustrates how to get Word up and running on your computer. Chapter 2 fills you in on starting Word and the various options available. Chapter 3 covers the basics of editing. Finally, Chapter 4 will help you configure Word for your printer.

Content

Part II of this book is called "Content" and is intended to help you become a better writer. The techniques you will be taught are the same ones I teach in seminars on magazine writing and legal writing. To be honest, would-be article writers and practicing lawyers are taught almost identical courses because the same techniques work for both groups. In other words, good writing technique doesn't vary.

Part II contains five chapters. Chapter 5 introduces you to the "process" approach to writing. Chapter 6 shows you how to use Word's integrated outlining function as an "invention" tool that can help you become a better writer. Chapter 7 provides tips on how to draft your document. Chapter 8 introduces the ideas and techniques behind a systematic approach to revising what you have written. And Chapter 9 shows you how Word can help revise your document through its Outliner, Thesaurus, Spell Checker, and other features.

Form

Part III of this book covers what most books seem to treat as the essence of word processing: form (the look of your document on the page). These four chapters discuss the use of Word as desktop publishing software. In Chapter 10, you will examine in more detail direct formatting of a document and learn to use running headers and footers. Chapter 11 covers how to use two kinds of multiple-column formats. In Chapter 12, you will learn the advanced formatting power of Word's style sheets. In Chapter 13, you will learn to use a combination of style sheets and Word's Outliner to format an impressive document.

Academia

Part IV, "Word and the Academic," covers three topics dear to students and professors everywhere. Chapter 14 illustrates how to easily and automatically include footnotes in your documents. Chapter 15 covers procedures for indices, and Chapter 16 teaches you to use Word to automatically generate tables such as a table of contents or a table of illustrations.

Office Specialties

Part V of this book is entitled "Word and the Office." In this section, you will learn about Word's special features that can help businesspeople with the day-to-day writing jobs needed in any company. Chapter 17 discusses how to create forms and form letters by using Word's merge facility. In Chapter 18, you will learn about Word's glossary, in which you can store thousands of words of "boilerplate" text that can be called up with a few keystrokes. The glossary also holds Word macros, which are series of commands you can invoke with just one or two keystrokes. Chapter 19 demonstrates that Word is not only smart with words but also with numbers; it can perform simple math functions as well as automatically number an outline or sections of a document you are writing. Finally, in Chapter 20, you will learn how Word can be used as a powerful tool for maintaining client lists or any material that must be sorted into numerical or alphabetical order. Chapter 21 covers how to quickly find the document you want from the mass of information on your hard disk; this process is easy with Word's document retrieval features.

Printers

Finally, Part VI is called "Word and Printers." You may not need to read this section. Microsoft's support of printers is legendary; the company provides competent printer "drivers" for almost every printer made. If you own a rare printer or a printer with special capabilities, this section teaches you to help Word take full advantage of your printer's capabilities. Chapter 22 is an introduction to concepts behind printer drivers and the functions they perform. Chapter 23 illustrates how to use Word's MAKEPRD program to customize a printer driver for your particular printer.

Complex but not Difficult

This book covers a wealth of material. Word would not be so highly regarded if it did not perform diverse functions, and any computer program that performs many functions is necessarily complex.

Remember, complexity and difficulty are not the same, however. Word *is* complex, but it is also easy to use. There are often two or three methods for performing a single task. One method uses Word's menu driver command line. The second system uses "shorthand" commands that bypass the menu. For many functions, you can also use the mouse. As you become accustomed to Word, you will learn which command techniques are easiest for you, and you will find that the more you ask Word to do, the easier it is to use Word.

Word's Help function is excellent; it provides help for current tasks, and you can also choose at any time to start a Word tutorial system to teach you about the basic features of Word.

To begin, read Chapter 1 to learn how to get started with Word.

PART I

WORD FUNDAMENTALS

CHAPTER 1

INSTALLING MICROSOFT WORD

This chapter will help you install Microsoft Word on your computer. Installing Word involves preparing working disks from which you will run the program. If you have a hard disk, part of installation involves copying the program from the distribution disks to the hard disk. You must also indicate whether or not you are using a mouse, the kind of printer you will be using, and other details about your computer system.

IF YOU DON'T LIKE TO READ INSTRUCTIONS

If you would rather avoid reading instructions, the following sequence is the fastest way to get Word up and running on your system.

Put the Word Utilities disk in drive A of your computer. Type

SETUP < return >

< return > represents an instruction to press the key labeled Return or Enter (or with an arrow pointing down and to the left). Follow the on-screen instructions, answering questions as they are asked and changing disks as requested. This procedure creates working Word disks (for a floppy disk system) or copies the Word files to your hard disk.

Next, if you have a floppy disk system, insert the Word Program disk in drive A and a blank, formatted disk in drive B. If you are working with a hard disk system, change directories to the subdirectory containing your Word files by typing

cd\word < return >

Then, in either case, type

WORD < return >

Your computer will load Microsoft Word.

If this procedure works, you can skip to Chapter 2 and read the sections "The Word Menu," "Quitting Word," and "Getting Help." Then, move on to Chapter 3, "Editing Basics."

If, for some reason, Word does not run on your system, return to this chapter and make sure that your computer meets the program's hardware requirements. This chapter also teaches you to run Word more quickly on your computer and, if necessary, to set up a Word system without using the SETUP program. Read Chapter 2 in detail to help Word take full advantage of your video display system.

HARDWARE REQUIREMENTS

Before you can run Microsoft Word, you must have the right kind of computer. Fortunately, Microsoft has ensured that the program runs on a wide variety of machines. This book covers releases 4.0, 3.1, and 3.0 of the IBM PC (and compatible) version of Word.

Versions 3.0 and 3.1 of Word are similar; they will collectively be referred to as version 3 unless there is an important difference.

Computer and Operating System

The PC version of Word is not particular about hardware; it can run on nearly any computer that uses the MS-DOS operating system. This group includes the IBM PC family, PC compatibles, and even a few machines that are not particularly compatible.

Word version 3 requires MS-DOS (or PC-DOS) 2.0 or later. Version 4.0 of Word requires MS-DOS 3.1 or later.

Throughout this book, both MS-DOS and PC-DOS will be referred to as MS-DOS.

Memory

A fair amount of memory is required to take full advantage of Word.

Word 4.0 requires at least 320K of memory with at least 256K available for running Word. Word version 3 requires 256K with 192K available for running Word.

The amount of memory available for running Word is the amount of memory remaining after you have loaded the operating system, its extensions, and any memory-resident programs. Operating system extensions may include special device drivers and additional file buffers. These extensions are loaded by the computer as it starts up and are listed in a file called CONFIG.SYS, which is on the diskette you use to boot your system or in the root directory of your hard drive. Memory-resident programs are programs loaded into memory so as to be instantly accessible; they include such products as Sidekick, Polywindows, ProKey, and many others.

If you are not sure how much memory your computer system has available, use the CHKDSK.EXE program on your DOS disk. At the DOS prompt, type

CHKDSK <return>

After a moment, your screen should resemble the following:

```
C:\>chkdsk
 33409024 bytes total disk space
    83968 bytes in 4 hidden files
   161792 bytes in 73 directories
 20838400 bytes in 1120 user files
 12324864 bytes available on disk

   649936 bytes total memory
   127360 bytes free
```

The last two lines — "bytes total memory" and "bytes free" — are essential for evaluating system memory. For Word 4.0, the bytes total memory should be at least 327,680 bytes (320K × 1024 bytes/K), and the bytes free should be at least 262,144. For Word version 3, the bytes total memory should be at least 262,144 bytes, and the bytes free must be at least 196,608. To accomodate Word's tutorial system, add about 92K (94,208 bytes) to these totals.

If your system lacks enough available memory and you have already removed all memory-resident programs and DOS extensions, you must add memory to your computer. Consult your dealer about adding memory chips to your computer's mother board (if possible) or adding a memory expansion board to your system.

Disk Drives

You will need at least two double-density, double-sided, 5.25" floppy disk drives to run Word on your computer. A hard disk will considerably improve program speed.

For laptop computers using 3.5" disks, you must request the smaller disks from Microsoft or transfer the files from a 5.25"-drive system to the laptop using a cable and file transfer software. After obtaining the program on the smaller disks, you can (theoretically) get away with one disk drive, but this would require that you place Word on every disk used to store data. A better method is to use two drives or at least a physical drive and a second RAM drive (a portion of memory that the system interprets as a disk drive).

Video

Word will run in character mode with virtually any MS-DOS computer system. In character mode, Word uses variations in the character and background colors and intensities to indicate on the screen a character's traits (bold, italics, underlining, and so on).

Taking full advantage of Word's WYSIWYG (What You See Is What You Get) abilities, however, requires a computer system that can display graphics. On a graphics system, bold characters appear brighter, underlined characters are underlined, italics characters are italicized, and so on.

Word runs with all common combinations of IBM-compatible graphics cards and monitors. Version 3 specifically runs with the following:

- IBM Enhanced Graphics Adapter (EGA) and compatible graphics cards

- IBM Color Graphics Adapter (CGA) and compatible graphics cards

- Hercules Graphics Card (HGC) and compatible monochrome graphics cards

Version 4.0 of Word runs with all of the previous graphics cards as well as the following:

- IBM Personal System/2 VGA graphics card

- Genius graphics card

Nearly all video cards for IBM-compatible systems emulate one or more of these video standards. For example, if you run Word version 3 on a Personal System/2 machine, the MCGA, VGA, and 8514/A video systems sold with the IBM PS/2 machines can emulate CGA and EGA modes.

If your computer is IBM-compatible and comes with a built-in graphics card or monitor, it is probably a CGA- or Hercules-compatible system.

In addition, manufacturers of nonstandard video cards or monitors may also supply screen drivers with their products. A **driver** is a file that contains information Word must know to work with these systems. Before you buy a nonstandard video system, check to make sure it will run Word properly and easily. Demand that your dealer promise *in writing* that the system you are buying will run Word.

Monitors

Each graphics card requires a compatible monitor. Remember, a monitor that runs with one video system will usually *not* run with another; for example, a CGA monitor usually cannot run with an EGA system. A TTL monochrome monitor that will run with Hercules monochrome cards will not run with a CGA or EGA system.

Some monitors, such as the NEC Multisync, are designed to run with almost any video card; however, these monitors are expensive. Unless you know you will be changing video systems soon or must move one monitor between two computers using incompatible video cards, you are probably better off getting a less expensive monitor that runs only with the video card you will be using.

There are also some graphics cards that will run with any monitor, such as the ATI EGA Wonder. Again, unless you plan on changing monitors soon, there is little reason to buy one.

A recommended choice for a graphics card is a Hercules Graphics Card Plus. Hercules cards have a screen resolution of 720 × 348 dots, which is the best resolution of any graphic systems using standard monitors. The Graphics Card Plus provides the added bonus of allowing you to run Word in character mode (about four times faster than graphics mode) but, through a sophisticated system, it still allows on-screen formatting of italics, bold, and other text formats. Also, if you do a lot of word processing with Word or other systems, you'll find that a Hercules-compatible monochrome system is very easy on the eyes.

CGA systems work, but character resolution is mediocre at best (640 x 200). On a color monitor, characters are fuzzy. It is actually better to run a CGA on a good low-resolution monochrome monitor, which will be considerably crisper; however, by the end of a day of writing, your eyes will need a rest.

An EGA system is expensive. Unless you use graphics software that greatly benefits from color—and few packages do—you'll be spending too much money. If you use an EGA with 64K of memory and a monochrome monitor, the resolution will be slightly lower than a Hercules card (640 × 350). A 64K EGA with a color monitor is not recommended. To obtain high resolution (640 × 350), you must work in monochrome mode. If you want color, you must settle for 640 × 200 resolution. An EGA card with 128K, however, can give you high resolution (640 × 350) in 16 colors on an EGA-compatible monitor.

Hercules also makes a color graphics card — the InColor card — that provides 720 × 348 resolution in sixteen colors in an EGA-compatible mode. Like the Graphics Plus card, it can also run Word in character mode while providing full on-screen formatting.

Choose your monitor and video cards carefully. Changes are expensive.

The Mouse and Other Pointing Devices

For many functions, Word works better with a mouse or some other pointing device, such as a track ball, joy stick, or digitizer pad.

Word expects a Microsoft mouse, but it is not the only pointer you can use with Word. Most pointers come with drivers that can emulate the Microsoft Mouse.

There are two ways to inform the computer that your system includes a mouse (or other pointing device). One method involves using a system driver like Microsoft's MOUSE.SYS, which must be listed in a file called CONFIG.SYS in the root directory of the disk used to boot your computer system. Make sure the following line is in the CONFIG.SYS file:

DEVICE = MOUSE.SYS

If MOUSE.SYS itself is not in the root directory, be sure to list the path to MOUSE.SYS in the DEVICE statement as follows:

DEVICE = C:\MOUSE1\MOUSE.SYS

Replace C:\MOUSE1 with the path to the MOUSE.SYS file on your computer.

The second way to inform the computer (and Word) that you have a mouse is with a program such as Microsoft's MOUSE.COM, which you load before you load Word. For example, you can use a batch file called MW.BAT to load MOUSE.COM and Word. The batch file must contain the following statements:

C:\MOUSE1\MOUSE.COM
C:\WORD\WORD

Either system loads the mouse driver. Check the documentation that came with your mouse or other pointing device to find out exactly how to use it.

Options for Speed

Word performs many diverse functions, so it may seem to run slowly on a standard PC (with an 8088 chip running at 4.77 MHz) because Word normally runs in graphics mode. Rather than telling the computer to place a particular character on the screen, Word actually tells the computer exactly how to draw the character. This way, when Word wants italics (*A*) or bold (**A**) or both (*A*), it can display these formats on the screen. It takes much more information, however, to instruct the computer to paint a character on the screen than to tell it to place a character on the screen. There are several ways you can increase this speed.

First, make sure you have the latest version of Word. Version 4 is faster than version 3, and version 3 is faster than version 2. If you are working with an older version, write to Microsoft for upgrade information.

Second, and least expensive, is Word's option that allows you to run it in character mode (see "Options for Starting Word" in Chapter 2). In character mode, Word simply instructs the computer to place a character on the screen and uses some of the computer's internal screen attributes to show the formatting. Since most computers can display a bold character on the screen, bold characters will appear bold; however, underlining, italics, small caps, and other types of characters will usually appear as different colors, with inverse video backgrounds, or with various combinations of different colors or backgrounds. You must give up some screen formatting to make gains in speed.

Word 4.0 allows you to toggle between graphics and character modes by pressing Alt-F9 (press the F9 key while holding down the Alt key). As a result, with 4.0, you can use character mode to enter the text, do basic formatting, and then switch to graphics mode to see just how it looks.

The third way to speed up Word is with a faster computer — the faster the better. A computer built around Intel's 80386 chip is 15 to 20 times as fast as a standard IBM PC. Examples of 80386 machines include the IBM PS/2 Model 80 and the Compaq Deskpro 386. Machines that use the 80286 chip are also quite speedy. The PS/2 Models 50 and 60 use the 286, as do dozens of AT-class machines (named after IBM's PC AT, which was the first computer to use the 80286). ATs run 8 to 15 times faster than a standard IBM PC. There are also "turbo" XTs and PCs, which run special high-speed versions of Intel's 8088 and 8086 chips or NEC's V20 or V30 chips; they run approximately twice as fast as the PC.

In addition to a faster computer, there are several other ways to speed up elements of Word's performance. For example, a hard disk (sometimes called a fixed disk) can hold the contents of dozens of floppy disks and can read and write information very quickly. A hard disk won't speed up Word's screen display, but it will do away with disk saves that seem to provide enough time for a coffee break.

Finally, Hercules Computer Technology of Berkeley, California, makes a pair of graphics cards for the PC that use a system called RAMfont. One card runs in monochrome (the Graphics Card Plus), and the other runs in color (the InColor Card). RAMfont allows a computer to run Word in the faster character mode but still provide full on-screen formatting.

BACKING UP DISTRIBUTION DISKS

Before continuing, be sure to back up your Word distribution disks (the original disks you purchased). You should *never* do anything with your original distribution disks except make copies of them. After they are copied, put them away in a safe place, preferably away from where you work.

To copy your Word distribution disks, put the working copy of your DOS disk in drive A of a floppy disk system or change directories to the subdirectory on your hard disk that contains the program DISKCOPY.COM. Then, at the DOS prompt, type

DISKCOPY A: B: <return>

DISKCOPY will prompt you to place each of your Word distribution disks in drive A (one at a time) and then copy those disks to drive B. If your computer has only one disk drive, it serves as both drives A and B. From time to time, the screen will tell you to put "disk B: in drive A:" or "disk A: in drive A:," which is your cue to swap disks.

When you have made copies of all your Word distribution disks, you are ready to proceed with setting up your system.

THE SETUP PROGRAM

Word versions 3 and 4.0 come with a program called SETUP.EXE that you can use for copying your original copy of Word to a set of working disks or your hard disk. It is not entirely necessary to use SETUP, but it makes the process much easier.

SETUP automatically examines your system, analyzes what kind of equipment you have, and copies the necessary files to your working floppy disks or the Word subdirectory of your hard disk. If SETUP is not sure exactly what kind of equipment you have, it will request additional information. For example, it will ask about your printer because there is no way for Word to know what printer you are using.

SETUP is completely menu-driven and will ask you for each disk as needed.

If you are using floppy disks, you must have several formatted disks handy, but don't worry if you run out. One choice on the SETUP menu allows you to format more disks.

If you have a mouse, SETUP creates or modifies the file CONFIG.SYS to include the line necessary to load the mouse driver.

MANUAL SETUP ON A FLOPPY DISK SYSTEM

If you choose not to use the SETUP program, you can prepare your own working disks. The Word program disk must contain at least the following files:

- WORD.COM (from the Word distribution disk labeled "Program Disk")

- MW.PGM (also from the Program Disk)

- MOUSE.COM, MOUSE.SYS, or a comparable mouse driver if you are using a mouse or other pointing device (MOUSE.COM and MOUSE.SYS are both found on your Microsoft Mouse program disks). Both Word 3.1 and 4.0 come with new MOUSE.SYS files that improve mouse performance with those versions; the files are on the Utilities Disk of your Word distribution package.

- COMMAND.COM (from your DOS disk)

- a printer driver compatible with your printer (see the Word *Printer Information* manual for details on which printer drivers to copy; printer drivers are found on the disks labeled "Printer Disk 1," "Printer Disk 2," and "Utilities").

Unfortunately, there is not enough room on a standard 5.25" floppy disk for these files and the hidden operating system files, which means that if you have a floppy disk system, you must use one disk containing the system files to start your computer. Then, you must take that disk out of drive A and insert the Word program disk. If you try to copy all required Word files to a disk that contains the system files (one that has been formatted with the command FORMAT /S or that has had the system files added to it with the command SYS), you will receive a "disk full" error message.

To prepare a working disk for the Word spell checker, copy all the files on the distribution disk labeled "Microsoft Spell." At the very least, your speller disk should contain the following files:

Version 3	Version 4
HIGHFREQ.CMP	SPELL-AM.LEX
MAINDICT.CMP (the dictionaries)	SPELL-AM.EXE
LOOKUP.COM	
MARKFIX.COM	
PROOF.COM	

A working thesaurus disk must contain the WFBG.SYN file, which is the only file on the distribution disk labeled "Thesaurus." The Thesaurus was first included in version 3.1 of Word.

You will also want a copy of the appropriate "Learning Microsoft Word" disk. There is one learning disk for using Word with a mouse and another for working strictly with a keyboard.

Of course, if you have high-capacity disks, such as the AT-style 1.2-megabyte disks or the 720K 3.5" disks, you can maintain a more complete system on your main disk and avoid swapping disks later.

MANUAL SETUP ON A HARD DISK SYSTEM

If you have a hard disk system, the easiest way to install Word is to use SETUP, answering the questions as asked and inserting disks as requested; however, if you want to install Word manually, begin by creating a separate directory for your Word files. At the DOS prompt, type

MD \WORD <return>

Then, change to the \WORD subdirectory with the following command:

CD \WORD <return>

Finally, use the DOS COPY Command to copy all files from the Word Program disk, Microsoft Spell disk, Thesaurus disk, and the appropriate Learning Word disk. Insert each disk into drive A: and type

COPY A:*.* C:\WORD <return>

Next, you must copy some (but not all) of the files on the Word Utilities disk. The easiest way to perform this task is to copy all the files and then erase those you don't need. Insert the Utilities disk in drive A: and type

COPY A:*.* C:\WORD <return>

Then, delete the printer drivers (files with the extension .PRD). Type

DEL *.PRD <return>

Finally, use the *Printer Information* manual to determine which printer driver supports your printer. Use the DOS DIR command to find the appropriate printer driver file and copy it to your \WORD subdirectory. Word printer drivers are found on the distribution disks labeled "Printer 1," "Printer 2," and "Utilities."

If your printer uses downloaded "soft" fonts, you also need an .EXE file with the same name as your printer driver. For example, if you use the driver for Hewlett-Packard downloaded portrait fonts (HPDWNSFP.PRD), you also need the HPDWNSFP.EXE file, which will automatically download fonts the printer requires to print a document.

CHAPTER 2

RUNNING MICROSOFT WORD

STARTING WORD

If your computer isn't already running, turn it on. On a floppy disk system, insert your Word Program disk in drive A and a blank floppy disk in drive B. If you are working with a hard disk, change directories to the subdirectory containing your Word files by typing

CD\WORD <return>

Then type

WORD <return>

Within a few seconds, you should see the program begin to appear on your screen. Depending on how you started the program, you may or may not see a sign-on screen with the Microsoft logo. The screen will clear and you will see the standard Word edit screen. The following illustration shows the screen in Word version 3:

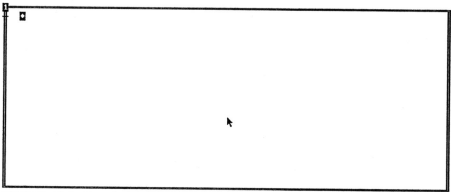

```
COMMAND: Alpha Copy Delete Format Gallery Help Insert Jump Library
          Options Print Quit Replace Search Transfer Undo Window
Edit document or press Esc to use menu
Page 1    {}                         ?              Microsoft Word:
```

Figure 2.1a

The following illustration shows the screen in version 4:

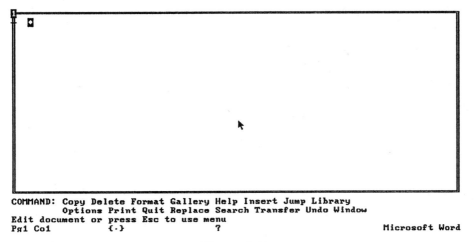

```
COMMAND: Copy Delete Format Gallery Help Insert Jump Library
         Options Print Quit Replace Search Transfer Undo Window
Edit document or press Esc to use menu
Pg1 Co1              {·}                 ?                 Microsoft Word
```

Figure 2.1b

THE WORD MENU

At the bottom of the Word edit screen is the Word menu. The menus of versions 3 and 4 differ slightly; version 3 has one extra command – Alpha – and, in version 4, both the page number and the column number are indicated in the bottom left corner of the screen. The functions of these differences will be covered in detail in Chapter 3.

When the highlight is in the menu, you can select menu choices. To move the highlight to the menu, press the Escape key, usually labeled **Esc** and found either at the top left corner of the keyboard or at the top left corner of the numeric keypad.

Once the highlight is in the menu, you can make a selection in one of three ways. First, you can press an uppercase letter of any of the menu items; usually, but not always, this will be the first letter of each item listed. Second, you can point to a choice with the mouse and click the left mouse button. Third, you can advance the highlight to the next choice and press Return. In version 3, use the Tab key to move the highlight to the right; hold down the Shift key and press the Tab key to move the highlight to the left. In version 4, you can also use the arrow keys to move around the menu.

If you want to explore, this is an appropriate time. Write a few lines of text. Try a few options to see where they lead. See what they do. Don't worry; there's nothing you can do with a keyboard or a mouse that will harm Word or the computer.

The specific functions of each menu choice will be detailed later in this book.

THE PATH

If you are using a hard disk, you must put the \WORD subdirectory in your path statement. This way, you will be able to start Word at any time, from any subdirectory. For example, you could place a book manuscript in a subdirectory called C:\BOOKS\WORD. To work on it, first log on to the subdirectory by typing

CD\BOOKS\WORD <return>

Then, type

WORD <return>

to start Word. Because the subdirectory where Word program files are stored is in the path, the computer can find the program and load it even though you are logged into another directory.

To add the \WORD subdirectory to your path, include the statement

PATH = C:\WORD

in the AUTOEXEC.BAT file in the root directory of your hard disk. If your AUTOEXEC.BAT file already contains a path statement, add the Word sub-directory to the end of it, preceded with a semicolon as follows:

PATH = C:\OTHERS;C:\WORD

Consult your DOS manual for a more detailed explanation of paths and the AUTOEXEC.BAT file.

FILE HANDLES

If you will be using Word and the Word spell-checking program at the same time, your computer must be able to simultaneously handle at least fifteen open files. Make sure there is a line reading

FILES = 15

in the CONFIG.SYS file in the root directory of the disk used to boot your system (either a floppy disk or the hard disk.) You may use a value greater than 15 if other software requires it.

STARTUP OPTIONS

When Word is started, five **switches** affect the way the program performs. These switches are typed on the command line that starts the program. Switches are represented by a slash followed by a single letter, such as /h, and they may be either uppercase or lowercase. For example, to load Word with the /h switch, type

WORD /h <return>

WORD /L

The /l switch automatically loads the last document on which you were working and returns you to the point in the document at which you were working. It's an effective time-saver when you are working on a large project to
which you must return every day.

WORD /C

The /c switch starts word in character mode, which is much faster than normal graphics mode; however, in character mode you must sacrifice on-screen
formatting such as italics and underlining. These traits are indicated by different colors, different backgrounds, or different print attributes.

You do gain scrolling speed in character mode, however. If you have an
older IBM PC or clone that does not have a "turbo" mode, this switch can
make quite a difference.

If you are using an IBM PC AT, an AT clone, or an IBM PS/2 model 50, 60,
70, or 80, don't bother with the /c switch. These machines are fast enough
that scrolling speed is not a concern.

The Hercules Graphics Plus Board

If you are using a Hercules Graphics Plus video card, use the /c switch to
start Word. Due to some fancy footwork in the video card, you will obtain
both on-screen formatting *and* fast scrolling; however, the mouse pointer will
be a box (not an arrow) and won't take other fancy shapes on the screen, but
the trade-off is worth it.

If you use the Hercules Plus card and DESQview with version 4 of Word,
however, start in graphics mode and do *not* toggle display modes (Alt-F9).
If you do, you will see strange screen displays in other programs running
under DESQview. This is not a problem with version 3 because it cannot
toggle display modes.

WORD /H

If you use a Hercules Graphics Card, an IBM Enhanced Graphics Adapter (EGA), or a video card compatible with either, the /h switch starts Word with 43 lines on the screen rather than 25, which allows you to see more of your document at once. The characters, of course, are smaller.

WORD /M

If you are using an EGA card (or compatible) with only 64K memory and an EGA compatible monitor, the /m switch starts Word in high-resolution mode (640 × 350) but with a black-and-white display. On a 64K EGA without the /m switch, Word normally runs in a low-resolution (640 × 200) mode with a 16-color display. On an EGA card with 128K memory, Word normally loads in high-resolution mode with a 16-color display, so the /m switch is not needed.

WORD /K

If you have an enhanced keyboard with 12 function keys, all 12 keys should function; however, some keyboards and computers are not entirely compatible with IBM, and the F11 and F12 keys don't work properly. Also, some memory-resident programs, particularly foreign keyboard drivers, can cause problems. In such cases, use the /k switch to run as if you had a normal keyboard with only ten function keys.

Switch Summary

Following is a chart showing how the /c, /h, and /m switches work together when Word is used with an EGA card:

64K EGA Card

Switches	EGA Monitor	Monochrome Monitor	RGB Monitor
no switch	640 × 200 25 lines 16 colors	640 × 350 25 lines monochrome	640 × 200 25 lines 16 colors
/c	text mode 25 lines 16 colors	text mode 25 lines monochrome	text mode 25 lines monochrome
/m	640 × 350 25 lines monochrome	not valid	not valid
/h	640 × 350 43 lines monochrome	text mode 43 lines monochrome	not valid
/h/m	640 × 350 43 lines monochrome	not valid	not valid
/h/c	text mode 43 lines 16 colors	text mode 43 lines monochrome	not valid

continued...

128K EGA Card

no switch	640 × 200 25 lines 16 colors	640 × 350 25 lines monochrome	640 × 200 25 lines 16 colors
/c	text mode 25 lines 16 colors	text mode 25 lines monochrome	text mode 25 lines 16 colors
/h	640 × 350 43 lines 16 colors	text mode 43 lines monochrome	not valid
/h/c	text mode 43 lines 16 colors	text mode 43 lines monochrome	not valid

QUITTING WORD

To quit Word, press the Escape key. If you have done any editing, Word will prompt you to save your work by highlighting everything on the screen and displaying the following message:

```
Enter Y to save, N to lose edits, ESC to cancel.
```

GETTING HELP

When you have a question about how to do something in Word, help is never more than a few keystrokes or one mouse click away.

To obtain context-sensitive help, i.e., help with the task you are currently performing, press Alt-H (press the H key while holding down the Alt key). Word will switch to its Help program and display a screen appropriate to the task at hand.

For more general help, press the Escape key, and then press H for help. With a mouse, click on the question mark at the bottom center of your screen. Either method leads you to the first of many screens of help information. At the bottom of the Help screen is the Help menu. In version 3, it resembles the following:

```
HELP: Resume Next Previous
      Introduction Commands Editing Keyboard Mouse Selection Tutorial
```

In version 4, it resembles the following:

```
HELP: Resume Next Previous
      Basics Index Tutorial
```

There are three ways to select a Help category. First, you can use the Tab/Shift-Tab keys (or the arrow keys in version 4) to advance the highlight to the category in which you need help, and then press Return. In version 4, you can also use the arrow keys to move the highlight. You can also use the mouse to point to the category in which you need help, and then click the left mouse button. Finally, you can simply press the first letter of the category in which you need help.

The Help Index

The Index option in version 4 will display an extensive list of subjects for which you can obtain help:

```
HELP INDEX: Alignment     File-formats      Macros          Selection
            Character-format Footnotes       Margins         Spellchecker
            Columns          Form-letters     Mouse           Style-sheets
            Commands         Glossaries       Outlining       Tabs/Tables
            Customize-screen Indents          Page-numbers    Windows
            Divisions        Keyboard         Printing
            Doc-retrieval    Library-commands Running-heads
            Editing          Load/Open        Save
```

There are only five topics — Introduction, Commands, Editing, Keyboard, Mouse, and Selection — in the version 3 index. All are listed as part of the version 3 Help menu.

Regardless of how you choose the topic, Word's Help module will take you to the first of several pages of information on the topic you have chosen. To move to the next page, select Next (with the Tab key, the mouse, or by pressing N). To go back a page, select Previous.

When you are ready to resume editing, select Resume.

THE WORD TUTORIAL

For a lesson on how to use a particular Word feature, select the Tutorial command. You will see a two-item menu as follows:

```
TUTORIAL: Lesson Index
```

If you select the Lesson option, Word will start the Word tutorial at the beginning. If you select Index, Word will list the possible tutorial subjects. Select a subject, and Word will begin the tutorial on the chosen subject.

LIBRARY RUN OPTION

There is one other feature of Word you should be aware of before you begin learning editing fundamentals: the Library Run feature. This feature allows you to run another program temporarily and then easily return to Word.

Press the Escape key to get to the Word menu, and select L(ibrary) (press L, point and click on Library with the mouse, or move the highlight to Library and press Return). Select R(un) from the Library submenu. Word will display the following prompt:

```
Enter DOS command
```

Type the name of a program you want to run, and press Return. If the program is not in the current directory, be sure to specify the path to the program. See your DOS manual for a more detailed explanation of paths.

When the program is finished, you will receive the following message:

```
Press any key to return to Word
```

Pressing any key will return you to the point at which you were working in your document.

CHAPTER 3

EDITING BASICS

This chapter presumes that you have already learned how to get Word running on your computer and are ready to start editing. If you haven't been able to install Word on your system, see Chapter 1. If you completed the installation, but the program won't run for some reason, see Chapter 2. Eventually, you will want to go back to those chapters for some tips on how to make Word run faster and how to get the most out of your video display system.

LOOKING AT THE SCREEN

Figure 3.1a shows Word's normal edit screen for version 3.

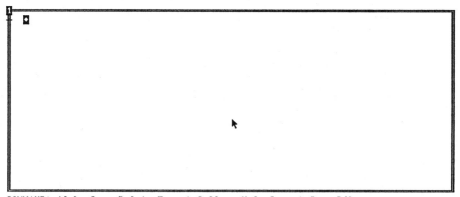

```
COMMAND: Alpha Copy Delete Format Gallery Help Insert Jump Library
         Options Print Quit Replace Search Transfer Undo Window
Edit document or press Esc to use menu
Page 1   {}                         ?              Microsoft Word:
```

Figure 3.1a

Figure 3.1b shows how the screen looks in version 4.

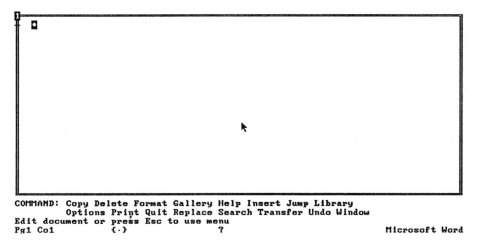

```
COMMAND: Copy Delete Format Gallery Help Insert Jump Library
         Options Print Quit Replace Search Transfer Undo Window
Edit document or press Esc to use menu
Pg1 Col          {·}              ?              Microsoft Word
```

Figure 3.1b

The Text Area

The portion of the screen inside the double lines is called the **text area**, which is where you do your writing and editing.

At the upper left corner of the screen is the number 1 on an inverse video field. The number tells you that this window is window number 1. Word can work with up to eight windows at a time. The inverse video behind the 1 indicates the active window.

Just below and to the right of the 1, you will see an inverse video block partially filled by a diamond shape. The block is called the **selection**. The diamond shape is the **end-of-file marker**.

The Selection

The **selection** is analogous to the cursor in other programs. Like the cursor, the selection shows you where the next character you type will appear on the screen; however, in Word, "cursor" is not an appropriate name. A cursor is just a position marker. The Word selection is much more versatile and important. In Word, the selection can be as short as one character or as long as an entire document. It is the key to all your editing because Word operates on a "select and act" basis. First, with the selection, you highlight the material you want to edit; then you tell Word what you want to do with that text. For example, you can select a word then delete it or select it then change its font. Later in this chapter you will see just how useful the selection can be. Right now, consider a few more features of the Word edit screen.

The End-of-File Marker

The **end-of-file marker** shows you where your document ends. As a general rule, there should be some space between the text you are editing and the end-of-file marker because when the selection is on the end-of-file marker, you won't be able to format your text as you type, a procedure explained later in this chapter. Create that space now. Press the Return key a few times, and then press the Up Arrow key until the selection moves back up to the corner. Now, the selection should be by itself in the top left corner of your screen, and the end-of-file marker should be by itself a few lines farther down the screen.

The Command Area

Below Word's text window is the **command area**. In version 3 of Word, the command area normally reads as follows:

```
COMMAND: Alpha Copy Delete Format Gallery Help Insert Jump Library
         Options Print Quit Replace Search Transfer Undo Window
Edit document or press Esc to use menu
Page 1 {}                        ?              Microsoft Word: FILENAME.EXT
```

In version 4, the command area reads somewhat differently:

```
COMMAND: Copy Delete Format Gallery Help Insert Jump Library
         Options Print Quit Replace Search Transfer Undo Window
Edit document or press Esc to use menu
Pg1 Col{}                      ?                 Microsoft Word
```

The command area has three elements: the menu, the message line, and the status line.

The **menu** fills the first two lines of the command area. It tells you what commands are currently available.

The **message line** is where Word prompts you in case you have forgotten what to do. When you are editing, Word's message line appears as follows:

```
Edit document or press Esc to use menu
```

The **Status line** is the last line on the screen and includes five pieces of information. First, it tells you which page in your document contains the selection. In version 4, it also tells you which column contains the last character in the selection and, as an option, can also tell you which line on a particular page contains the end of the selection. Second, the status line shows you what text is in the **scrap**, a portion of memory that holds the most recently deleted text; the scrap contents are shown within the curly brackets ({}). Third, if you use a mouse, Word will put a question mark in the middle of the status line; for help, you can click on that question mark with your mouse. Fourth, in a space just ahead of the word "Mircosoft," Word will display messages about special keys you have pressed. For instance, press the Num Lock key on your numeric keypad, and the letters "NL" will appear (press the key again and the letters disappear). Finally, at the right side of the screen, Word displays its name. In version 3, this name is followed by the name of the file on which you are working; in version 4, the name of the file on which you are working is superimposed over the bottom right corner of the border. (Since you just loaded Word, there will be no file name on your screen.)

Switching Between Text and Command Areas

Use the Escape key to switch Word's attention from the text area of the screen to the command area. To switch back to the text area, use the A(lpha) command in version 3, or, in version 4, just press the Escape key again. When you are working in the text area, press the Escape key, and the first command at the bottom of the screen will be highlighted. In version 3, the first command is the Alpha command; in version 4, it is the Copy command.

CHOOSING COMMANDS

When Word's attention is in the command area, you can select commands three ways:

1.	by pointing to the command with the mouse and clicking the left mouse button.

2.	by entering the uppercase letter in the command.

3.	by moving the highlight to the command and pressing the Return key. To move the highlight to the command in version 3, use the Tab key to move to the right, and use Shift-Tab (hold down a Shift key and simultaneously press the Tab key) to move left. In version 4, you can use the Tab key, Shift-Tab combination, or you can use the arrow keys to move around the menu choices.

These three techniques work with any menu in Word.

Try selecting commands now. Press Escape (usually at the upper left corner of the keyboard, but sometimes at the upper left corner of the numeric keypad). The first command in the command area should be highlighted. In version 3 this command will be Alpha. If you press the Return key, the highlight will disappear, and you will be able to edit again. In version 4, the highlighted command will be Copy. If you press Escape, you will be able to edit again.

Express Commands with the Mouse

Many of the choices on Word's main menu lead to other menus. If you are using a mouse, by pressing the right button, you select not only a command in the main menu but also the first choice in the submenu. For example, select the Print command from the command menu. Do so by pointing to the Print command with the mouse and clicking the left mouse button, by pressing P on the keyboard, or by moving the highlight to the Print command and pressing the Return key. What you will see is another menu that reads as follows:

```
PRINT: Printer Direct File Glossary Merge Options Queue Repaginate
```

The first choice on the Printer submenu will be highlighted because most of the time, when you chose the Print menu, you want to print a file.

Had you used the *right* mouse button to select Print on the main menu, you would have also selected Printer on the submenu. Using the right mouse button selects a main menu command *and* the first command on the submenu.

Two Kinds of Menu Choices

Note that there are two kinds of choices in Word: fill-in-the-blank choices and short menu choices. These kinds of choices are found in all Word menus, and you use the same techniques for making your selections.

Fill in the Blank Choices

Some menu items ask you to enter a value in a field, as does *default Tab width* in the Options submenu. If you are happy with the choice already on the screen, just press Tab (or an arrow key in version 4) to move on to the next field. If you press any number or letter key, the existing value will disappear, and the new one you enter will take its place.

Short Menu Choices

If a choice gives you a short menu, as does the *visible* field in the Options submenu, press the first letter of your choice or use the Space Bar to cycle through the choices to the one you want. When you move the highlight away from the field in which you are working, your choice will be surrounded by parentheses.

Implementing or Cancelling Your Choices

When you have finalized your choices, press the Return key to implement them.

The methods of cancelling your choices are slightly different in versions 3 and 4. In version 3, you would press Escape, which will take you back to the main menu with the highlight on Alpha. Press the Return key to resume editing. In version 4, pressing Escape will take you directly back to editing. If you want to return to the main menu, press Shift-Escape.

ENTERING TEXT

Now that you are familiar with parts of the edit screen, how to move from editing to issuing commands, and the basics of issuing commands, you are ready to learn how to enter and manipulate text with Word.

Start by making sure you are ready to edit. The command area at the bottom of the screen should show the main menu with none of the commands highlighted. If it shows a submenu or anything else other than the main menu, press Escape. In version 3, this action will take you back to the main menu with the Alpha command highlighted. Press the Return key to move back to the text area. In version 4, pressing Escape at any time when Word's attention is in the command area will take you immediately back to editing.

Now you need some text to work with. First, give yourself some room before the end-of-file marker. Remember, it is not a good idea to be working too close to the end-of-file marker because when the selection is on the end-of-file marker, you can't format your text as you go. So press the Return key a few times to move the end-of-file marker down, and then use the Up Arrow key to move the selection back to the top of the screen. Now, type in a half a dozen lines, perhaps this paragraph. The only difference is that you should put the number 1 and a period at the beginning of the paragraph. When you are finished, your screen should resemble the following:

```
1.    Now you need some text to work with.  First, give
yourself some room ahead of the end-of-file marker.
Remember, it is not a good idea to be working too close to
the end-of-file marker because when the selection is on the
end-of-file marker, you can't format your text as you go.
So press the Return key a few times to move the end-of-file
marker down then use the Up Arrow key to move the selection
back to the top of the screen.  Now, type in a half a dozen
lines, perhaps this paragraph.  The only difference is that
you should put the number 1 and a period at the beginning of
the paragraph.  When you're done, your screen should
resemble the following: ¶


     ◘


                                                 3-2.DOC
COMMAND: Copy Delete Format Gallery Help Insert Jump Library
         Options Print Quit Replace Search Transfer Undo Window
Key code not defined
Pg1 Co6         {}              ?                  Microsoft Word
```

Figure 3.2

(If you are using version 3 of Word, your screen may not look exactly like Figure 3.2, but the differences are minor.)

To give yourself more text to work with, you need to quickly create a large document by copying this paragraph several times; then, automatically number the resulting paragraphs so you have some idea where you are in your document. Following is the cookbook recipe for how to number the paragraphs. This process will be covered in detail later in the book.

Press the function key labeled F10. **Function keys** are at the left side of the keyboard on many computers or in a row across the top on others. Pressing F10 extends the selection to include all of the current paragraph. Now, press the Delete key (usually at the bottom of the position control keys or on the numeric keypad). Don't panic when the text disappears from the screen. It is supposed to disappear. Now, press the Insert key (usually found next to the Delete key). Press it again until you've done so ten or twelve times.

Now you should have a dozen identical paragraphs in your document, each beginning with the number 1. To give each paragraph a unique number, press Escape to switch Word's attention to the command area. Press L for the Library command, and then press N for Number. You will be given two choices with the word "Update" highlighted. You want "Update," so just press the Return key. The number 1 at the head of each paragraph will be changed to reflect the sequence of paragraphs in your new document, running from 1 to however many paragraphs you created.

Now that you have a document that is more than one screen long and has numbers on the paragraphs so you can tell whether you are at the beginning, middle, or end, you need to learn how to move around Word's editing screen.

MOVING AROUND THE SCREEN

One of the most common editing moves is to simply move the selection around the screen. There are several ways you can move the selection. The easiest way is to use the arrow keys and other position control keys. But if you want to move in bigger steps, you will find that the mouse and the function keys come in handy. When you really must move a long way, you can move in even larger steps using the Jump command (discussed later in this chapter) or Word's integrated Outliner (see Chapter 6).

Position Control Keys

One of the easiest ways to move around your document is to use the arrow keys and other position control keys. These keys are located on the right-hand side of your keyboard.

The Up Arrow key moves the selection up one line; the Down Arrow key moves the selection down one line. Not surprisingly, the Right and Left arrow keys move the selection one character at a time to the right and left respectively. If you are using the arrow keys to move the selection and the selection moves off the screen in any direction, the screen will scroll to keep the selection in sight.

The Home key moves the selection to the left end of the current line while the End key moves it to the right end. The Page Up and Page Down keys move the selection up and down the document one screen at a time.

The Control Key

You can also use the Control key and keys on the position control pad to move in larger chunks. The Control key is usually on the left side of the keyboard by the letter A and labeled **Ctrl**. Sometimes, it is in the bottom row of the keyboard near the Space Bar. Some keyboards even have two Control keys.

You use the Control key as you would a Shift key: you hold it down while simultaneously pressing another key. So, hold down the Control key and, at the same time, press the Home key. The selection will jump to the top of the screen. Hold down the Control key and press the End key, and the selection will jump to the bottom of the screen. The Control-Page Up key combination moves the selection to the top of the document while the Control-Page Down key combination moves the selection to the end-of-file marker.

In version 4, there are four other commands that use the Control key. Control and the Right or Left Arrow key combination moves the selection to the beginning of the next or previous word respectively. The Control and Up or Down arrow key combination moves the selection to the first character of the previous or next paragraph respectively.

Following is a summary of the actions executed by the position control keys.

Key	Version 3	Version 4
Left	left	left
Right	right	right
Up	up	up
Down	down	down
Ctrl-Left	-	previous word
Ctrl-Right	-	next word
Ctrl-Up	-	previous paragraph
Ctrl-Down	-	next paragraph
Home	beginning of line	beginning of line
End	end of line	end of line
Ctrl-Home	top of window	top of window
Ctrl-End	bottom of window	bottom of window
PgUp	scroll up one screen	scroll up one screen
PgDn	scroll down one screen	scroll down one screen
Ctrl-PgUp	beginning of document	beginning of document
Ctrl-PgDn	end of document	end of document

Function Keys

You can also use several of the function keys to move quickly through your document; however, the version 3 and version 4 function keys operate quite a bit differently.

Version 3 Function Keys

In version 3, the function keys F7 and F8 move the selection one word at a time to the left and right respectively, highlighting the entire word. The F10 key first selects the current paragraph then moves forward through the document one paragraph at a time for each time you press it. The F10 key always selects an entire paragraph. The F9 key selects the current sentence but, unlike F10, pressing it again will *not* move the selection to the next sentence.

Following is a summary of the Version 3 Function keys.

Version 3 Function Key	Selects
F7	word left
F8	word right
F9	current sentence
F10	current paragraph

Version 4 Function Keys

In version 4, the F7 and F8 keys move the selection one word at a time to the left and right respectively, selecting the entire word. This action is similar to the action of Ctrl-Left Arrow and Ctrl-Right Arrow key combinations. The difference is that the F7 and F8 keys move the selection and highlight the entire word. The Ctrl-Left Arrow and Ctrl-Right Arrow key combinations move the selection but leave the selection on the first character of the word.

The Shift-F7 key combination selects the current sentence then moves back one sentence each time you press it. The Shift-F8 key combination also first selects the current sentence then moves forward one sentence each time you press it. Both Shift-F7 and Shift-F8 always select an entire sentence.

The F10 key first selects the current paragraph then moves forward through your document one paragraph at a time each time you press it. The F9 key also first selects the current paragraph but then moves backward through the document one paragraph at a time. Both the F9 and F10 keys always select an entire paragraph.

The Shift-F9 key combination selects all lines that already contain part of the selection. So, for example, if the selection started at the end of one line and ended near the beginning of the next line, Shift-F9 would expand the selection to include all of both lines. The Shift-F10 key combination selects the entire document.

Following is a summary of the Version 4 Function keys.

Version 4 Function Key	Selects
F7	word left
F8	word right
Shift-F7	current then previous sentence
Shift-F8	current then next sentence
F9	current then previous paragraph
F10	current then next paragraph
Shift-F9	any line containing any part of selection
Shift-F10	entire document

Moving with the Mouse

You can use the mouse to move the selection anywhere in the document. If the position you want is on the screen, just point and click the mouse button. If you click the left mouse button, the selection will move to the *character* nearest where you are pointing. Clicking the right button moves the selection to the *word* nearest the pointer. Clicking both buttons together selects the *sentence* nearest the pointer.

The Scroll Bar

To move to a position no more than one screen above or below your current position in the document, move the mouse pointer until it rests on the double line at the left side of the screen. This double line is the **scroll bar**. If you click the left mouse button, the screen will scroll down. Click the right button and the screen will scroll up. The number of lines it scrolls will be the number of lines the mouse pointer is positioned from the top. For example, if you position the mouse pointer in the scroll bar next to the tenth line from the top and click the left mouse button, the screen will scroll down ten lines. Click the right mouse button and the screen will scroll up ten lines. So, to scroll up or down one full screen at a time, position the mouse pointer at the very bottom of the scroll bar and press the left button (for down) or the right button (for up).

Note that in version 4, you can set Word so that the window border does not appear when there is only one window on the screen; however, if the border does not appear, you cannot use the scroll bar since the scroll bar is part of the border.

To scroll farther, position the mouse pointer anywhere on the screen; then press *and hold* the left mouse button. Now, when you move the mouse, the selection will extend, changing the background of the characters from black to white. To move down your document, move the mouse down until it lies on the double line at the bottom of the text area; to move up your document, move the mouse up to the top double line. In version 4, if you have turned the window border off, just move the mouse to the very top or bottom of the screen. As long as you keep the mouse pointer at the top or bottom of the window, the screen will scroll. When you arrive at the desired position, let go of the mouse button. To return to a single-character selection, position the mouse pointer at the exact spot on the screen where you want the selection to be and click the mouse button once. The long extended selection will disappear and be replaced by a single-character selection.

The Thumb

On the scroll bar at the left side of the screen, you will see a short horizontal line. This line is the **thumb**. The thumb simply tells you where you are in your document. If the thumb is near the top of the line, you are near the top of your document. If it is near the bottom of the line, you are near the bottom of your document.

The Jump Command

The Jump command gives you the power to move through your document to any designated page. But first your document must have pages in it. Word does not paginate a document until you print the document or until Word is instructed to work out the page breaks.

Repagination

Later in this chapter, you will learn how to print a file. For now, you will learn how to compute the page breaks using the Print Repaginate command. Just press Escape to move Word's attention to the command area. Now select Print (by pressing P, by pointing with the mouse and clicking with the left mouse button, or by moving the highlight and pressing the Return key). The Print command submenu should appear:

PRINT: Printer Direct File Glossary Merge Options Queue Repaginate

Select the Repaginate command. You will then be asked if you want to "confirm page breaks." Press the Return key to select the highlighted choice, "No." In the bottom left portion of the screen, Word will count off the pages as it computes the locations of the page breaks.

Now, if you scroll through your document, you will see little page markers at the end of each page. In version 3, the page markers appear as double arrows in the left margin. In version 4, the page marker appears as a line of dots across the screen. The page markers mark the first line of each new page. As you move from one page to the next, the message in the lower left corner of your screen will tell you which page contains the selection.

Jumping

Once Word has paginated the document, you can use the Jump command to move to a particular page. Press Escape to move to the command menu. Select the Jump command. You can then choose between "Page" and "Footnote." Footnotes will be covered in Chapter 17. For now, just press the Return key to select "Page," and Word will ask you for a page number. Enter the number, press Return, and Word will magically transport you to the beginning of that page.

In version 4, you can also press the Shift-F5 key combination, and Word will ask for a page number then jump there when you press Return.

The Outliner

One other way to move quickly through a document is by using Word's **integrated Outliner**, which is covered in Chapter 8, "Drafting" (also see Chapter 6).

BLOCK MANEUVERS

Now that you know how to enter text and how to move around your document, it is time to learn about one of the nicest features of Word: the ability to operate on large blocks of text; you can delete them, format them, or move them easily with just a few keystrokes.

Extending the Selection

Before you can perform an editing function on a block of text, you need to select the text block. You do so by extending the selection one of several ways.

The Extend Select Key—F6

The function key labeled F6 is the **Extend Selection** function key. When you press it, the letters "EX" appear at the bottom of the screen next to the words "Microsoft Word." This message tells you that the EXtension mode is on. As you use the arrow keys, the selection extends.

Alternatively, you can use the mouse in conjunction with the F6 key to extend the selection. Press F6, point to a spot on the screen, click either the right or left mouse button, and the selection will extend from where it previously was located to the location at which you are pointing.

You can cancel the F6 selection extension mode with any of the position control keys (arrows, Home, End, PgUp or PgDn) or by pressing any letter, number, or punctuation key. If you start typing again, what you type will appear at the *front* of the selection.

Shift and Arrow Keys

In version 4, you can also extend the selection by holding down either Shift key and using the arrow keys, the PgUp key, or the PgDn key.

Other Function Keys

You can also use the F6 key in conjunction with the function keys F7, F8, F9, and F10 to select text. For example, as you learned earlier in this chapter, the F7 and F8 keys move the selection one word at a time to the left and right respectively. If you press F6 before you press F7 or F8, the selection extends one word at a time each time you press F7 or F8. Or, as another example, you can use the F10 key to select one paragraph at a time. Press F6 then F10 to select the current paragraph. Then each time you press F10 again, the selection will extend by another paragraph.

The Mouse and the Selection Bar

In the left portion of the screen is a two-column clear area called the **selection bar**. If you use a mouse, you can use the selection bar to select large quantities of text.

When you move the mouse pointer into the selection bar, its shape changes. If you are running Word in graphics mode, the mouse pointer will be an arrowhead to the left, and it will become an arrowhead to the right. If you are operating Word in character mode, the mouse pointer will be a blinking block, and it will change to a larger blinking box.

Following is what the mouse selects when it is in the selection bar:

Click	To Select
Left Mouse Button	Line next to mouse pointer
Right Mouse Button	Paragraph next to mouse pointer
Both Mouse Buttons	Entire document

Dragging the Mouse

You can select varying amounts of text by "dragging" the mouse in the selection bar. To drag the mouse, hold down a mouse button and move the mouse up or down. The selection will be extended as the mouse pointer moves. If you are holding down the left mouse button, the selection will extend one line at a time. If you are holding down the right mouse button, the selection will extend one paragraph at a time.

You can also select text by dragging the mouse within the body of the text itself. Point to the first character of the text you want to select. Press and hold the mouse button while moving the mouse pointer to the last character you want included in the selection, and then release the mouse button. If you hold down the left button, the selection will extend one character at a time. If you hold down the right button, the selection will extend one word at a time. If you hold down both buttons, the selection will extend one sentence at a time. If the spot where you want to end the selection is off the screen to the top or bottom, just move the mouse pointer to the top or bottom of the screen, and the screen will scroll to bring your desired end point into view.

Column Selection

Word can also select text by columns. This feature is covered in Chapter 16, "Tables."

The Scrap and Delete

Now that you have an extended selection, what can you do with it? Because Word operates on the Select-Act principle, after you extend a selection, the next editing command you issue will apply to that entire block. For example, if you press some character formatting keys (which will be covered later in this chapter), all the text in the selection will be formatted. But most often, you delete or copy a block of text to the **scrap** or **glossary** (see Chapter 21, "The Glossary and Macros," for a detailed discussion of the glossary).

When you press the Delete key, Word copies whatever is selected to a special section of memory called the **scrap**. For example, mark a short piece of text using the F6 Extend Selection key and the arrow keys. Then press the Delete key. The selection disappears, but not entirely. Look at the bottom of your screen. Just to the right of the page number is a pair of curly brackets ({}), and between them you can see the beginning and end of the text you just deleted.

The curly brackets contain the scrap, which holds only one deleted (or copied) item at a time.

You can also delete text to the scrap by choosing the Delete command from the Word main menu and then pressing the Return key in response to Word's suggestion that you use the scrap (marked with the curly brackets) as the destination for your selection.

The Scrap and Copy

Remember that you can delete *or* copy to the Scrap. To copy selected text to the scrap, press Escape to move to the command area, and then select C(opy). In the command area, you will see the following:

```
Copy to: {}

Enter glossary name or select from list
```

To *copy* the selection to the Scrap, that is, to leave it on the screen *and* to place it in the scrap, just press the Return key.

The Scrap and Insert

To place the contents of the scrap back into your document in a different location, move the selection to the destination for your text and press the Insert key. Alternatively, you can select the Insert command from the Word main menu. Word will take the contents of the scrap and insert them into the document at the location of the selection.

By using Delete to Scrap, Copy to Scrap, and Insert, you can quickly and easily move large blocks of text to different parts of your document.

SAVING YOUR WORK

One of the vagaries of modern life is electricity. You rely on it and just when you've relied on it too much, somebody in Fargo, North Dakota, shorts out a toaster trying to retrieve a slice of bread with a knife. The power transformer on the pole outside the house goes down, taking with it the neighborhood substation, which then overloads an old capacitor in Duluth, which shorts out the major transmission line carrying power from James Bay, Quebec, to your house. Suddenly, your computer screen goes blank, and that 100,000 word novel you've been writing since this morning disappears into the ether.

While the above situation may be extreme, electrical problems such as sudden power surges and system failures do occur, so you need to get into the habit of periodically saving your work. Some users save every five minutes, some every 15 minutes. Do save your work often so you will be able to recover from such near tragedies.

Once you have named your file, it takes just four keystrokes in version 3 and only two in version 4 to save your work. Those keystrokes should soon become second nature to you. If you haven't yet named the file, you will need to use just a few more keystrokes.

Saving in Version 3

To save a file in version 3, press Escape to move to the command area, and then select the Transfer option. From the Transfer submenu, select Save. If the file already has a name, that name, complete with its path, will appear. Just press Return. If you have not previously given the file a name, fill in a name (see "The File Name" later in this chapter) and press Return.

Saving in Version 4

It is even easier to save a file in version 4. Just press the Ctrl-F10 key combination, which is the same as pressing < Esc > T(ransfer) S(ave) < return >.

The Version 4 Document Summary

In version 4, the first time you try to save a document, Word will ask for a **document summary**. The document summary fields resemble the following:

```
title:                              version number:
author:                             creation date: 9/25/87
operator:                           revision date: 9/25/87
keywords:
comments:
```

In Chapter 21, "Document Retrieval," you will learn how to use the information in this document summary to select documents that meet certain criteria. If you produce a lot of files — and you will sooner or later — it is important to fill in the document summary with the kind of information that will help you identify documents later when you've forgotten the contents of the file named BOBLET.DOC or some other file with an equally forgettable name.

For example, the document summary for this chapter reads as follows:

```
title: Word book - chapter 3        version number: 2
author: tp                          creation date: 7/16/87
operator: tp                        revision date: 9/25/87
keywords: edit load save format paragraph character
comments:
```

To later update a document summary with new or changed information, use the L(ibrary) D(ocument-retrieval) U(pdate) command sequence and select the file you want to update from the list on the screen.

The File Name

In all versions of Word, the first time you try to save a file, Word will ask you for a file name. If you have not yet named your file, Word will ask you for a name. A Word document file name follows the standard rules for naming files under MS-DOS. It can have a file name up to eight letters long with an optional file type up to three letters long. The file name and file type must be separated by a period. For example,

FILENAME.TYP

is a legitimate file name.

Unless told differently, Word presumes that the file type (or file name extension) of any document file is .DOC. All you must do is assign a file name up to eight characters long, and Word will automatically append to it the file type .DOC. So if you type a file name of "CHAP03," Word will save the file as "CHAP03.DOC." If you want to save a file name without a file type, for example TIMLET, include the period on the Transfer Save command line as follows:

TRANSFER SAVE filename: TIMLET.

If you don't include the period, Word will assume you want to save a file named "TIMLET.DOC."

If there is a conflict between the name you assign to a file and an existing file, Word will ask if it should overwrite (erase) the file on the disk before saving your new file. If there is no conflict, Word will immediately save the file.

After you work in Word for a while, the <Esc>, T(ransfer), S(ave), <return> sequence or Ctrl-F10 key combination will become second nature. Make it a habit to save your work every time you stop to think or take a deep breath. You can never save too often, but it is easy to save too infrequently.

If you forget to save periodically, Word will eventually display the message "SAVE" at the bottom of the screen to let you know it is time to save your work to disk.

Formatted or Unformatted

Word also gives you the choice of saving a file as a formatted or unformatted file. A **formatted** file includes all the information Word needs to know about paragraph, character, and division formatting. An **unformatted** file is stored without that information. Files that are stored unformatted can be transferred to virtually any other word processing program but will have lost all their formatting features.

TRANSFER OPTIONS

There is one other choice on the Transfer submenu with which you should be familiar, the Options command. Press Escape and then select T(ransfer) and O(ptions). Word will list its Transfer Options Setup, which is the current default drive and directory for saving and retrieving document files.

If you have a floppy disk system, the default will be the root directory of drive B. If you have a hard disk system, the default will be the directory you were in when you first started Word. For example, if you were writing this book, the chapter files would be stored in a subdirectory on drive C. The Transfer Options *setup* field would then look like the following:

```
TRANSFER OPTIONS setup: C:\BOOKS\WORD
```

You can change this default drive and directory by changing the value in the Transfer Options Setup field. The new value will stay in effect for the remainder of your Word session, unless you change it again. The new value will also be saved by Word for use the next time you start the program. (If you don't understand the directory structure of MS-DOS, see your DOS documentation.)

Loading an Existing File

To load an existing file, you again select the T(ransfer) command, this time selecting L(oad) from the submenu. Word will ask you for the name of the file you want. If it is in the default directory (as specified by the Transfer Options Setup command above), then just enter the file name. Again, Word presumes a file type of .DOC unless you specify otherwise. Press Return, and Word will load the file you specify.

When a file name has no extension (for example TIMLET), be sure to include the period when you give Word its name, for example,

TRANSFER LOAD filename: TIMLET.

Otherwise, Word will presume that you want a file named TIMLET.DOC.

A List of Files

If you can't remember the name of the file you want to load, when you select the T(ransfer) L(oad) command, Word can give you a list of document files in the default directory. In version 3, press any of the arrow keys for a list. In version 4, press the F1 key. Word will display a list of the files in the default directory with the file type .DOC.

If you want to see a list of other files, type a standard MS-DOS ambiguous file name in the field calling for the file name, and then press an arrow key or the F1 key. (If you don't know what an ambiguous file name is, see your DOS manual.) For example, for a list of all the files in the current default directory, enter *.* where Word is asking for a file name. The screen should resemble the following just before you press an arrow key or F1:

```
TRANSFER LOAD Filename: *.*                    read only: Yes(No)
```

For a list of files in another directory or on another drive, be sure to specify the drive and directory:

```
TRANSFER LOAD Filename: C:\BOOKS\WORD\*.*      read only: Yes(No)
```

Once you have the list of files on the screen, use the arrow keys to move the highlight to the file you want to load. Press the Return key to load that file.

Read Only

When you are loading a file, at the right side of the command area the following field appears:

```
read only: Yes(No)
```

You can move the highlight to that field by pressing the Tab key. In version 4, you can also use the arrow keys to move to that field. Then use the Space Bar to select between the choices, press Y or N on the keyboard, or point and click at your choice with the left mouse button.

When you select Yes for Read Only, Word will load the file but will not allow you to save it under the same file name. You will need to specify a new name to protect the integrity of your original file. You should normally just leave this field set to No.

Last Chance to Save

If you try to load a file into a window that already contains a file, Word will highlight the existing file and prompt you with the following message:

```
Y to save, N to lose edits, ESC to cancel
```

This prompt is Word's way of giving you a chance to save the file you've been working on before it loads a new file. Press Y to save the file you've been working on, and then load the new file. If you press N, Word will abandon the file you've been working on and load the new file. Any changes made since you last saved the first file will be lost. If you press Escape, the Load command will be canceled.

Merging Two Files

Sometimes you might want to add the contents of a previously existing file to the file already in the window. In other words, you want to merge the two files. Word's Transfer Merge command performs this operation.

Press Escape to move to the command area, and then select T(ransfer) and M(erge). Word will ask for the name of the file. Enter the file name, press the Return key, and Word will load that file into the current window, starting at the beginning of the selection.

If you want a list of files displayed before you specify a file, press one of the arrow keys for a list of the .DOC files in the current Transfer Options default directory. Enter a DOS ambiguous file name for a list of other files. Use the arrow keys to move the highlight to the file you want to select, and press the Return key to merge that file with the file in the currently active window.

DOCUMENT RETRIEVAL

Version 4 of Word allows you to search for documents that contain certain information in their document summaries or certain words in their text. For example, you could find all documents that contain the name "Perrin." Chapter 21, "Document Retrieval," contains detailed instructions on how to use the document retrieval features of Word 4.0 to search and display documents.

DISASTER INSURANCE—THE UNDO COMMAND

Before going any farther, you should know about one of Word's most ingratiating features: its ability to undo what it has done. The Undo command is simple and will save you from grief countless times. Just press Escape and chose the Undo command with the mouse, with the Tab key, or by pressing U on the keyboard. In version 4, the Shift-F1 key combination is a shortcut version of the Undo command.

The Undo command reverses the last editing act and restores the document to the way it was before the last editing command was executed. For example, you might delete something to the scrap with the intention of moving it to another part of the document; however, you might then forget and delete something else into the scrap before inserting the material you wanted to move. Using Undo can omit the second delete command and insert your lost text back into the scrap.

Remember to use the Undelete command: <Esc> U(ndo) or Shift-F1. It will rescue you from your editing mistakes more than once.

THE GLOSSARY

The scrap holds only one block of text at a time; however, you can copy or delete many blocks of text to the **glossary**. Then, you can restore each block of text by simply typing a short descriptive name and pressing F3, the Expand Glossary Name key.

The Glossary is covered in detail in Chapter 21, "The Glossary and Macros."

THE OPTIONS COMMAND

The Options command on the main menu allows you to control the way Word presents itself. You can change elements of the screen display and other characteristics of the program. Word saves your choices in a file called WORD.INI, which is stored on your Word working disk or in your Word subdirectory on your hard disk. The program then uses these values for every Word session until you change them.

You can call up the Options screen by pressing Escape and then selecting O(ptions). The Options screen in version 3 resembles the following:

```
OPTIONS visible: (None)Partial Complete  printer display: Yes(No)  menu (Yes)No
     default tab width: 0.5"       measure:(In)Cm P10 P12 Pt           mute: Yes(No)
     date format:(MDY)DMY          time format:(12)24    decimal character:(.),
```

In version 4, the options screen contains a few more fields:

```
OPTIONS visible: None Partial Complete        printer display: Yes(No)
  menu: Yes(No)                menu color: 1   mute: Yes(No)
  display: Graphics(Text)   screen borders: Yes(No)   line numbers:(Yes)No
  date format:(MDY)DMY      time format:(12)24   decimal character:(.),
  default tab width: 0.5"   measure:(In)Cm P10 P12 Pt   linedraw character: ()
  summary sheet:(Yes)No     cursor speed: 0   speller: C:\WORD
```

You can use the Tab/Shift-Tab keys to move through the various choices. Tab moves you forward; Shift-Tab moves you backwards. In version 4, you can also use the arrow keys.

Options Menu Choices

Each of the choices on the Options menu is described in the following sections. Options features that are new with version 4 of Word are marked with an asterisk (*).

Visible

The *visible* option controls which special characters are displayed on your screen. If you choose None, then no special characters will be displayed. If you choose Partial, then paragraph ends are indicated by the paragraph symbol; new lines started with the newline command are displayed as down arrows, and optional hyphens are displayed as hyphens. Choosing Complete adds spaces (shown as dots at midline height), Tab characters (shown as right arrows), and hidden text (shown as a double-headed arrow).

Each of these characters is important for a different reason, and there may be times when you will want them visible on the screen.

You insert a **paragraph symbol** into your document by pressing the Return key. The paragraph symbol not only marks the end of a paragraph but also contains the formatting information for that paragraph. If you delete the paragraph symbol at the end of a paragraph, the paragraph joins with the following paragraph and assumes the same formatting.

Newline characters start a new line without starting a new paragraph. You put a newline character in your document by holding down the Shift key and pressing the Return key. A newline character does not contain paragraph formatting information; it only starts a new line.

Optional hyphens are hyphens that only appear when a word is broken at the end of a line. For example, "upright" is not normally a hyphenated word, but if it appeared at the end of a line, you might want to hyphenate it. You enter optional hyphens by holding down the Control key and simultaneously pressing the hyphen key or by using the L(ibrary) H(yphenate) command from the main menu.

You enter a **space character** in your document each time you press the Space Bar. To Word, a space is a character just like the letter a, b, or c. In fact, it is the most frequently used character in a document. You will want to see the space character when you need to know whether what appears as blank space on the screen is actually made up of space characters, tabs, or built-in paragraph formatting. Text being held in the scrap always has the spaces and tabs showing.

Tab characters are what you enter into your document each time you press the Tab key. Like the space character, the tab character normally shows on screen as blank space, usually several spaces wide. But the tab character is a single character. Its effect is to move the next text entered to the next tab stop on the screen.

You enter **hidden text** into your document by using the F(ormat) C(haracter) command to set the attribute of that text to hidden, as you will see in detail in Chapter 13, "Direct Formatting." You can use this option to leave nonprinting notes in your text or for letting Word know that certain text should be part of a table of contents or index.

Printer Display

When *printer display* is set to Yes, Word formats the screen to show exactly which characters will be on which line. Just how your screen will look depends on the printer you are using and the fonts you have selected for your text.

In version 4, Alt-F7 is a shortcut for toggling the printer display on and off.

For example, if you were working on a document, Word would normally show 60 characters on each line on the screen. But if you were using a laser printer with proportional spacing to print the document, you could fit a lot more than 60 characters on each line. When you set the Printer Display mode to Yes, Word will rearrange the text on your screen to show you exactly where each line would end on the page. With some fonts, the lines extend right off the screen to the right, but that is no problem. If you want to see them, just scroll to the right using the Right Arrow key, the F8 key, or the End key.

Menu

When the *menu* field is set to No, Word clears the menu and the message line from the command area at the bottom of the screen, leaving only the status line. This action gives you another three lines in the text area. To restore the menu, press Escape or click either mouse button with the pointer on the bottom borderline (version 3) or on the status line (version 4).

Menu Color*

If you have a color monitor, Word will let you display the menu in a color different from the rest of the screen color. Move the highlight to the *color* field, and then press F1 for a list of the colors available on your system. Move the highlight to the color you want, and then press Return to implement the choice.

Mute

Normally, Word beeps at you when you try to do something you are not supposed to do. If you don't want to be reminded, set the *mute* field to Yes.

Display*

Version 4 of Word allows you to switch back and forth between the faster text display and the slower but more complete graphics display. You can use the *display* field to set this feature, but it is much easier to use the Alt-F9 key combination to switch back and forth.

Screen Borders*

In version 4, Word allows you to clear the screen borders from the edit area. If you set the borders and the menu both to Off, Word will give you a full 24 lines in which to work. The only extraneous information left on the screen is the status line with the page and column number, the scrap, and the name of the file on which you are working.

When you open another window (see Chapter 7, "Drafting"), Word automatically restores the borders.

If you are learning Word after having worked with another word processing program, you may find this cleaner screen more familiar.

Line Numbers*

When you set the *line numbers* field to Yes, Word includes the line number along with the page and column number in the status line.

Date Format

Word allows you to easily and quickly insert the date into your documents using the glossary. All you need to do is type the word "date" and press the F3 key. Word will expand the word "date" into the current date (presuming you have properly set the system date on your computer). The Dateprint command also inserts dates into documents as they print. Both are explained in Chapter 18, "The Glossary and Macros."

The *date format* field controls the format of those dates. If set to MDY, the date will print in the format Month Day, Year, for example, July 11, 1988. If set to DMY the date prints as Day Month Year, for example, 11 July 1988.

Time Format

The glossary commands Time and Timeprint work like the Date and Dateprint commands. When this field is set to 12, the time is printed in 12-hour format (e.g., 1:13 PM). When set to 24, Word uses a military style 24-hour clock (e.g., 13:13).

Decimal Character

In some countries, notably Sweden, Norway, Finland, Denmark, Germany, and France, the comma is used as a decimal character in numbers. So, for example, what a North American would write as 98.6 degrees, people in some other countries might write as 98,6 degrees. You can set this field to use a comma as a decimal separator if you are working in or writing to those countries.

You only need to change the decimal character if you are using decimal tab stops, which are tab stops you use to align numbers in tables. If you just enter a number with a comma as decimal character in the middle of a sentence, you don't need to change the *decimal character* field.

If you set this field to make your decimal character the comma, there are several other places in Word that will be affected, specifically, commands that normally use commas to separate the elements of a list such as when you want to print only part of a document. Normally, you would tell Word that the pages you want are 1,5,7,11, meaning pages 1, 5, 7, and 11 but not 2-4, 6, 8-10, or anything past 11; however, if you have previously set the decimal character to a comma, you would need to list those pages as 1;5;7;11.

Default Tab Width

Word presumes that you want tab stops set every one-half inch across the page (and the screen); however, you can change this setting with the *default tab width* field. You can set the distance to any of the allowable measurements (see the next otion, "Measure").

Measure

Word will accept measurements in any of five measuring systems: inches, centimeters, 1/10-inch units (10 Pitch or P10), 1/12-inch units (12 pitch or P12), or points (1/72 inch units). When you enter measurements in any field that requires them, you can use any of the units. For example, when setting the default tab width, you could use any of the following measurements and all would equal the same value: 0.5", 1.27 cm, 5 p10, 6 p12, 36 pt. All are one-half inch; however, if you don't indicate which unit you are using, Word will presume it is the unit you have designated in the *measure* field. Word converts all displays of measurements to the current default measurement unit so you can always know which units to use.

When you use the Windows Option command, Word will allow you to display a ruler across the top of the screen. The ruler shows the position of tabs, margins, and other features. In version 4, if you have set the default measure to inches, centimeters, or P10, the ruler shows 10 marks to the inch. If you set the default measure to Points or P12, the ruler shows 12 units to an inch.

Line Draw Character*

In version 4, Word allows you to draw lines around, above, below, or beside paragraphs. The *line draw character* field lets you select the characters that are used to draw those boxes. Move the highlight to this menu choice and press F1 for a display of the characters you can use.

Summary Speed*

When you set this field to No, Word does not ask you for a summary sheet when you first save a document.

Cursor Speed*

Use this field to set the speed of Word's cursor. The best speed for you will depend on your computer. For example, you would set it to the slowest speed, 0, if you had an AT class computer. At the top speed, 9, the cursor would scroll right off the screen before you could get your finger off the arrow key; however, if you are running Word on a PC or XT class computer, you may want to set the cursor to a higher speed.

Speller*

The final Options field lets you store Word's speller on a drive/directory other than the drive/directory containing the Word program files. You can also use this field to specify a foreign language speller stored in another drive/directory.

CHARACTER FORMATTING

Word wouldn't be much good if it didn't let you format your text, and Word's formatting features allow you to do that job very well. In this section, you are going to look at Word's character formatting capabilities. In Chapter 10, "Direct Formatting," you will study these capabilities in greater detail, and in Chapter 12, "Formatting with Style Sheets," you will look at another way to format characters. But for those projects that you must finish right away, there are easier ways to make Word give you all kinds of fancy print effects such as *italics*, **bold print**, <u>underlining</u>, and more.

Format Character Command

One way to format characters is to use Word's Format Character command to select both character styles and fonts. Remember Word's select-act principle: you select text with the selection, then you act (execute a command). If the selection is one character long, the action affects that one character. If the selection is longer, the entire selection is affected. If it includes the entire document, then the action affects the entire document.

To display the Format Character fields, press Escape to move to the command area and then select the F(ormat) command. From the Format submenu, select C(haracter). The command area of your screen should resemble the following:

```
FORMAT CHARACTER: bold: Yes(No)   italic: Yes(No)      underline: Yes(No)
        strikethrough: Yes(No)   uppercase: Yes(No)  small caps: Yes(No)
        double underline: Yes(No)  position: (Normal)Superscript Subscript
        font name: Courier        font size: 12          hidden: Yes(No)
```

The main character formats are Yes/No choices. Pick any combination of them that you want; however, some combinations may not print on your printer; it depends on your printer's capabilities and the formats supported by the print driver you selected when installing Word in Chapter 1.

Fonts

The fonts available also depend on your print driver. Use the Tab key (or the arrow keys in version 4) to advance the highlight to the *font name* field, and then press F1 (or an arrow key in version 3) to see the names of the fonts available with your print driver. In version 4, you can use the Alt-F8 key combination to go directly from editing to the Font Name field.

You can learn more about the fonts available on your printer by looking in the *Microsoft Word Printer Information* manual that comes with the Word software. To select any of the fonts, move the highlight to that font and press the Tab key to advance to the *font size* field. Again, press F1 (or an arrow key in version 3) to display a list of the font sizes available for that font. Once you are familiar with the font names and font sizes available for your printer, you can enter their names directly into these fields.

Word automatically compensates for changes in font size when determining the number of characters it can fit on a line, when centering a line, or when performing other formatting functions both on screen or when printing.

Built-in Formats

An easier way to format characters is to use Word's 11 built-in character formats. As you type, you can call for one of these formats with a quick two- or three-keystroke command. For example, to assign *italic* type, hold down the Alt key (usually at the lower left corner of the keyboard) and simultaneously press the letter i. To cancel the italic command and return to regular text, simultaneously press the Alt key and the Space Bar.

You may add formats on top of formats. Word doesn't care. You can specify italics, double-underlined, bold, and small caps if you want. Then, press the Alt-Space Bar key combination, and all the special formats disappear.

If you are using a style sheet, using the built-in formats takes one extra keystroke. You press the Alt-x key combination and then the character for the format you want. For example, you would press Alt-x then i for *italic* and Alt-x then the Space Bar to switch back.

Following are the keystrokes for Word's built-in character formats:

Character Format	Press Alt and this Key (Alt-x and this key if using a style sheet)
Italic	i
Bold	b
Underline	u
Double	Underline d
Strikethrough	s
Small Caps	k
Superscript	+ or =
Subscript	- (hyphen)
Normal	Space Bar
Uppercase	no built-in format
Hidden	e

Don't forget, if you are using a style sheet (see Chapter 12), you need to press Alt-x and then the code key.

Style Sheets

You can control the format of characters in a paragraph using Word style sheets. For details, see Chapter 15, "Formatting with Style Sheets."

PARAGRAPH FORMATTING

Formatting paragraphs is similar to formatting characters. You can use the Format Paragraph command, or you can use Word's ten built-in paragraph formats.

Format Paragraph Command

The Format Paragraph command works like the Format Character command. It allows you to specify the characteristics of the paragraph containing the selection. You need not select the entire paragraph. If the selection includes all or part of two or more paragraphs, the format applies to all of them.

When you select the Format Paragraph command, the command area of the screen should resemble the following:

```
FORMAT PARAGRAPH alignment: (Left)Centered Right Justified
     left indent: 0"           first line: 0"         right indent: 0"
     line spacing: 1 li    space before: 0 li      space after: 0 li
     keep together:(Yes)No   keep follow: Yes(No)  side by side: Yes(No)
```

The following sections describe what each field does.

Alignment

In **left-aligned** paragraphs, the first letter of each line is flush with the left margin. This style is sometimes called "flush left" formatting. In a **centered** paragraph, each line is centered between the margins. A **right-aligned** paragraph is the opposite of a left-aligned paragraph; the last letter of each line is aligned with the right margin, and the left side is "ragged." In a **justified** paragraph (a paragraph in this book, for example), both the right and left ends of each line are flush with the margins.

Left Indent

Entering a value in the *left indent* field indents the body of the paragraph. The indent is measured from the left margin (set with the Format Division Margins command discussed later in this chapter). Use this field when you want a paragraph to be "set in," for example, a long quote.

First Line

The *first line indent* field determines the distance the first line of the paragraph is indented from the left margin. You can use a negative number in the *first line indent* field to produce a "hanging indent" effect where the first line of a paragraph extends farther to the left than the body of the text. For example, set the left indent to 0.5 inches; then set the first line indent to -0.5 inches to hang the first line at the left margin; the rest of the paragraph will then be indented 0.5".

Right Indent

Use a *right indent* when you want the right side of the paragraph to be indented from the right margin.

Line Spacing

You can specify the *line spacing* in lines as any of the five standard measures or as AUTO.

When you specify the line spacing in lines, Word uses six lines to an inch. Word presumes that if you enter a number in this field, you mean to specify the line spacing in lines. If you want to specify spacing in any of the standard measures, you must specifically include them. For example, all of these measures are equal to Word's standard line spacing of six lines per inch: .16", .42 cm, 1.7 p10, 2 p12, 12 pt.

AUTO sets the line spacing to the size of the largest typeface on that line. Be careful when using AUTO line spacing. The results may not look as you expected. For example, it often looks better to use a bit more line spacing than the font would at first call for. For example, a book set in 10 point type should have the line spacing set at 12 point. The extra two points of spacing makes the type much easier to read. Such extra space between lines is called **leading**. In the days before computerized typesetting, type was cast in lead. When you wanted to add extra space, you inserted thin lead spacers between the lines of type.

Space Before

The *space before* field sets the space that will be left clear before a paragraph. Typically, you would set the space before paragraphs to one line.

Space After

Space after is the opposite of space before. It sets the amount of clear space after a paragraph. The total space between paragraphs is the combination of the line spacing — the space *after* the first paragraph and the space *before* the second paragraph. As a rule, use only space before *or* space after but not both, and you won't see strange formats appearing seemingly out of nowhere.

Keep Together

Keep together set to Yes keeps the entire paragraph on the same page; if one line would print on a second page or in a second column, Word moves the entire paragraph.

Keep Follow

When you set *keep follow* to Yes, Word prints a paragraph on the same page or column with at least the first two lines of the next paragraph. You can use the *keep follow* attribute to keep tables together, to keep section headings on the same page as the paragraphs they head, or to keep the closing of a letter on a page with at least one paragraph of text.

Side by Side

Use *side by side* to print two (or more) paragraphs next to each other. This format is one method of printing in columns.

For side-by-side formatting to work, this field must be set to Yes in all paragraphs involved, and the left and right indents of those paragraphs must be adjusted so they don't overlap. Chapter 11, "Multicolumn Formats," covers side-by-side formatting in detail.

Built-in Formats

Just as Word has built-in character formats, it also has built-in paragraph formats. You use them much the same way you use the built-in character formats by pressing the Alt key and simultaneously pressing a code key. If you are using a style sheet, you press Alt-x and the code key.

As with character formats, you can select several paragraph formats at once, and as long as they are not mutually exclusive, they will all be implemented in that paragraph. For example, you can select double-spaced (Alt-2), justified (Alt-j), and hanging indent (Alt-t) all at the same time with no problems.

Because paragraph formatting is kept in the paragraph character at the end of each paragraph, each time you press Return, you will create a new paragraph with the same formatting as the one from which it is split.

Following are Word's built-in paragraph formats:

- **Justified.** In justified paragraphs, the lines end evenly at both the right and left margins. Use Alt-j for a justified paragraph.

- **Left Indent 1/2".** The Alt-n command indents the paragraph one-half inch each time you press that key combination.

- **Reduce Left Indent 1/2".** The Alt-m command is the opposite of Alt-n; it reduces the paragraph's indent by 1/2 inch each time you press that key combination.

- **First Line Indent.** Alt-f indents the first line one-half inch; however, pressing it several times will not increase the indent. 0.5" is all you can indent.

- **Flush Left.** Alt-l makes a paragraph left-aligned.

- **Hanging Indent.** In a paragraph with an hanging indent, the first line runs all the way to the left margin, but the subsequent lines are indented. The command Alt-t produces a hanging indent paragraph, and each time you press Alt-t, the lower lines of the paragraph will indent another 1/2 inch.

- **Flush Right.** Alt-r produces a paragraph that is flush right, ragged left.

- **Double-Space.** Alt-2 sets the spacing for the paragraph containing the selection to double-spacing.

- **Open Spacing.** An open space paragraph has the line before attribute set to 1 line. Use Alt-o to specify open spacing.

- **Standard Paragraph.** A standard paragraph is left-aligned. It sets *left indent, first line indent,* and *right indent* all to zero. The *line spacing* is single line while the *line before* and *line after* fields are both set to zero. *Keep together, keep follow,* and *side by side* are all set to No.

The following table lists the codes for the built-in paragraph formats:

Paragraph Format	Press Alt and this Key (Alt-x and this key if using a style sheet)
Italic	i
Justified	j
Left Indent 1/2"	n
Reduce Left Indent 1/2"	m
First Line Indent	f
Flush Left	l
Hanging Indent	t
Flush Right	r
Double Spaced	2
Open Spacing	o
Standard Paragraph	p
Centered (version 4 only)	c

Tabs

One of the important tools of paragraph formatting is the tab character. You enter a tab character into your document each time you press the Tab key, which is located in the upper left corner of your keyboard.

Tabs can be confusing because they are both document form and content. The tab character is a single character (content), but it appears on the screen or page as anything from one to an entire line of spaces (form).

The magic of tabs is that they can be used to keep columns neatly arranged on the screen and on the page because a tab "stop" is an absolute position measured from the left margin. It does not move when you change fonts or print spacing. If a tab stop is set at 1 inch from the left margin, text printed at that stop will be one inch from the left margin whether you are using 24 point Optima or 6 point Times Roman. The tab stop does not move.

Tab Alignment

Both version 3 and version 4 offer four varieties of horizontal tabs. When the alignment of a tab stop is left-aligned, text starts at the tab stop and reads to the right. But Word also allows you to use right-aligned tabs (where the text ends at the tab stop), centered tabs (where the text is centered on the tab stop), and decimal tabs, which you can use to line up columns of figures.

Following are examples of these four types of tabs.

- A left-aligned tab:

        10,000,000.0
        1,000.05
        100.125

- A right-aligned tab:

    10,000,000.0
       1,000.05
        100.125

- A center-aligned tab:

        10,000,000.0
         1,000.05
          100.125

- A decimal-aligned tab:

    10,000,000.0
       1,000.05
          100.125

Default Tab Width

Tabs in Word come preset every one-half inch. You learned earlier in this chapter that by using the *default tab width* field of the Options command, you could vary that setting. Just change the value in the *default tab width* field, and the placement of standard tabs will change. Tabs set this way are all left-aligned tabs.

Format Tab Command

For more sophisticated tab control, use the Format Tabs command. This command allows you to set specific tabs for a paragraph.

To use the Format Tabs command, press Escape then select F(ormat) from the main menu and T(abs) from the submenu. The command area of your screen should resemble the following:

```
FORMAT TABS: Set Clear Reset-All
```

Use Clear to clear an individual tab stop; you will be asked for the location of the stop. If you can't remember the tab's placement, turn on the ruler line at the top of the screen to see them. Use the Window Options command, and set the *ruler* field to Yes, or place the mouse pointer at the top right corner of the window and click the left mouse button.

Use Reset-All to clear tab stops you've set for that paragraph, and reinstitute the default tabs.

Use the Tabs Set option to set tab stops for the current paragraph. In version 3, when you choose Set, the command area of your screen should resemble the following:

```
FORMAT TABS SET: position:
     alignment:(Left)Center Right Decimal     leader char:(blank). - _
```

In version 4, there is an additional type of tab, a vertical tab:

```
FORMAT TABS SET: position:
 alignment:(Left)Center Right Decimal Vertical leader char:(blank). - _
```

Enter the position where you want the tab stop, as measured from the left margin. You can use any of the standard measures; if you don't specify a measurement, Word uses the default measure set with the Options command.

Press the Tab key to advance to the *alignment* field. Use the Space Bar to cycle through the choices or press the first letter of your choice.

Occasionally, you will want to vary the **leader character**. This field specifies which character, if any, you want Word to print between the last character printed on the line and the first character aligned with the tab. For example, to do a table of contents with the chapter titles on the left side of the page and the page numbers on the right, you would set a right-aligned tab at the right margin and specify a period as the leader character.

Vertical Tabs

When you set a vertical tab stop in a paragraph, Word draws a vertical line for the height of that paragraph at the distance you have specified. For more details, see the section "Drawing Lines" in Chapter 16, "Tables."

Setting and Clearing Tabs with a Mouse

You can use the mouse to set and clear tabs. To set tabs with the mouse, select the Format Tab Set command, make your alignment and leader choices, then point to the position on the ruler where you want the tab and press the left mouse button. To clear tabs with the mouse, select Format Tab Set, point to the tab marker on the ruler, and click both mouse buttons.

DIVISION FORMATTING

Besides character and paragraph formatting, Word also allows you to format **divisions.** A division is a block of text that shares the same page format: margins, columns, and other basic layout features. It ends with a **division mark,** which holds the division formatting (as a paragraph mark holds a paragraph's formatting). A division mark appears as a series of colons stretching across the screen. Like a paragraph mark, it is a single character even though it appears on the screen as a group of colons.

Format Division Command

You format a division using the F(ormat) D(ivision) command. In version 3, when you chose this command, you will be given three choices:

```
FORMAT DIVISION: Margins Page-Numbers Layout
```

Version 4 offers an additional choice:

```
FORMAT DIVISION: Margins Page-Numbers Layout line-Numbers
```

Format Division Margins

When you select F(ormat) D(ivision) M(argins), the command area of the screen should resemble the following:

```
FORMAT DIVISION MARGINS top: 1"   bottom: 1"   left: 1.25"  right: 1.25"
              page length: 11"   width: 8.5"   gutter margin: 0"
         running-head position from top: 0.5"   from bottom: 0.5"
```

Each field expects you to fill in a unit of measurement. If you don't specify units, Word presumes you mean the current default units (as set with the Options command). Acceptable units (and their abbreviations) are inches ("), centimeters (cm), 10-pitch units (p10), 12-pitch units (p12), points (pt), and lines (li).

Following are descriptions of each Margins field:

- *Top*: the top margin or the distance from the top of the sheet of paper to the first line of text on the page.

- *Bottom*: the bottom margin; not surprisingly, it is the distance from the bottom of the sheet of paper to the last line of text on the page.

- *Left*: the left margin or the distance from the left edge of the paper to the beginning of text. Don't confuse the left margin with left *indent,* which is measured from the left margin to the beginning of text in particular paragraphs. Also, remember that the left and right margins do *not* affect running headers; for a header to match the margins, it needs to have its indents set to the same value as the margins.

- *Right*: the right margin or the distance from the end of text to the right side of the paper.

  The area between the margins is sometimes called the **print column**. All text (except running headers) falls within the print column and between the top and bottom margins.

- *Page Length*: the length of the paper you are using.

- *Width*: the width of the paper you are using.

- *Gutter Margin*: When your document is going to be printed and bound, you want to specify a **gutter margin**, which is extra space added to the left side of odd-numbered (right side) pages and to the right side of even-numbered (left side) pages to allow for space used by the binding.

- *Running Head Position From Top*: the distance from the top of the page to the first line of the running header. Note the interaction between top margin and running head position. If you have a multi-line header, you could overlay your header on your text.

- *From Bottom*: the distance from the bottom of the page to a running header, or footer, set to appear at the bottom of the page.

Format Division Page-numbers

If you chose F(ormat) D(ivision) P(age-numbers), the command area of your screen should resemble the following:

```
FORMAT DIVISION PAGE-NUMBERS: Yes(No)  from top: 0.5"  from left: 7.25"
   numbering:(Continuous)Start     at:          number format:(1)I i A a
```

As usual, you advance to the various fields with the Tab key. You select between alternate choices with the Space Bar, or you fill in choices in command fields.

If you select Yes in the first field, the pages will be numbered in the position you indicate with *from top* and *from left*. These fields expect their entries to be in any of the measuring systems acceptable to Word. If you don't specify units, Word will presume you want to use the default units set with the Options command.

Continuous numbering starts the numbering at 1 if you are working from the first page in a document or continues the numbering scheme of the previous division if there is one. If you tell Word to Start numbering, it will use the number you specify in the field on the first page of the division. The number format sets the style of numbers Word will use. Choose "1" and word uses Arabic numerals (1, 2, 3). Choose "I" and Word will use uppercase Roman numerals (I, II, III); choose "i" and Word uses lowercase Roman numerals (i, ii, iii). Choose "A" if you want Word to number your pages with uppercase letters (A, B, C), and choose "a" to number them with lowercase letters (a, b, c).

Page Numbers in Headers and Footers

To insert a page number in a header or footer (a running head), type the word "page" and immediately press the F3 key. Page will become "(page)" on the screen but will print as the page number. If you want to put the word "page" in front of the page number, on your screen, it will resemble the following:

```
Page (page)
```

Usually, you do not want to include a page number command in a header *and* use the Format Division Page-Number command except to specify a new starting number for pages or to specify a different numbering character. Both of these choices will be reflected in (page) when it appears in a header.

Format Division Layout

The Format Division Layout command allows you to control the position of footnotes, the number of columns on a page, and when a new division starts. When you use the F(ormat) D(ivision) L(ayout) command, the command area of your screen should resemble the following:

```
FORMAT DIVISION LAYOUT footnotes:(Same-page)End
          number of columns: 1       space between columns: 0.5"
               division break:(Page)Continuous Column Even Odd
```

The *footnotes* field sets the location of footnotes (see Chapter 14, "Foot-notes"). If you choose Same-page, the footnotes will appear at the bottom of the page on which they are cited. If you choose End, the footnotes will all be bunched together at the end of the division.

The *number of columns* field is where you enter the number of newspaper-style columns you want on a page. You can specify up to five columns. In the *space between columns* field, fill in the space you want between the columns. In newspaper-style columns, text runs down the page to the end of the column then jumps to the top of the next column.

Word can also format side-by-side columns. Use the F(ormat) P(aragraph) command and set paragraph attributes to side by side. For details on using columns, see Chapter 11, "Multicolumn Formats."

The *division break* field tells Word where to start the new division format. The Page option tells Word to immediately start a new page and to use the new division format on that page. If you specify Continuous, Word will start the new formatting at the top of the next page, filling in the remainder of the current page with the old format; use this option if, for instance, the first page of the office newsletter has two columns but interior pages have three. For a continuous division break to work, you must set the *division break* field to Continuous for both divisions involved. Column is the command to start the new formatting immediately on a new page in the first column. If there is only one column in the format, it operates the same as Page. Use Even and Odd to start the new division on the next even- or odd-numbered page. Use Odd to, for example, ensure that a new chapter starts on a right-hand (odd-numbered) page.

Format Division Line-numbers

In Word version 4, there is a new format division command, Format Division line-Numbers. Its command fields resemble the following:

```
FORMAT DIVISION LINE-NUMBERS: Yes No            from text: 0"
         restart at:(Page)Division Continuous   increments: 0
```

When you turn this feature on, it numbers the lines on your page. Lawyers, in particular, like this feature. It allows them to quickly and easily direct a judge to the right place in a written submission.

To turn this feature on, set the first field to Yes. The *from text* field specifies how far to the left of the left margin the numbers will appear. Restart can be used to start the line numbering anew on each page, at the beginning of a new division, or to keep the same line numbering scheme going continuously, regardless of new divisions or pages.

SUMMARY

In this chapter, you have learned all the basics of Word. You have learned about the layout of Word's editing screen and the difference between the text area and command area. You have learned how to enter text, move it around, save it, and then reload it to work on it again. And, finally, you have learned how to format characters, paragraphs, and divisions.

In the next chapter, you will learn the basics of printing a document using Microsoft Word, and, with that skill under your belt, you will be able to do 90% of the word processing tasks that come your way.

But stopping here is like eating half the pie. The really good information comes in Part II of this book. So read on.

CHAPTER 4

PRINTING BASICS

Chapter 3 discusses how to use Microsoft Word to create documents and perform basic editing tasks. In this chapter, you will learn to print documents you create.

THE PRINT COMMAND

The key to Microsoft Word's printing power is the Print command on Word's main menu. The Print command leads to a submenu of eight choices:

```
PRINT: Printer Direct File Glossary Merge Options Queue Repaginate
```

Six of these options — Printer, Direct, File, Options, Queue, and Repaginate — are covered in this chapter. Discussion of the Print Glossary command is included in Chapter 18, "The Glossary and Macros." The Print Merge command is explained in Chapter 17, "Merge and Forms."

Print Printer

The Print Printer command instructs Word to begin printing the document in the currently selected window.

Remember, if you select a menu option with the right mouse button, both the selection on the screen and the default choice on the submenu are selected, so selecting the Print command with the right mouse button will also select Printer on the submenu and start the print job.

In version 4, you can also press Ctrl-F8 to start a print.

Print Direct

The Print Direct command allows you to directly send characters from the keyboard to the printer. Whether or not those characters print immediately depends on the printer in use. A daisy wheel printer works much like a typewriter; each character is printed as it is received. Most dot matrix printers, on the other hand, require a full line ending with the Return key before printing. Laser printers require an entire page ending with the Form Feed character before printing.

Cancel the Print Direct command by pressing the Escape key.

Print File

The Print File command will send formatted printer output to a file rather than to a printer. Formatted output includes all special commands to the printer.

When you chose Print File, Word displays the following:

```
PRINT FILE name:
```

Type the name of the file that is to receive the formatted output.

Use the Print File command to prepare a file that users without Word can print with full formatting on another printer.

You can also use Print File to prepare a file formatted with only carriage returns marking the end of lines. Such files can be sent over electronic mail services or used by most other word processors. There are three steps: first, choose the PLAIN.PRD driver with the Print Options command (discussed in the following section); second, set the top and bottom margins to 0 with the Format Division Layout command; third, choose Print File and name the file that is to receive the output.

Print Options

The Print Options command lets you set printing preferences.

When you select Print Options in version 3, the following choices are displayed:

```
PRINT OPTIONS printer: MT910
            draft: Yes(No)    queued: Yes(No)      copies:1
            Range:(All)Selection Pages     page numbers:
            feed: Manual(Continuous)Bin1 Bin2 Bin3 Mixed
            widow/orphan control:(Yes)No          setup: LPT1:
```

Version 4 includes two additional choices, and the menu has been reorganized:

```
PRINT OPTIONS printer: MT910                setup: LPT1:
      copies: 1                             draft: Yes(No)
      hidden text: Yes(No)                  summary sheet: Yes(No)
      range: All Selection(Pages)          page numbers:
      widow/orphan control:(Yes)No         queued: Yes(No)
      feed: Manual(Continuous)Bin1 Bin2 Bin3 Mixed
```

Word version 3 stores five of these fields — *printer, draft, feed, widow/orphan control*, and *setup* — in the file MW.INI, and the program will reload the options for later Word sessions. Version 4 stores these five options and the setting of the *hidden text* field. Whenever you change one of these settings, the change is saved and remains in effect until you change it again. The other fields are reset to default values each time Word is started.

Following are descriptions of each of the choices on the Print Options menu.

Printer

Set the *printer* field to the name of your printer driver. If you used the SETUP program to install Word (see Chapter 1, "Installing Microsoft Word"), this field should already contain the name of the chosen printer driver. The example reads MT910, the name of a custom printer driver developed for a Mannesmann-Tally MT910 laser printer. (For information on writing your own printer drivers or modifying existing printer drivers, see Chapter 23, "MAKEPRD and How To Use It.")

If no driver exists for your printer and you are not sure which printer your printer emulates, try one of the four TTY printer drivers. TTY.PRD is a no-frills printer driver that works with almost any printer, and it usually provides boldfacing and underlining. If you can't obtain underlining, try TTYBS.PRD. TTYWHEEL.PRD is designed for daisy wheel printers, and TTYFF.PRD is for printers with cut-sheet feeders.

Setup

The *setup* field is used to inform Word which output port is connected to the printer. Valid answers are LPT1:, LPT2:, LPT3:, COM1:, and COM2:. You must include the colon, although your responses need not be in uppercase letters.

LPT1:, LPT2:, and LPT3: are parallel printer ports. Most printers use LPT1:.

COM1: and COM2: are serial ports. If you are using COM1: or COM2:, you must use the DOS MODE command to configure the serial port. (See Chapter 22, "Word and Printers," for an explanation of parallel and serial interfaces and how to determine which interface to use.)

If you have more than one printer connected to your computer (for example, a high-speed, dot matrix machine connected to LPT1: and a slower, daisy wheel printer connected to COM1:, simply change the *printer* field and *setup* field to switch printers.

Copies

If you want more than one copy of a document, enter the number of copies in this field. Word prints a complete copy of the document and then starts over, eliminating the need for collating.

Draft

If you set the *draft* field to Yes, Word prints the document without some requested special effects, but it also prints it more quickly. For example, if you use a dot matrix printer, such as an Epson or a Roland, Word drops microspace justification, a method of justifying a line by inserting many small spaces between the words. If you use a daisy wheel printer, such as a Diablo or Qume, Word drops the font changes. Draft mode eliminates these special effects, but it does display the correct line and page breaks.

Hidden Text

Text is hidden with the built-in, Alt-E formatting command (see Chapter 3, "Editing Basics") or by selecting *hidden* in the Format Character command.

Hidden text printing varies in versions 3 and 4; as a result, the Hidden Text field appears only in the Print Options menu of version 4.

In version 4, hidden text will print only if the *hidden text* field is set to Yes. Hidden text will only appear on the screen if the *show hidden text* field of the Window Options command is set to Yes. These two functions are completely independent. For example, hidden text can show on the screen but not print, and text can be hidden on the screen but still print. The setup depends on how you set the Window Options *show hidden text* and the Print Options *hidden text* fields.

In version 3, if hidden text is displayed on the screen, it prints; if it is not displayed, it does not print. It's that simple. The Window Options *show hidden text* field handles the entire procedure.

Summary Sheet

When the *summary sheet* field in Version 4 is set to Yes, Word also prints a copy of each document's summary sheet, which is useful in an office where several users share a single laser printer. Word includes a copy of the summary sheet with each document, indicating to which person each document belongs.

Range and Page Numbers

The *range* field allows you to print any part of a document. Selecting All prints the entire document; Selection prints only the highlighted portion of the document, and Page allows you to print selected pages. List the pages you want to print in the *page numbers* field. To print a range of pages, use a hyphen or colon to separate the first and last page numbers. To print non-contiguous pages, separate the page numbers with commas (or semicolons if you set the decimal character to comma with the Options command). You can mix ranges and individual pages. For example, 1, 3, 5-9,12 prints pages 1, 3, 5, 6, 7, 8, 9 and 12 (so does 1,3,5:9,12). If your document contains more than one division and repeats page numbers, specify the division containing the pages by including an uppercase D and the division number as follows: 1D1, 1D2, 2D5. This particular combination prints the first page of the first division, the first page of the second division, and the second page of the fifth division.

Widow/Orphan Control

When Widow/Orphan Control is set to Yes, Word adjusts the page breaks in a document to ensure that the last line (or lines) of a paragraph is not printed as the first line on a new page (widow) or that the first line of a paragraph is not printed as the last line of a page (orphan).

Queued

The *queued* field controls whether or not Word sends printer information directly to the printer (No) or sends it to a disk file to be parsed out to the printer as you continue to edit (Yes). When queuing, Word formats the document as if it were sending the appropriate electrical signals to the printer, but it instead stores those signals in a file on your disk. Because your computer computes much faster than you type, Word uses the time between your keystrokes to send the contents of that file to the printer. As a result, you can print and edit at the same time.

Whether or not you want queued printing depends on several factors. If you have a slow printer, such as a 15- or 20-character-per-second daisy wheel, you will probably want to queue printing as a matter of course; however, when using a laser printer, which can print even the longest documents in a few moments, it's not worth it.

Use the Print Queue command (see following section) to control the operation of the print queue.

Feed

Use the *feed* field to control paper flow in the printer. When Manual *feed control* is selected, Word stops at the end of each page so you can change paper if necessary. Continuous *feed control* works well with printers loaded with continuous-feed paper, with a single-bin, cut-sheet feeder, or with a laser printer using only one paper bin. Bin1, Bin2, and Bin3 all feed from the corresponding paper bins on printers with multiple-feed bins. Check your printer's documentation to determine the different bins (or experiment on your own). Use "Mixed" if you keep your letterhead in Bin1 and plain paper in Bin2; the Mixed option feeds the first page from Bin1 and the rest of the document from Bin2.

Print Queue

When you set *queued* to Yes on the Print Options menu, Word queues your printing jobs, printing them to disk and then sending them to the printer between keystrokes. As a result, you can print and edit at the same time.

If you decide to use the print queue, this command lets you control it. When you choose Print Queue from Print's main menu, you are offered the following four choices:

```
PRINT QUEUE: Continue Pause Restart Stop
```

Select Continue to resume printing that has been paused with the Pause command. Restart will restart printing a document from the top; use this command if you've had a paper jam or other printer malfunction. Stop halts any printing in progress and erases the temporary file Word creates for print spooling. It may take a while for printing to stop if your printer stores a large number of characters.

Also, if you place more than one document into the print queue, you must use the Continue command to print the second document after the first is finished.

Print Repaginate

The Print Repaginate command can provide a better idea of how your Word document is going to look on the page. Unlike some other word processors, Word does not keep track of the breaks between pages until you print a document or use the Print Repaginate command.

When you instruct Word to repaginate, it computes all page breaks, taking into account changes in page formatting, varying font sizes, and all factors that can influence where one page ends and another begins. When this computation is done, Word marks the page breaks on the screen. In version 3, Word marks page breaks with a double arrowhead in the scroll bar on the left side of the screen. In version 4, page breaks appear as a single line of dots across the screen.

Of special interest to writers is the Repaginate command's ability to count the number of lines in your document and, in version 4, the number of words. Even if you are using version 3, you can work out a formula that will calculate a close estimate of the number of words from the number of lines.

If you select this command, there is only one option:

PRINT REPAGINATE: confirm page breaks: Yes(No)

If you instruct Word to confirm the page breaks, it will switch to printer display (and show you which characters are on which lines), stop at each proposed page break, and display the following prompt:

Enter Y to confirm or use direction keys

Press Y to proceed to the next break, or use the Up Arrow key to move up the page break. You cannot move the break down; the bottom margin would then be too small. Once you find the spot you want, press Y. Word will insert a hard page break.

When confirming page breaks while repaginating, Word also stops at each hard page break and displays the following:

Enter Y to confirm or R to remove

If you press R, Word removes the hard page break, recomputes the length of the page, and allows you to confirm the new page break. To insert a hard page break into your document while writing, press Ctrl-Shift-Return.

In version 4, Ctrl-F9 will start repagination with *confirm page breaks* set to Yes.

At any time during repagination, you can press Escape to cancel the operation.

The best method for assigning pages is to carefully think out your documents and perform pagination as you progress. If you use the *keep together* and *keep follow* fields of the Format Paragraph command and turn on *widow/orphan control*, you will rarely encounter wandering page breaks. Use hard page breaks only at the beginning of chapters or other breaks that require a new page; if you scatter them through your document, they will cause difficulties as you make changes.

Printing from the Document Retrieval Screen

Word version 4 also allows you to start printing from the Document Retrieval screen. See Chapter 21, "Document Retrieval."

SUMMARY

This chapter covers how to print Word documents using the Print Printer command, how to control printing using the Print Options and Print Queue commands, and how to preview and control page breaks using the Print Repaginate command.

This chapter and Chapter 3, "Editing Basics," cover the essentials of Word. The information in these two chapters could lead to many happy years of word processing but only to half of the benefits Word can provide. As previously mentioned, the next section of this book will help you use Word to actually become a better writer.

PART II

CONTENT-USING WORD AS A WRITING AID

In Part II of this book, you will examine the three-step writing analysis, which has come to be called the **process approach** to writing because it concentrates on the process, not the product, of writing. Chapter 5 provides a general overview of the process approach, and the remaining chapters in Part II provide greater detail. In Chapter 6, "Invention with Word's Integrated Outliner," you will learn to use Word's outlining function to help the creative process. In Chapter 7, drafting will be discussed as you examine how Word can augment the actual writing of your documents and how you can use multiple windows to assist in drafting. Chapter 8, "Revision: Some General Writing Tips," outlines how to revise your document in a organized manner. And Chapter 9, "Word's Revision Tools," will cover using Word's outliner for structural revision, finding the proper word with Word's Thesaurus, and when and how to use Word's built-in Spell program to eliminate spelling errors.

All writing is creative. Even projects as prosaic as a memo or a corporate annual report require much creativity. By applying techniques learned in the next few chapters, you can augment your creativity and improve *everything* you write.

CHAPTER 5

THE PROCESS APPROACH TO WRITING

Twenty years ago, college English professors held up samples of "good" writing and urged students to "write like this."

Those classes were a joke. Students knew it, and the professors knew it. Fortunately, some cared enough to try to find a better way. Starting in the 1960s, lead by people such as Gordon Rohman at Michigan State, teachers began applying techniques of social science to writing. They abandoned the English professors' obsession with *what* writers write and began to carefully examine *how* writers write.

The results of this research can help you write more quickly, more easily, and more enjoyably. It can make the *content* of your writing worth reading.

THE PROBLEM

Canadian humorist Stephen Leacock summed up the difficulty with writing when he said, "Writing is easy. You just write it down as it occurs to you. Yes, writing is easy. It's the occurring that's hard."

Writing calls on two contradictory skills: it asks that you be creative and insists that you be critical. Only when both skills are exercised in balance — and in turn — can you write well. Too much "creativity" may result in ignored readers. Too much critical thinking, especially early in a project, and you may not be able to write at all, frozen into inaction by fear of producing something less than perfect.

THE SOLUTION

While identifying the problem, researchers found the solution. They discovered that no matter the type of writing, successful writers divide writing into separate tasks: being creative and then using critical analysis to hone the creation. Researchers also found that almost all good writers use a variation of the same three-stage process: invention, drafting, and revision.

THE CREATIVE PROCESS

In his book, *The Creative Process* (New American Library, 1952), Brewster Ghiselin found a common pattern of four stages. The first stage is a period of hard work during which you put your mind to a topic, gather information, and generally "dig in." The second stage is a time of apparent quiescence when you seem to do nothing, but it is also a time during which your subconscious is actively sorting through the material you have gathered. The third step is a moment of inspiration or creative recognition where it all comes together in a flash (such as when you wake in the middle of the night with the answer to a problem that has bothered you). The final stage in the creative process is another period of hard work during which the creative product finally takes an organized form — the process of "getting it all down."

Implications of the Creative Process

Ghiselin's analysis provides hints as to how writing time should be organized. First, unless you allow your subconscious mind time to work, you will never enjoy moments of creative inspiration before a writing project is due. It helps to start a project early enough to allow for such "incubation" time. Don't punish yourself by always working on deadline. Of course, if all you must do is put together a short letter, you needn't wait; it's not that critical of a job. For major reports and other longer writing tasks, however, allow adequate time to properly do the job.

A second hint is to prepare for those moments of inspiration. Carry a notebook in a pocket or purse. Then, when you do experience a flash of insight, *write it down*. If you don't, it will disappear within seconds.

Third, try to schedule your writing time. In particular, if your job involves much writing, try to set aside a time each day to do your writing. Your mind will learn that this is the time for creativity.

Fourth, if you can, try to spread larger writing projects over more than one session. You write better if you put your work away and have a chance to return to it later.

Following is an overview of each stage in the writing process.

INVENTION

Many writers begin a writing job by sitting down, plunging into a turgid opening, stumbling into a trite middle, and dragging on to a hackneyed ending.

Instead, you must take time — lots of time — to be creative, to invent. You must figure out exactly what it is you have to say. It is at this point that "writer's block" usually appears.

Invention is hard work. It is difficult because most writers have been taught to maintain control, that there are proper and improper ways of doing things, and that letting your creative side express itself is often considered most improper. If you want to be a better writer, however, you must learn to express your creativity.

During the invention period, you must make a deal with yourself. You must let your creative "writer" write and keep your critical "editor" quiet. Sometimes this takes a conscious bargain that must be restruck each time your editor starts to interfere. Tell the side of your mind that may be saying "What you are doing is crazy" that it will assume full control during the revision process; for now, however, it's time to allow a little craziness.

In Chapter 6, "Invention With Word's Integrated Outliner," you wll learn some basic invention techniques you can use regularly, but first consider an example of such a technique.

Freewriting

Next time you sit down to a writing project, promise yourself that nothing you produce in the first hour will count. You have permission to make mistakes.

Spend only a second thinking about what you will write about. Then start writing. Write everything that comes to your mind. If you prefer typing, use the keyboard. If you find typing slows you down, write by hand.

There is only one rule. You must keep writing for ten minutes; you may not pause, go back, or correct your spelling and grammar.

If you get off the topic, just keep writing. Don't worry. There is no way to improperly perform this exercise except to stop, slow down, or go back to fix something. In fact, if you are using the computer, turn off your monitor or cover it with a piece of paper so you can't see what you are writing and won't be tempted to make it "right."

If you can't think of anything to say, repeat the last word or write "I can't think of anything to say" over and over again. Thoughts will start again quickly enough.

After ten minutes, stop. Read what you have written. Remember, this exercise is not meant to produce finished or even relevant writing. If a line or idea in the document strikes you, use it as the starting point for ten more minutes of writing. Then, take another short pause to let things "settle down," and write for another ten minutes.

This process is called **freewriting**, and its chief proponent is Peter Elbow of New York State University at Stony Brook, author of *Writing With Power* (Los Angeles: J.P. Tarcher, Inc., 1983). Freewriting is an intentionally unstructured activity, designed to force you out of your critical mode and into your creative mode. With the simple goal of writing for ten minutes without pausing, the conscious side of the brain is caught up in the immediate task of continung while the subconscious side of the brain takes over the job of deciding what to write. You may be surprised at what comes out of your subconscious mind. Often, of course, it will be trivial, but other times, you will find startling insights.

You can learn more about freewriting and other invention techniques through the suggested reading list in Chapter 6.

How Much Invention is Enough?

As a rule, use about half the time set aside for a particular writing task for invention. Invention is the most important part of writing; drafting and revision are actually rather mechanical. Treasure and nourish your invention time, and the quality of your writing will substantially improve.

Invention is difficult because you must take emotional and intellectual chances. It's OK to make mistakes. No one will ever know. Your mother will still love you.

DRAFTING

If the invention process is where most writing time is spent, drafting is where the least time is spent. Many writers use as little as 10% of their time for the drafting process.

Lewis Carroll had some of the best advice on drafting in *Alice in Wonderland*. At a point where Alice is trying to tell the Red Queen what has happened, she finds herself confused. The Queen advises, "Start at the beginning, go through to the end, and then stop."

For our purposes, modify these instructions to read "Start at *a* beginning, go through to *an* end, and then stop."

Don't spend too much time on your lead or conclusion; just write to include everything you want in your letter, report, term paper, story, or article. Let momentum carry you. There will be time later to start reorganizing and cleaning up your work, but for now, your writing needn't be perfect (or even close).

Consider these three critical questions:

- What am I trying to accomplish with this writing?

- To whom am I speaking?

- Why am I writing this?

Defining purpose, audience, and occasion will help bring your work into focus.

REVISION

The final writing phase is revision — the stage where your critical editor is king (almost). To make revision work for you, you must keep a rein on your editor while organizing and controlling your revision.

For example, do you find yourself correcting grammar, spelling, and punctuation as soon as you start to edit? Don't immediately make these corrections; instead, divide your editing into six or seven separate "passes" through the work. On each pass, look at one particular aspect of your writing.

The first editing pass is for truth and accuracy. Did the governor really say his opponent has a face like a ferrett? Why correct the spelling of ferret (only one t) if you will eliminate the whole sentence anyway?

Take a second run through your piece to reorganize the document's "building blocks." Did you include the discussion of revision before the section on drafting? The second pass is the time to put the elements in the proper places. Again, don't worry about little things. Move entire sections, and don't fiddle with the placement of words. Structural revision is a task in which Word is particularly strong. In Chapter 9, you will learn to use the Outliner to move large blocks of text with just a few keystrokes.

On a third and more detailed examination of your writing, carefully examine paragraph structure. In later sections, you will learn techniques for analyzing your paragraphs and making them more dynamic and effective.

In the fourth revision, examine each sentence, making sure it accomplishes your objectives. This book will teach you to find the critical core of a sentence and keep it active and powerful.

The fifth revision is for checking diction and word usage. Have you used "less" when you really mean "fewer"? Is it "eldest" or "oldest"? This revision is where the built-in Thesaurus included in Word 3.1 and 4.0 (and optional in 3.0) can help you find the right word. Use of the Thesaurus will be covered in Chapter 9.

On the last pass through your writing, clean up spelling, punctuation, and grammar. Again, Word can help; you will learn how to use Word's Spell program in Chapter 9.

SUMMARY

This chapter introduces you to the **process approach** to writing — a system to make your writing more powerful and effective — which can improve the *content* of what you write. You have learned how the mind functions during creativity and how this affects time management. You have learned that writing can be divided into a three-stage process: first, you must *invent*, determining content, freeing your mind, and searching for those strange synaptic synergies that only you can produce. Then, you must *draft* to get the thoughts on paper. Finally, you *revise*, and only then can you allow the critical side of your mind to influence your decisions.

The next chapter discusses how Microsoft Word can help you with the first step of this process — invention.

CHAPTER 6

INVENTION WITH WORD'S INTEGRATED OUTLINER

THE TRADITIONAL HIGH SCHOOL OUTLINE

In high school, your teachers probably asked you on occasion to turn in an outline along with your writing assignment. Like most students, you probably wrote the outlines *after* you had finised writing the paper, not before.

One reason many students resist outlining so strongly is that many teachers try to make outlining what it should not be: structured.

Remember the way it went? The first heading had to have a Roman numeral I in front of it. Then the next heading had to have an uppercase A followed by an Arabic number 1 and so on. If you didn't have at least two subtopics, you weren't allowed to use subheadings.

In other words, the outline assignment was full of structure and rules. You could easily spend more time doing a "correct" outline than you did writing a paper.

LESS STRUCTURE IS BETTER

You need to forget all about traditionally structured outlines. From now on, an outline can have any structure you want. It is *your* writing tool. If you want to do it in green ink on mauve paper in a half-uncial hand, go ahead. It's yours. No one needs to tell you how to structure it.

To be truly useful, an outline should be a tool to loosen you from rules, not impose more of them. So relax. Use your outlines as means of brainstorming and restructuring. Think of outlines as opening your vision to marvelous, unimpeded views, not restricting you to a single, closed room.

WHAT IS A COMPUTER OUTLINER?

A computer outliner, like the one built into Word, is a modern tool to help you create. It lets you jot down ideas, reorganize them to find new ways of looking at your topic, and, eventually, put them into an order that you find useful.

Scientist and author Jacob Bronowski, in his book *The Common Sense of Science* (Harvard Book Press, 1953), was writing about the way science describes the world in an orderly way. At the same time, he unintentionally laid out the only rule of good invention and outlining. "Nothing in this purpose," he wrote, "implies that the order must be of one kind rather than another. The order is what we find to work, conveniently and instructively. It is not something we can stipulate; it is not something we can dogmatize about. It is what we find; it is what we find useful."

In other words, relax. You can't do anything wrong except not to try. Let your mind go, and you will become a better writer.

HOW TO USE WORD'S OUTLINER

This chapter discusses the basics of Word's Outliner and, after describing the fundamentals, gives you some ideas on how you can make it work for you.

A Different View of the Document

The first thing you should know is that Word offers two ways of viewing a document. One is called **document view** and the other **outline view**. Think of them as the front view and back view of the same document. Though each looks a bit different, it is still the same principle. It's as if you see a friend walking down the sidewalk ahead of you. Even though you may only see his back, you might still recognize him. And you also might, for the first time, notice that he walks with a slight stoop. Because you are seeing him from a new angle, you have gained a new insight. Seeing a document from a different "angle" can also help you realize new insights.

TUTORIAL

If you don't already have Word running on your computer, start it now. If you have Word running and something appears on your screen, save it (if you want to) and clear the window (<**Esc**> **T**ransfer **C**lear **W**indow). Now you should have just a blank screen with the selection on the end-of-file marker in the upper left corner.

As you did previously, clear some space for yourself ahead of the end-of-file marker by pressing the Return key a few times, and then press the Up Arrow key to move the selection back to the beginning of the file.

Now, type the following few lines:

This is a major heading.
This is a second-level heading.
This is another secondary heading.
This one is tertiary.
This one is a major heading again.

At this point, all five lines should be flush with the left margin.

Shift-F2 to Switch Views

To switch between the document view of your writing and the outline view, hold down the Shift key and simultaneously press the F2 key. When you press Shift-F2—do so now—the message at the lower left corner of your screen will change. Instead of telling you that the selection is on page 1, it will say "Text." This message is one hint that you are in Outline view.

Note also that the letter "T" has appeared next to each line at the left side of the screen. The "T" means that Word is in Outline view and is treating the marked paragraphs as text paragraphs and not headings; however, it is plain from the wording of those five lines that they should be headings. You must make them into headings.

Levels

Outlining is a way of organizing ideas in hierarchical arrangements. You group ideas together in related categories and then assign "levels" to ideas to show areas of generality; the most general statements have "higher levels."

At first, however, ideas don't have any structure, just as the five sentences you typed on the screen don't have any structure. You just jot ideas down as they occur to you. Eventually, though, you will want to assign those ideas levels.

Text and Headings

The key combination Alt-9 (hold down the Alt key and press the number 9 at the top of the keyboard) changes a text paragraph into a heading paragraph. The combination of Alt-P (for Paragraph) changes a heading paragraph back into a text paragraph. (If you are using a style sheet, type Alt-XP.)

Now try these commands. Move the selection to anywhere in the first sentence. Hold down the Alt key and press the number 9 at the same time (the number 9 in the upper row of keys; do *not* use the number 9 on the numeric keypad). Notice that the "T" in front of that first line disappears, and the message in the lower left corner of the screen changes from "Text" to "Level 1." This message indicates that the paragraph is no longer a text paragraph but is now a heading at the highest level.

Now press Alt-P. The letter "T" should reappear, and the word "Text" should replace "Level 1" on the message line. The paragraph is a text paragraph again.

Assigning Levels

To change the level of a heading, use Alt-9 and Alt-0. Alt-9 raises the level of a heading (e.g., from level 2 to level 1) while Alt-0 lowers it (e.g., from level 1 to level 2).

Now try those commands. Again, place the selection anywhere in the first line and press Alt-9 to change the selection from a text paragraph into a heading. Now move down to each of the following lines and do the same, which will make them all into Level 1 headings.

Move the selection back up to the second line, the one that reads "This is a second-level heading." Press Alt-0 (again using the zero in the top row of your keyboard, *not* the zero on the numeric keypad). The line moves four spaces to the right, and the message at the bottom of the screen changes from "Level 1" to "Level 2." You have just changed that heading to a second-level heading.

No Skipping Levels

Try pressing Alt-0 again. Word beeps at you, but nothing else happens. Word won't let you skip from a first-level heading to a third-level heading.

Move the selection down to the next line. Press Alt-0 to turn it into a second-level heading.

Move down another line and press Alt-0 twice to turn the line into the tertiary heading it claims to be. Try pressing Alt-0 again, and Word will beep again. It cannot make this heading into a fourth-level heading without a third-level heading above it.

Adding to the Outline

An outline wouldn't be of much use if you couldn't add to it as you had new ideas, and it is easy to add both new headings and text to your outline.

To add to your outline, move the selection to the location where you would like to make your addition. Press the Return key, which will initially create a new paragraph with the same attributes as the paragraph from which it has been split. If it is split from a text paragraph, the new paragraph will also be a text paragraph. If it is split from a heading, the new paragraph will be a heading at the same level.

Adding Headings

If you have created a text paragraph and want a heading paragraph, press Alt-9 to convert from a heading paragraph to a text paragraph. Then type your heading and use Alt-9 and Alt-0 to assign it to the appropriate level. If you have created a heading paragraph, just type the heading and use Alt-9 and Alt-0 to move it to its appropriate level.

For example, move the selection to the last line of your outline, the one that reads "This one is a major heading again." Move the selection to the end of the line by pressing End. Press the Return key to create a new paragraph that is a heading at the same level as its parent, in this case, level 1. Type "This is yet another secondary heading." Now press Alt-0 to move the heading down to the second level.

Add another heading. Press Return again, and type "But this one is the last major heading." Now press Alt-9 to move it up one level to make it truly a first-level heading.

By now, your screen should resemble the following:

```
This is a major heading.
     This is a second-level heading.
     This is another secondary heading.
          This one is tertiary.
This one is a major heading again.
     This is yet another secondary heading.
But this one is the last major heading.
```

Adding Text

To add text, position the selection where you want to make your addition and press Return. If you are splitting the new paragraph from an existing text paragraph, just enter your new paragraph. You don't have to do anything special; however, if you are splitting your new paragraph from an existing heading, it will initially be a heading at the same level as its parent. Press Alt-P to change it into a text paragraph (press Alt-XP if you are using a style sheet). The letter "T" will appear again in the left margin, and the paragraph will stretch from margin to margin (unless you format it differently using the Format Paragraph command.) Now add your text.

To practice, move the selection back to the top of your outline (Ctrl-Page Up). Now move it down to the second heading ("This is a second-level heading"), and press End to move to the end of that line. Now press Return to create a new paragraph.

Initially, this paragraph will be a heading at the same level as the one from which it was split, but press Alt-P and turn it into a text paragraph. Now type some text, perhaps the first few lines from the "Gettysburg Address." When you are finished, your screen should resemble the following:

```
        This is a major heading.
            This is a second-level heading.
T       Fourscore and seven years ago our fathers brought forth on this
        continent a new nation, conceived in liberty, and dedicated to the
        proposition that all men are created equal.
            This is another secondary heading.
                This one is tertiary.
        This one is a major heading again.
            This is yet another secondary heading.
        But this one is the last major heading.
```

Collapsing and Expanding

Now that you can jot down your ideas, assign heading levels to them, add new headings, and add text to your outline, consider one of the best features of outlining: its ability to let you step back and look at the big picture by collapsing the outline and then expanding it again to let you dig back into the details.

Collapsing and Expanding Text

First, you need to learn how to collapse text from the screen so that you can concentrate on the structure of your outline by looking only at the headings.

The keys you use to collapse and expand text are Shift and the + and - keys on your numerical keypad (*not* the + and - keys at the top of the keyboard). These keys are called the Gray + and Gray - keys because on most keyboards they are gray keys.

Move the selection to the heading just above the paragraph of text you added to your outline. Now hold down a Shift key and press the Gray - key. The text will disappear from the screen, and a small "t" will appear before the heading to let you know that Word has collapsed text beneath it.

Now press Shift-Gray +. The text will reappear.

Collapse the text again before you move on to the next section.

Collapsing and Expanding Headings

Collapsing and expanding headings is even easier than collapsing and expanding text. You just use the Gray + and Gray - keys by themselves.

Move the selection to the first heading in your outline. Press the Gray - key. The headings subordinate to the first heading will collapse into the heading, and a "+" will appear in the left margin to let you know that the heading has collapsed the headings beneath it.

Notice that only the headings subordinate to the heading containing the selection collapsed. To collapse the entire outline to just its major (Level 1) headings, first press Shift-F10 to select the entire document, and then press Gray -. This command will collapse all subordinate headings and leave only Level 1 headings on the screen. This strategy allows you to back up and see the overall structure of what you are writing.

With the outline collapsed to just the major headings but the entire document still selected, press the asterisk (*) on your numeric keypad (Gray *). It is usually on the same key as the PrtSc (Print Screen) function. This command will expand the entire outline, including all subordinate headings (but not text).

Now press Gray - to collapse the outline again. Press the Up Arrow. This command will move the selection to the first character of the outline. Press Gray +, which expands one level of headings under the heading containing the selection. Press Gray * and *all* the headings and subheadings under the heading containing the selection will expand.

In version 4, you can also expand the headings down to a certain level by pressing Ctrl and the number on the numeric keypad of the lowest level you want to see.

Following is a summary showing in outline view the action of each collapsing and expanding key.

Collapsing Keys:

<u>Normally</u>

Gray -	Collapses headings subordinate to heading containing selection.
Shift Gray -	Collapses text paragraphs subordinate to heading containing selection.

<u>When Entire Document is Selected (Shift-F10)</u>

Gray -	Collapses all subordinate headings, leaving only Level 1 headings.
Shift Gray -	Collapses all text paragraphs into their headings.

Expanding Keys:

<u>Normally</u>

Gray +	Expands one level of headings under the heading containing the selection.
Shift Gray +	Expands text (if any) under the heading containing the selection.
Gray *	Expands all headings subordinate to the heading containing the selection.
CTRL-n (on numeric keypad)	Expands all headings to level n.

<u>When Entire Document is Selected (Shift-F10)</u>

Gray +	Expands one level below the existing headings.
Shift Gray +	Expands text immediately subordinate to the headings currently displayed.
Gray *	Expands the entire outline, showing all headings at all levels but not text.

Outline Organize Mode

The Word Outliner has two modes. Until now, you have been working in Outline Edit mode (called Outline View in version 3). In this mode, you can move freely around the outline, editing as much as you would normally edit in Text mode. But there is another mode called Outline Organize mode (confusingly called Outline Edit in version 3). This mode allows you to quickly move entire sections of the outline so you can easily organize it.

Because of the confusion over names, version 4 nomenclature will be referred to in the following sections.

Shift-F5

When you first switch to the Outliner with the Shift-F2 key, you are in Outline Edit mode. You move in and out of Outline Organize mode by pressing Shift-F5. You can only switch to Outline Organize mode when you are already in Outline Edit mode. When you are in Outline Organize mode, the message in the lower left corner of the screen reads "ORGANIZE" ("OUTLINE" is displayed in version 3).

Minimum Selection of a Paragraph

In Outline Organize mode, the minimum size of the selection is a paragraph. Subordinate headings and text are part of a heading *if* they are collapsed; you can use Outline Organize mode to move large blocks of text and headings in just a few keystrokes.

So you can see how Outline Organize mode works, make sure that your outline is fully expanded. If necessary, select the entire document (Shift-F10), and then collapse all of it (Gray -) and re-expand it all (Gray *).

Now move the selection to the top of the outline (Ctrl-PgUp) and collapse the headings subordinate to the first heading (Gray -). At this point, your screen should resemble the following:

```
+    This is a major heading.
     This one is a major heading again.
        This is yet another secondary heading.
     But this one is the last major heading.
```

The " + " before the first heading indicates that it has subordinate headings collapsed beneath it.

Move the selection to the end of the last line of the outline, and press Return to create a new, blank heading; then move the selection back to any spot in the first line.

Press Shift-F5 to change from Outline Edit to Outline Organize mode. The message in the lower left corner of the screen should read "ORGANIZE" ("OUTLINE" in version 3). The selection will expand to cover the entire first heading. What you can't see is that the selection also includes all of the outline structure subordinate to that heading, including the two secondary headings, the text, and the tertiary heading.

Press the Del key to delete the heading to the scrap. Use the Right Arrow key to move the selection through the outline to the blank heading you created a moment ago. Press Ins to insert the first heading back into your document at the very end. Now, with the selection still on that heading, press Gray * to expand it again. You will see that you not only moved the heading, but you also moved everything under it.

The Outline Organize mode is a feature of Word's Outliner that is very useful as a revision tool. It is also discussed in Chapter 9, "Word's Revision Tools."

PRINTING FROM THE OUTLINER

If you print a file while Word is in Outline Edit or Outline Organize mode, what you will receive is the outline as it appears on the screen, not the entire document. Occasionally, it may be useful to run off a copy of the current state of your outline, particularly if it has become rather long, just so you can keep yourself apprised of the big picture. It is easier to see the entire outline on a few sheets of paper you can spread out next to each other on a desk top.

USING WORD'S OUTLINER FOR INVENTION

Now that you know the mechanics of using Word's Outliner, you can use it as an invention tool. Because the Outliner gives you new freedom to reorganize and rearrange your ideas, you are freed from any constraints. If you don't like the way you first arrange ideas on the screen, you can always change them around.

In fact, one of the most useful steps you can take *is* to change things around. By rearranging the order of categories, occasionally randomly, you can sometimes come up with new ways of viewing the issue or topic about which you are writing.

Brainstorming

One of the best and easiest invention techniques is **brainstorming**. Brainstorming is a way of thinking about your topic and then jotting down any idea that pops into your head. Remember, the key to useful invention is turning off your critical "editor" and letting your creative "writer" do the work. In brainstorming, that is the approach you must take. You cannot reject an idea just because it sounds dumb to you. Simply jot it down on a line by itself and move on.

Brainstorming Practice

For this exercise, you need a clear screen. To clear your screen, use the Transfer Clear Window command (<**Esc**> **T C W**), and a clear window will appear in which you can work.

Now develop a new outline about a real topic: Uses for Cats.

When you brainstorm, you want to work in Outline Edit, and you want each line to be a heading automatically so you don't have to go back to make each one into a heading with Alt-9. Press Return and the Up Arrow key to move the end-of-file marker out of your way. Then press Alt-9 to turn the first paragraph into a heading. Now, each paragraph you split from this one by pressing Return will also be a heading.

Now start brainstorming. Following is a sample list of quick ideas about uses for cats:

- digging in the flower boxes on the balcony
- Eating
- distracting you from your work
- punching tiny holes in your waterbed
- friend to kids
- none — cats are useless
- friend to strangers

continued...

...from previous page
- filling cat box with unmentionables
- keeping up the allergy levels
- taking up the covers on the bed particularly in winter
- Loving
- Petting
- littering the house with dead birds and mice
- keeping your lap warm in winter
- Keeping down the mouse population
- increasing your indebtedness to the vet
- shedding on your best suit
- sitting on your work
- watchcat

Randomly Sorting Your Outline

Logically, the next thing you should do with the outline is to switch to Outline Organize mode and start rearranging your ideas; however, remember that you are trying *not* to be logical and linear, but analogical and lateral in your thinking. Rather than trying to introduce some order to this outline, first introduce some disorder. Scramble the order of the entries and see if positioning completely unrelated ideas next to each other gives you any new insights.

Library Autosort Command

Word has a sorting function that sorts paragraphs into alphabetic or numeric order. Normally, Word performs its sorts starting with the first character in the paragraph, but you can also make Word sort on other characters that will result in different sequences for your ideas.

To use Word's sorting ability, select the Library command, which brings up a submenu of specialized programs. In version 3, that menu reads as follows:

```
LIBRARY: Autosort Hyphenate Index Number Run Spell Table
```

In version 4, the menu offers a few more choices:

```
LIBRARY:   Autosort Document-retrieval Hyphenate Index  Link Number Run Spell
           Table thEsaurus
```

The choice you want from the menu is A(utosort), which will call up the following set of fields:

```
LIBRARY AUTOSORT by:(Alphanumeric)Numeric sequence:(Ascending)Descending
            case: Yes(No)              column only: Yes(No)
```

If you pick an **Alphanumeric** sort, Word will sort your paragraphs based on both numbers and letters. Paragraphs beginning with punctuation will come first, followed by those beginning with numbers and finally those beginning with letters. In an alphanumeric sort, paragraphs beginning with numbers are sorted on the sequence of characters, not the value of the numbers, so a paragraph beginning with 100 would come before one that begins with 20 because 1 is smaller than 2.

In **Numeric** sort mode, Word only uses the digits 0 through 9 and certain punctuation characters associated with numbers (.-,%$ and parentheses). In this mode, Word pays attention to the numeric value of numbers, so 20 comes before 100 because 20 is smaller than 100.

In **Ascending** order, the paragraphs are arranged from 0 to 9 and from A to Z. In **Descending** order, the priorities are reversed.

If you tell Word to pay attention to the **case** of words, paragraphs that begin with uppercase letters (A,B,C) are all sorted together ahead of the paragraphs that begin with lowercase letters (a,b,c).

Finally, in the *column only* mode, Autosort will sort *only* the contents of a marked column, leaving everything on either side of the marked column intact.

A Standard Sort

First, you need to perform a standard sort based on the first characters in the paragraph.

Select the entire document (Shift-F10); then chose L(ibrary) A(utosort) and press Return, which will perform a standard Alphanumeric sort. The results should look like the following:

```
digging in the flower boxes on the balcony
distracting you from your work
Eating
filling cat box with unmentionables
friend to kids
friend to strangers
increasing your indebtedness to the vet
Keeping down the mouse population
keeping up the allergy levels
keeping your lap warm in winter
littering the house with dead birds and mice
Loving
none-cats are useless
Petting
punching tiny holes in your waterbed
shedding on your best suit
sitting on your work
taking up the covers on the bed particularly in winter
watchcat
```

To show you how a sort by case differs, repeat the search, but this time set the case field to Yes. If you have mixed the uppercase and lowercase letters at the beginning of the lines, as was done in the example list, the results should resemble the following:

```
Eating
Keeping down the mouse population
Loving
Petting
digging in the flower boxes on the balcony
distracting you from your work
filling cat box with unmentionables
friend to kids
friend to strangers
increasing your indebtedness to the vet
keeping up the allergy levels
```

continued...

...from previous page

```
keeping your lap warm in winter
littering the house with dead birds and mice
none-cats are useless
punching tiny holes in your waterbed
shedding on your best suit
sitting on your work
taking up the covers on the bed particularly in winter
watchcat
```

The difference in this list is the first four lines that begin with uppercase letters; when the case field is set to Yes, uppercase letters come first.

Sorting on a Column

Now use Word's ability to sort on a column so you can scramble the list of things you can do with a cat.

Move the selection to the letter "i" in the first item on the list, "Eating." Now press Shift-F6, which is the Column Selection mode. At the bottom of your screen, next to where it says "Microsoft Word," you should see the letters "CS," which tell you that you are in Column Select mode. Now use the arrow keys to move the selection, and it will expand as it moves. Select a column that is five characters wide all the way down your list.

Now, if you do a sort with *column only* set to No, Word will sort your list line by line and based on what is in the column, not by the first characters of the paragraph. The fact that it is a line-by-line sort means that paragraphs that are longer than one line on the screen will be scrambled, with each line moving to where the sort field positions it. In the example, since none of the paragraphs is longer than one line, the results will look like the following:

```
watchcat
punching tiny holes in your waterbed
shedding on your best suit
none-cats are useless
friend to kids
friend to strangers
digging in the flower boxes on the balcony
Eating
Loving
```

continued...

...from previous page

```
taking up the covers on the be
d particularly in winter
filling cat box with unmentionables
Keeping down the mouse population
keeping up the allergy levels
keeping your lap warm in winter
increasing your indebtedness to the vet
littering the house with dead birds and mice
Petting
sitting on your work
distracting you from your work
```

Note that "watchcat" has moved from the bottom of the list to the top. The sort started with the fourth letter, and the fourth letter in "watchcat" is a "c," which is near the beginning of the alphabet.

You can randomly reorder your ideas again by sorting on a column, starting with the fifth or sixth characters, each time generating a new list.

Be careful not to perform any sorts with the *column only* field set to Yes. This setting will sort the contents of the column but will leave the rest of each line unchanged.

What Do You Do with these Sorts?

Good question. You look at the various listings. You read them and see if the reordering of your ideas generates any more insights about your topic.

If such experimentation doesn't generate new ideas, fine. You have only spent a few minutes trying. No one can fault you for that. You can start structuring your outline now by switching to Outline Organize mode and moving the elements of your outline around into some kind of logical order.

But if, in the seeming *dis*order, your eye spots a particular *order* that you normally wouldn't see, then your writing will be richer as a result.

OTHER INVENTION TECHNIQUES

While Word's Outliner is a powerful invention tool, outlining is not the only invention technique you can use for writing. There is a panoply of them. Many are very unstructured; others have more organization. Choose those that work best for you.

Other invention techniques include freewriting and invisible writing, clustering, talking and writing, researching, heuristics (exploratory writing through question and answer techniques), and journal writing, to name a few. Following is a list of suggested books that cover a variety of invention techniques.

Suggested Reading

Benson, Herbert. *The Relaxation Response.* Morrow Publishers, 1975. Benson's book debunks the myth of mysticism surrounding meditation and makes it easy and accessible to everyone.

Coe, Richard. *Form and Substance: An Advanced Rhetoric.* New York: John Wiley and Son, 1981. A good introduction to the process approach to writing.

Elbow, Peter. *Writing With Power.* New York: Oxford University Press, 1981. Elbow, now at New York State University at Stony Brook, is one of the primary proponents of freewriting.

Lindemann, Erika. *A Rhetoric for Writing Teachers.* New York: Oxford University Press, 1982. Lindemann presents a good selection of heuristics in her chapter on prewriting techniques.

Rico, Gabrielle Luser. *Writing the Natural Way.* Los Angeles: J.P. Tarcher, Inc., 1983. Rico developed the "clustering" variation on brainstorming with which she has had great success with her students.

GOALS OF INVENTION

When you finish your invention period, you should be able to sum up your proposed document in four ways:

- Give it a title. It doesn't need to be flashy, just descriptive.

- Explicitly state your theme or major idea. Write it down.

- Explicitly state the purpose for which you are writing. Is it to inform your reader? To persuade him or her? Are you exploring a field with your writing, searching for insights yourself? Write this information down also.

- Finally, who is your audience? If necessary, refine your understanding of your audience: what do they want to know, and what do you want to tell them?

Now you are ready to draft your document.

CHAPTER 7

DRAFTING

The second stage of any writing project is **drafting**, the method by which you use the results of your invention to write the first draft of your document.

USING THE NUTSHELL

Remember that the last step in your invention process was to summarize the document in a nutshell: its title, its theme or major idea, the purpose for which you are writing, and the audience. Use that summary as a guide while you draft.

THE OLD ONE-TWO

You should note several points about drafting. First, you should have done a lot of work before ever putting pen to paper (or fingers to keyboard, as the case may be). About half of the time you set aside for a particular writing task should be spent on invention.

Second, you don't want to spend too much time on drafting. Only 10% of the time you have set aside for a particular writing project should go into drafting. Though that time limitation may sound difficult, you'll find it is easy to draft a document if you've done enough invention. You should have bits and pieces of your document lying around in the form of freewriting exercises, brainstorming ideas, and other fragments you previously jotted down. And, of course, if you developed an outline, your piece is organized: you should know what topics you want to discuss and may even have some notes written about those topics.

So begin drafting your document. Don't worry about getting just the right word yet. Also, don't be concerned at this stage if you decide you have listed the topics in the wrong order. Those are revision issues. At the most, make a note in your text so you'll be sure to remember to work on those areas at the appropriate stage of revision. *****Set notes to yourself off with a line of asterisks or some other character so you'll notice them when you go back through your draft during revision. *****

DRAFTING ASSISTANCE FROM WORD

When you are drafting, Word can help you. In particular, Word can assist you in moving quickly around your document, and it can show you the outline and the text on the screen at the same time.

There are two ways to move quickly around your document: using the Jump command and using the Outliner as a shortcut to where you want to go.

Moving Around Using the Jump Command

While you are drafting (or at any other time), you can jump to any page in your document using Word's Jump command.

Before you can jump to a page, your document must have pages; it must have been printed at least once, or you must use the Print Repaginate command.

When you select the J(ump) command, you will be offered two choices:

```
JUMP to: Page Footnote
```

Select Page by pressing Return, and then fill in the page number:

```
JUMP PAGE number: 1
```

Press Return again. Word will instantly "jump" the selection to the first character on that page.

In version 4 of Word, you can use the Alt-F5 key combination as a shortcut to the Jump Page command.

If you are revising a document, resist the urge to repaginate after printing a draft and then making some changes. That way, you will still be able to find your way around the document by the pages of your printout.

Moving Around Using the Outliner

An even easier way to move around your document is by using Word's built-in Outliner. For example, following is the outline for this chapter as the book was in progress. It is what the writer would see if he pressed Shift-F2 to switch from Document View, where he was working, to Outline View.

```
t    Chapter 7 ↓
     ↓
     Drafting ¶
t        Using the Nutshell¶
t        The Old One, Two¶
t        Drafting Assistance from Word¶
t            MOVING AROUND USING THE JUMP COMMAND¶
t            MOVING AROUND USING THE OUTLINER¶
+            USING WINDOWS¶
t                WINDOWS AND MICE¶
t                    Opening Windows with the Mouse¶
t                    Closing windows with the mouse¶
t                    Moving Windows with the Mouse¶
t                    Mouse Window Practice¶
t                WINDOWS AND THE KEYBOARD¶
t                    Opening Windows with the Keyboard¶
t                    Closing Windows with the Keyboard¶
t                    Moving Windows with the Keyboard ¶
t                    Zooming a Window¶

                                                          CHAP07.DOC
COMMAND: Copy Delete Format Gallery Help Insert Jump Library
         Options Print Quit Replace Search Transfer Undo Window
Edit document or press Esc to use menu
Level 2          {¶}              ?              Microsoft Word
```

Figure 7.1

Once you are in Outline View, you can move the selection anywhere in the outline. Then, when you change back to Document View, the selection will be on the heading you've selected in Outline mode.

For example, if you were writing this book, and you wanted to move to the very first section in this chapter, you would switch to Outline View, move the cursor to the line that says "Using The Nutshell," and then when you switched back to document view, the selection would be positioned at that heading. To move back to this section, you would switch back to Outline View, move the selection to the heading "Moving Around Using the Outliner," and switch out of Outline View; you would then be back at the head of this section.

As you can see, the more headings you include in your outline, the more you can control where the selection is positioned or moving to.

The Outliner is a particularly easy and convenient way to move around long documents.

USING WINDOWS

A third Word tool that is useful when drafting is the program's ability to simultaneously display up to eight document windows on the screen. All eight windows can show different views of the same document, or each can hold a different document.

For example, you can use Word windows to display the outline of a document in one window and the document itself in the other. That way, you can keep an eye on the big picture in the outline window while you take care of details in the document window. If both windows are displaying the same part of the document, when you make changes in one window, those changes show up simultaneously in the other window.

Another trick is to display notes from an interview or research in one window while you work up an outline or draft in the other window.

Switching Windows

To move between windows, press the F1 key, which will move the selection to the next window in numerical order.

Windows and the Mouse

Though Word windows are fairly straightforward, they are one aspect of Word that definitely benefits from a mouse. When you use a mouse, actions such as opening, closing, moving, and reshaping windows are as simple as clicking and pointing.

If you don't have a mouse, you can skip ahead to the section titled "Windows and the Keyboard." If you have a mouse, read the following sections.

Opening Windows with the Mouse

To open a window, position the mouse pointer on the top or right window border or on the ruler line at the top of the screen, and press either the left or right mouse button. To open a vertical window, position the mouse pointer on the top border or on the ruler line, and press either mouse button. To open a horizontal window, position the mouse pointer on the right window border, and press either mouse button.

When you open a window with the left mouse button, the new window contains the same document as the window from which it was split. When you open a window with the right mouse button, the new window is empty.

If you are running version 4 without a border or a ruler line, you cannot use the mouse to create a new window.

Closing Windows with the Mouse

To close a window using the mouse, position the mouse pointer on either the top or right window border, and press *both* mouse buttons.

Moving Windows with the Mouse

To move or resize a window with the mouse, position the pointer over the lower right corner of the window, hold down the left mouse button, move the mouse pointer to where you want the lower right corner to be, and release the mouse button.

Note that to make a window near the right side of the screen larger, you would make the window to its left smaller, since you can only control the location of the bottom and right borders of a window.

Mouse Window Practice

Now try each of the previously discussed functions. Move the mouse pointer to the top window border, and press the *left* mouse button. This action will open a vertical window containing the same document as the window from which it was split.

Now move the mouse pointer to the right border of your new window, and press the *right* mouse button. Word will open a third window in the lower right corner of the screen, but this window will be empty because you used the right mouse button to open a clear window.

Finally, move the mouse pointer to the right border of the large window on the left of the screen, and press the right mouse button to open up another clear window.

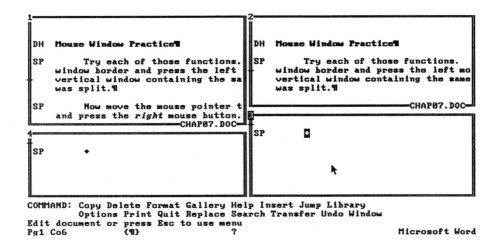

Figure 7.2

Next, you are going to close a window, but not in the same order as it was opened. You are going to close window number 1, which is the original window but is now just the top left corner of the screen.

Position the mouse pointer on the top border of window number one, and press both mouse buttons at the same time. The window will close; the window at the bottom left will expand and become window number 1. Word did not bother to remind you to save your file because the document in the window you just closed is the same as the document in window 2.

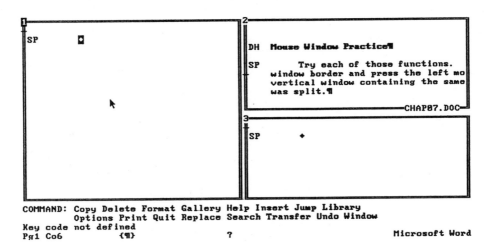

Figure 7.3

Now, move and resize the windows.

Move the pointer to the lower right corner of window 1, the large vertical window on the left of the screen. Press and hold down the left mouse button and *drag* the mouse across the screen. Release the mouse button when you've moved all the way to the left side of the screen. Window 1 will move to the extreme left side of the screen and be about five characters wide (which is the minimum window width).

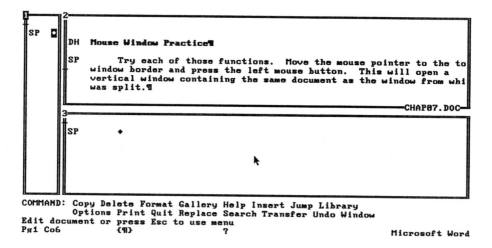

Figure 7.4

Next, move the mouse pointer to the lower right corner of the window that stretches across the bottom of the screen. Hold down the left mouse button and drag the mouse. Nothing will happen because you can't move the lower right corner of that window without shrinking the program screen.

Close the remaining windows with the mouse and leave only one window containing your document. Remember, to close a window with the mouse, position the mouse pointer on the top or right border and click both mouse buttons.

Windows and the Keyboard

Using Windows with keyboard control works just as well as windowing with the mouse. It just takes a few keystrokes; however, if you are a quick touch typist, you may well find the keyboard more convenient than working with the mouse.

When you select the Window command, you are given four choices:

```
WINDOW: Split Close Move Options
```

Opening Windows with the Keyboard

Use the Window Split command to open a new window. When you split off a window by entering a command from the keyboard, the window is automatically split from the window that contains the selection.

When you choose W(indow) S(plit), Word asks you whether you want a horizontal or vertical split, or whether you want to open a footnote window. Footnotes are covered in Chapter 17. For now, standard document windows will be addressed.

If you choose a horizontal window split, Word will ask for the row at which to perform the split.

```
SPLIT WINDOW HORIZONTAL at line: 13   clear new window: Yes(No)
```

The line at which Word suggests the window be split is the line above the current selection position. If that position is not satisfactory, you can specify any line you want for the split.

If you set the *clear new window* field to Yes, the new window will be empty. If you set it to No, the new window will contain the same document as the window from which it was split.

You create vertical windows almost identically. Select W(indow) S(plit) V(ertical), and you will receive the following message at the bottom of the screen:

```
WINDOW SPLIT VERTICAL at column: 24    clear new window: Yes(No)
```

All the options work just as they would for horizontal window splits.

Closing Windows with the Keyboard

To close a window with the keyboard, select W(indow) C(lose), and Word will ask you for the number of the window to close.

```
WINDOW CLOSE window number: 1
```

Enter the number of the window you want to close and press Return. If you have unsaved changes in that window, Word will offer you an opportunity to save them before closing the window.

Moving Windows with the Keyboard

Moving and resizing windows from the keyboard are also quite straightforward actions. You just specify to which window you want to move and give the new coordinates of the lower right corner. For example, the menu specifications might resemble the following:

```
WINDOW MOVE move lower right corner of window #: 1 to row: 20 column: 40
```

You only need to specify the number of the window and where you want the corner to be positioned. If you specify coordinates that would not leave enough room for an existing window, Word will move the window as far as it can in the direction you specify.

Zooming a Window

A new feature of Word version 4 is the ability to **zoom** a window so it takes over the entire screen. Press Ctrl-F1 to zoom the current window up or down. When one window is zoomed, the remaining windows are zoomed, and pressing F1 will cycle you through them, each window choice taking up the entire screen.

The Window Options Command

The W(indow) O(ptions) command allows you to control several window display parameters. The choices you make are stored on disk and stay in effect until you change them.

The Window Options command calls up the following fields:

```
WINDOW OPTIONS window number: 1  outline: Yes(No)  show hidden text: Yes(No)
               background color: 0  style bar: Yes(No)        ruler: Yes(No)
```

The parameters set with the above set of fields will affect only the window with the *window number* you designate.

Setting *outline* to Yes is the same as pressing Shift-F2. It switches to the outline view of the document in the window.

When the *show hidden text* parameter is set to Yes, hidden text is displayed on the screen. If you are running Word in a normal graphics mode, hidden text will appear on the screen with a dotted underline; in character mode, it appears with a solid underline or a different background color. In version 3, hidden text that shows on the screen also prints. In version 4, hidden text only prints when the *hidden text* field of the Printer Options command is set to Yes.

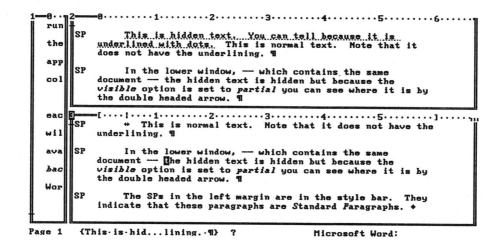

Figure 7.5

The *background color* field lets you separately adjust the color of each window. Depending on your hardware, you will have up to 64 choices. To see what colors are available on your system, advance the selection to the *background color* field, and press one of the arrow keys (in version 3) or F1 (in version 4). Word will display the colors.

When the *style bar* field is set to Yes, Word will clear a two-column space at the left of the screen for style sheet information. This feature is covered in detail in Chapter 12, "Formatting with Style Sheets."

Finally, the *ruler* field lets you change the top window border into a ruler that indicates the location of tabs and margins. You can also turn on the ruler by pointing to the upper right corner of the window with the mouse and clicking with the left mouse button. Pointing to the same spot and clicking with both mouse buttons will turn the ruler off. The ruler can be very useful, so you might want to leave it on.

Clearing an Existing Window

Use the T(ransfer) C(lear) W(indow) command to clear an existing window. If you have made changes to your document since it was last saved, you will be offered a final chance to save the file before the window is cleared.

Working with Windows

Once you become more familiar with windows, you will wonder how you lived without them. For example, if you suddenly have one of those moments of creative inspiration, but for a project other than the one on which you are working, you can quickly open another window, jot down your idea, and save it.

Or, as mentioned previously, you can put your notes for a project in one window and the text in the other. Or you can display the outline view in one window and the normal view in the other.

Windows and Macros

If you use a macro program like Prokey or Superkey, you will also want to develop a few macros for quick window manipulation. For example, you could have one macro set for Ctrl-1 that makes window number 1 as large as possible, another macro set for Ctrl-2 that makes window number 2 as large as possible, and yet another macro set for Ctrl-5 that splits the screen evenly between the two windows.

Once you work with Word's windowing power, you'll be hooked.

CHAPTER 8

REVISION—SOME GENERAL WRITING TIPS

Once you have written the initial draft of your document, you can let your editor out of its cage. **Revision** is the time when your critical side should take hold as you start rewriting, reshaping, reviewing, and generally polishing your document for your reader.

But rather than just haphazardly revising, you should try to revise systematically, going through your document several times, each time looking at a particular aspect of revision. The first time, you might check it over for truth and accuracy. Then, you might look at the overall structure of the piece. Follow up with a review of your paragraphs, and then check your sentences. For the fifth revision, you could check for diction to make sure you are using words correctly, and, finally, you should make one last pass through your document to correct punctuation, spelling, and grammar.

This chapter will cover how to make this kind of systematic revision work effectively to improve your writing. But Word can be of particular help with certain parts of revision, specifically structural revision, diction, and spelling. Chapter 9 will explain how to use the particular abilities of Word to assist in your revision.

THE OVERRIDING CONCERNS

When you are revising, you need to keep two goals firmly in mind: clarity and brevity.

Clarity comes first. Writing is an intimate art. You are attempting to take ideas from your head and implant them in your reader's head. For such a transfer to occur, your reader must be able to understand exactly what you are saying. You must be clear at all times.

Second, you must keep your document as short as possible. Your reader doesn't have time to waste reading unnecessary verbiage. Your job is to cut out the nonessentials. Almost any first draft can be cut in half during revision. Make that percentage your goal. Avoid making excuses as Abraham Lincoln is credited with doing when he wrote, "Please forgive me for writing such a long letter. I didn't have time to make it short."

Of the two, clarity is more important. If you have to choose between making it clear and making it short, make it clear.

All through your revision, remember those two principles: clarity and brevity. Anytime you make any change, ask yourself, "Does this change make my writing clearer or shorter?" If it does not, rethink the change.

REVISION #1—TRUTH AND ACCURACY

The first time you read through your document, concentrate on the truth and accuracy of what you are saying. The terms truth and accuracy do not share the same meaning. Something may be true—"He shot at me with a gun!"—but not really accurate—"Well, yes it was a BB gun." So read through your document, and for every statement of fact ask yourself, "Is this statement true?" "Can I prove it?" "What is my source?" Then also ask yourself, "Even if true, does this statement give an accurate and honest picture?"

Also, make sure that your document doesn't contradict itself. It is common, particularly in a long piece of writing, to catch yourself near the end making a statement that is the opposite of what you said at the beginning. Watch for such contradictions.

There are two times during the revision process when you could check for truth and accuracy: the first pass through your document or the last pass. If you do it last, you may discover that you have spent time polishing a paragraph that is wrong and must ultimately be cut. If you do it first, you may take time verifying facts that eventually get cut for space or aesthetic considerations. Either way, you take a chance. You might prefer to check for truth and accuracy first just to get that step out of the way.

Is a truth and accuracy check important? Consider the example of a prominent lawyer in a large firm who submits a letter in which he presents an offer to settle a lawsuit for wrongful dismissal. In the second paragraph the letter states, "Gross bimonthly pay in the amount of $1,750.00 less withholding tax at 27% which amounts to a net payment of $1,220.00." Suppose the recipient of the letter quickly grabs a calculator to check the numbers and finds that total is wrong: $1,750 minus 27% is $1,277.50. The lawyer in question had never noticed the mistake because he had not reread the letter for truth and accuracy. At the least, it could be an embarrassment; at the most, it could jeopardize some important settlement negotiations.

REVISION #2—STRUCTURE

The second time you read through your document, concentrate on its overall structure, its backbone. During this revision, you want to stand back from your writing and take the big view. Does this paragraph really belong at the beginning? This one at the end? Is this paragraph a nice one but ultimately a paragraph that really belongs in another document entirely? Those are the kinds of questions you should ask during structural revision.

You will find that Word's Outliner is a perfect tool for handling structural revision. Its ability to let you move outline headings around and carry all the attached text with them can make revision quick and painless. Details on how to use Word's Outliner for structural revision are covered in Chapter 9 (also see Chapter 6).

The Basic Structure

In reviewing your document's structure, go back to basics. Does your piece have a beginning, a middle, and an end? You would be surprised how often people write documents that don't. Just to make sure, identify those parts of your document and mark where one part ends and the next begins.

In the writing business, these three parts are called the **lead**, the **middle**, and the **close**.

The Lead

The lead is really a special kind of transition. Transitions, in general, let your reader know that there's been a change in person, place, time, or topic, and they help your reader make the intellectual transition from one situation to the next. The lead, as a transition, should help your reader make the adjustment from his or her reality into the document you have written.

Leads are a specialized art because the lead determines whether your reader will want to finish what you have written. If your lead is interesting and fulfills its function as a transition, it will encourage the reader to keep reading. If it is dull and provokes more questions than it answers, your reader won't continue.

Leads need not be fancy. They can be as simple as, "Thank you for your letter of last Tuesday in which you asked me if I could visit your office with my book of samples." What a lead *must* do is inform the reader of the people, the place, the time, and the topic about which you are writing, which is why "Thank you for your letter of last week," is not adequate as a lead. It forces your reader to return to his or her files to find the specific letter to which you are referring.

Four Types of Leads

Professional writers use various kinds of leads that you can adapt to your work. Examples are the **anecdote**, the **scene setter**, the **bullet**, and the **startling assertion**. These four types of leads are designed to make the reader want to continue reading, to seduce him or her into your document.

There are many types of leads, however. The only absolute about leads is that they entice the reader from where he or she is into your writing. Most of the time, a simple introduction is enough; you hardly need an anecdotal lead on a two-page letter. But whenever your document is long enough to possibly put the reader off, try using a little seduction.

The Anecdote

An anecdotal lead is just a short story that typifies the person about whom you are writing.

Consider the following example:

> When Rex the Wonder Horse was but a colt, his dam once called him to the stable. "Did you gnaw down this cherry tree?" she asked him. "Yes, dam. I cannot tell a lie. It was I who gnawed down that cherry tree."
>
> According to those who know him, this story is typical of Rex, even as a youngster.

An anecdotal lead usually reveals something about one of the people (or horses) you are writing about. Such a lead should show the reader an essential side to this subject's character. An anecdote is a versatile type of lead that can fit almost any kind of writing because it is just story-telling; however, when the topic of your document is a story or a person, the anecdotal lead can also be used in business correspondence and in reports as well.

The Scene Setter

A scene-setter lead, on the other hand, focuses not as much on the people in your writing as on the surroundings:

> In Fantasmagoria Stables, home of Rex the Wonder Horse, the morning sunlight dapples lightly on the hay in Rex's stall. As the 42-year-old veteran of more than 100 Hollywood oaters shakes his now gray mane, his trainer, Old Gabby, slaps his favorite mount on the rump, raising a cloud of dust. But, though the surroundings look comfortable, retirement for the horse that once earned $1 million a year is not easy.

A scene-setter lead is similar to an anecdotal lead in mood, but it is not a story. It provides your reader with information about who is there, but in addition to telling about those people, it also tells about their surroundings.

The Bullet

A bullet lead uses three specific examples to illustrate a general point. Consider the following bullet lead:

> Rex the Wonder Horse, now 42, has been denied Social Security benefits by the government.

> Tag, Buster Brown's dog who spent countless years lying under the stinky heels of millions of kids, has been cut off welfare.

> Cheetah, the chimp who saved Tarzan in dozens of jungle epics, is now living on skid row in Los Angeles.

These are not isolated examples but just three of the tragic cases of animal stars cast aside by society once their usefulness had expired.

Why does a bullet lead always use three examples? Not for any magical reason, just because three examples tend to have the most impact. Try using two or four examples, and you'll see the difference in effect.

The Assertion

The startling assertion lead is designed to surprise your reader so much that he or she will be curious enough to continue reading. For example, consider the following lead:

> *Grazing and Herding News* has learned that Rex the Wonder Horse, throughout his years in Hollywood, has been actively engaged in espionage on behalf of the French film industry. When confronted with the accusation, Rex replied, "Neigh!" and refused to say more without talking to a lawyer.
>
> But the Rex scandal is just a glimmer of what some equine experts suspect is a well-organized plot to undermine American values by degrading the quintessentially American film, the western.

The General Statement

Note that all four types of leads end with some kind of general statement. This sentence serves as a transition that tells the reader how the details of this particular lead apply to a larger picture. For example, in the first lead about Rex the Wonder Horse, the general statement tells how Rex's honesty was not confined to this one situation, saying something about his character. In the scene setter, the general statement tells that the story is going to be about hard times at Fantasmagoria Stables.

The general statement is critical. Without it, your reader will wonder how the lead relates to the rest of your document.

The Middle

When you revise the middle or main body of your document, look for logical sequence and small units. Logical sequence and small units are important because reading is like eating. Most people can actually eat quite a bit as long as they take small bites and chew their food thoroughly before swallowing. It's the same with reading. Most readers can understand some fairly difficult concepts as long as they receive them in small chunks and have time to think about each concept before moving on to the next one.

When reviewing the middle of your document, make sure you have included all the details. If you are arguing a specific point, make sure you have actually made your point and not presumed that your reader would agree. It is a greater sin to skip over details than to slow the pace of your writing down a bit to make sure everything necessary is on the page.

The Close

In the close of your document, you can reiterate your main points. If possible, have your close resonate with the opening: use an allusion, a reference, or a metaphor. Consider the following close:

> Life today for Rex the Wonder Horse may not be a bed of cherries, but at least he's getting back to those honest roots that made him America's favorite equine star.

Resonant closes give your reader a sense of completeness. The close of a piece of writing is a bit like the nice, solid clomp you like to hear when you slam a car door. If it sounds tinny and lightweight, you don't feel good about the car. A close that just leaves what you've written simply hanging in air effects your reader in the same way.

Table of Contents

While you are closely checking the structure of your document, decide if it needs a table of contents. For almost any document that is more than three of four pages long, you will want to include a quick list of what information is to come in the document and where that information can be found. While such a list is called a "table of contents" here, don't confuse it with the table of contents of a book.

This table of contents is part of the prose; it is not in true table format. For example, in this book, you will find a prose table of contents in the introduction under the heading "How this Book is Organized."

In a letter or short report, the table of contents could read as follows:

> In your letter, you raised several issues. I deal with the first one, whether or not my client is responsible for his actions, starting on the next page of this letter. The second issue, the appropriate penalty, is covered starting on page five.

While such brief foreshadowing may not seem crucial, your harried reader will thank you.

Signpost Turns: Transitions

While you are checking the structure of your document, make sure you are "signposting" the turns with transitions. As mentioned previously, the function of a transition is to let your reader know that you have changed mental directions. Whenever the players, the scene, the time, or the topic changes, you need a transition.

A transition can be as simple as "Meanwhile, back at the ranch . . . ," or as long as an entire chapter. Don't be too subtle, however. Billy Wilder, the director of such films as *The Apartment* and *Some Like It Hot*, once said, "It's alright to be subtle as long as you're obvious about it." You won't impress your reader with a subtle change in direction if the reader misses it. Don't be afraid to say, "That finishes my discussion of art in 18th century Bosnia. Now I turn to the same period in neighboring Montenegro."

Headings and Numbers

One type of transition tool — one that it is almost impossible to overuse — is the heading. Headings, like the one above this paragraph, serve both as transitions and as navigational aids to the reader later when he or she reads your document for a second (or third) time. Headings also make it easy to rearrange the structure of your document with Word's Outliner, as you'll see in Chapter 9.

Make your headings informative, and make them stand out from the text with bolding, capitalization, underlining, or a different typeface.

Reconsider the Audience

While you are reading through your document with an eye to structure, check whether you have paid enough attention to your audience. After spending all that invention time thinking about your audience, you don't want to discover that you've forgotten your audience in the drafting.

Read with two questions in mind: Have I addressed the concerns of my audience? Have I considered my audience? Again, those two questions are similar but different.

"Have I addressed the concerns of my audience?" could be restated, "Does my document answer my reader's questions?" Again, consider an example from the legal field. In a letter to a client, a lawyer will often detail his or her trip to the library and what the law says about the client's problem. What the lawyer often forgets to do is what a lawyer is usually paid to do: tell the client what he or she should do. The client is reading the letter for advice, not for the legal research. In this case, the lawyer doesn't deliver because he or she hasn't addressed the concerns of the intended audience.

Considering your audience is a bit different. Here, an appreciation of the person or persons who will be reading your document is important. Is your reader a formal person, someone who expects old fashioned courtesies rather than modern breeziness? If so, you'd better drop the line that says, "That's about it," and replace it with "I trust this meets your needs."

REVISION #3—PARAGRAPHS

On your third reading of your document, pay particular attention to your paragraphs. The paragraph is the basic unit of writing, yet many writers, even experienced ones, are unclear on just what a paragraph is and how it functions.

In English, you discuss ideas by moving from general concepts to more specific ones, much the way outlines are arranged. A paragraph, as the essential unit of thought in English, works the same way. It consists of a general statement, the **topic sentence**, followed by a group of ideas (sentences) all related to the general statement (theme). That much you probably already know.

Professor Francis Christensen, however, has developed a system for analyzing paragraphs. In Christensen's analysis, you label the most general statement in the paragraph, the topic sentence, with a 1. Ideas (sentences) that are one level of generality more specific you label 2. The next level down, ideas even more specific, you label 3, and so on.

When you "chart" a paragraph this way, you receive an instant picture of its structure. If you find charting a paragraph difficult, it is usually a good sign that there are big problems with the paragraph.

The following example details a **subordinate** paragraph structure. Each sentence in the paragraph is more specific than the sentence that comes before it.

1.   In English, you discuss ideas by moving from general concepts to more specific ones, much the way outlines are arranged.

    2.   A paragraph, as the essential unit of thought in English, works the same way.

        3.   It consists of a general statement, the **topic sentence**, followed by a group of ideas (sentences) all related to the general statement (theme).

            4.   That much you probably already know.

Note how each sentence relates to the topic sentence through the sentence that comes before it. Remove any sentence from the sequence, and the paragraph won't make as much sense.

Following is an example of the other main paragraph structure, a **coordinate** paragraph.

1.   Don't be too subtle, however.

     2.   Billy Wilder, the director of such films as *The Apartment* and *Some Like It Hot* once said, "It's alright to be subtle as long as you're obvious about it."

     2.   You won't impress your reader with a subtle change in direction if the reader misses it.

     2.   Don't be afraid to say, "That finishes my discussion of art in 18th century Bosnia. Now I turn to the same period in neighboring Montenegro."

Note that each of the sentences labeled "2" could directly follow the first; they could appear in almost any order, which is one mark of a coordinate structure.

Of course, life, and writing, is not that simple. Usually paragraphs have some kind of combined structure such as the following:

1.   Things work differently in Outline Organize mode.

     2.   The minimum selection is a paragraph.

          3.   If that paragraph is a heading, the selection includes all subordinate headings and text.

     2.   The arrow keys also work differently.

          3.   The Up and Down Arrow keys move to the next paragraph *at the same* level.

continued...

4.   If the selection is currently on a level 1 heading, the Up Arrow key will take you to the next level 1 heading up the document; the Down Arrow key will take you to the next level 1 heading down the document.

3.   The Left Arrow key will take you to the next paragraph up the outline, regardless of level, and the Right Arrow key will take you to the next paragraph down the visible outline.

You certainly don't need to analyze each of your paragraphs as they are examined here. Such examination would take much too long; however, when you are having trouble with a paragraph, perhaps wondering whether or not to start a new paragraph at a particular place, this method can help you.

REVISION #4—SENTENCES

For your fourth reading, carefully review your sentences. Watch for four main factors:

- First, make sure all your sentences are, in fact, sentences.

- Second, check that the central action of the sentence is expressed with a verb and not a noun.

- Third, make sure the verb is in the **active** voice.

- Finally, bring all the central elements of the sentence together in one place.

Is It a Sentence?

Remember the two crucial requirements of every sentence:

- Each sentence must have a subject and a verb.

- Each sentence should express *one* idea.

By making sure that each sentence includes at least a subject and a verb, you will avoid sentence fragments. A **sentence fragment** is a collection of words on the page that is punctuated like a sentence but which lacks one of the essential elements of a sentence.

Some sentences, the shortest sentences, seem to break the first rule and lack a subject. They are just one word long: Stop. Go. Read. All three of these sentences contain just a verb; however, each *does* have a subject, an implied "you," so they do follow the rule.

The second rule, making sure each sentence contains only one idea, will help you avoid the common problem of **run-on sentences**, which are sentences that seem to read on and on and on and on for pages. They are the mark of an inexperienced and undisciplined writer. They are also easy to spot. They have more than one idea in them; more specifically, they have more than one verb in them. Now, multiple verbs are not always bad. Many good sentences are **compound** or **complex** sentences, but if you spot more than one verb in your sentence, look it over carefully and ask whether it is legitimately compound or complex or whether it just seems to wander on too long. (By the way, the previous sentence is a perfect example of a compound/complex sentence; it contains six verbs, "are," "spot," "look," "ask," "is," and "seems," yet works just fine.)

Some computerized grammar checking programs automatically flag sentences over a certain length on the premise that these sentences are more likely to be run-on sentences.

Is the Central Action in a Verb?

The verb is the central action around which the rest of the sentence is built; it is the most critical word in any sentence. Yet often, you will see sentences where this central action has been turned into a noun, a *thing* word. Sentences where the central action is expressed in a noun are flat and lifeless. Turn the central action back into a verb, and you will make the sentence much more readable.

Following is an example of a sentence where the central action is in a noun: "We made a decision to have a discussion of the subject." This sentence actually contains two perfectly good verbs: "decide" and "discuss"; however, those verbs have been turned into nouns. Turn them back into verbs, and the sentence becomes more readable and, as a bonus, shorter: "We decided to discuss the subject."

The way to spot verbs that have been turned into nouns is to look for the *ion* ending on words. Later in this chapter, you will see how you can use Word's search ability to find *ion* endings. Then you can check those words to make sure you heven't needlessly turned a noun into a verb.

Is the Sentence in the Active Voice?

In the **active voice**, the action is conveyed from a doer, the **subject** of the sentence, through the verb to a goal, the **object** of the sentence. For example: "The boy hit the ball." In that sentence, the boy, the subject of the sentence, carries the action of hitting through to his goal, the ball, which is the object of the sentence.

Another way to write that sentence would be to use the **passive voice**: "The ball was hit by the boy." Note that the object of the action, "ball," has been turned into the grammatical subject of the sentence.

The passive voice has two hallmarks: a form of the verb *to be* attached to other verbs and the word *by*. Look at the example again. "The ball *was* hit *by* the boy."

You must watch for forms of *to be* when revising your document, but you can use Word's search function (see Chapter 9) to search for "by." When Word stops at the word "by," check the sentence carefully. If the sentence in the passive voice, see if you can convert it to the active voice.

Advantages of Active Voice

The best advantage of the active voice is that it is clearer. In an active sentence, you know exactly who is doing what. Passive sentences are impersonal and lack vigor. They can lead to fuzziness, wordiness, awkwardness, and even grammatical error.

For example, in a lease for a house, you might find a sentence that reads, "The pool shall be cleaned once a week." Who is to do the cleaning? Is it the responsibility of the tenant or the landlord? Or is that sentence merely a statement of fact; the neighbor does it as a good deed every Saturday? In that passive sentence, the person responsible for cleaning the pool is never made clear.

Certainly there are occasions where the passive voice is appropriate, but those occasions are rare. As a general rule, use the active voice.

Is the Core Together?

Finally, bring all of the central elements of the sentence, its core, together in one place. The core of the sentence contains those elements central to the understanding of the sentence: the subject, the verb, and the object. They should be right next to each other. The following sentence has its core elements spread all over the place:

> The boy, after swinging mightily as no one in Pawtucket County had ever swung before, hit, with such a force that it knocked off the cover, the ball.

Now, admittedly, that sentence is an extreme example but not as extreme as it may seem. Just listen to how it reads when you put the core elements together and position the extraneous information before and after the core.

> After swinging mightily as no one in Pawtucket County had ever swung before, the boy hit the ball with such a force that it knocked off the cover.

A clumsy, hard-to-understand sentence can easily be changed into one that is clear and easy to understand.

When you review your sentences, literally check each sentence against your short checklist. Is it a sentence? Is the central action a verb? Is it in active voice? Is the core together?

REVISION #5—DICTION

When you check for **diction**, you are checking your word choices—have you chosen just the right word to express a particular thought?

There is one basic rule for diction: if you have any doubt about the meaning of a word, then *look it up*.

Recall the previous example of the lawyer's letter offering to settle a wrongful dismissal claim for "Gross bimonthly pay in the amount of $1,750.00 less withholding tax at 27% which amounts to a net payment of $1,220.00." Not only do the numbers in that sentence fail to add up, but the author has also misused the word "bimonthly." Bimonthly means once every two months (bi = two). It is doubtful that the person in question made only $1,750 for two months work, particularly since this person was an executive. What the author of that letter probably meant was "semimonthly," which means twice a month (semi = half). And semimonthly is not the same as "biweekly," which means every two weeks.

The English language is extremely rich in vocabulary. Somewhere out there is the *one* word to exactly express the idea that is in your head. Don't give up until you find it. As Mark Twain once said, "The difference between the right word and the almost right word is the difference between lightning and lightning bug."

Simpler is Better

Whenever you have the choice between two words, a polysyllabic monster and a simple, one-syllable cretin, choose the cretin. Your writing should not be used as a forum to show off your expansive vocabulary. Stick to the simple, everyday words the majority of your readers will understand. If you feel you simply must use a big word, make absolutely certain that its meaning is plain from its context. *Do not* distract your readers by making them reach for the dictionary.

Other Diction Problems

In addition to selecting just the right word, review your document for three other diction problems: ambiguity, abstraction, and inappropriate use of foreign words.

Ambiguity

An ambiguous word is a word that can have more than one meaning. It is not the same as a vague word. Think of those terms in the following way. A vague word is like a fence around an intellectual ranch. It defines a group of ideas. An ambiguous word is really two fences around two ranches that may or may not be related. A vague word simply surrounds a very large ranch.

For example, the word "plane" is ambiguous. It can mean an airplane, a flat surface, a carpentry tool for smoothing boards, or a variety of sycamore tree. The meaning is only made clear by the context of the word.

The word "aircraft," on the other hand, is vague. It includes not only airplanes but also helicopters, sailplanes, gyrocopters, and manned balloons.

Vagueness is acceptable in some circumstances; ambiguity is never acceptable. You may choose to cast the wide net of a vague word if you want to encompass all the different ideas included in that word. But ambiguity is just inviting your reader to pick the wrong category and come to the wrong conclusion. If you say that you will sell someone your plane for $100, you are offering a good deal for an airplane but not so good a deal if you're really offering the block plane your father used in his garage workshop.

Abstractions vs. Concreteness

Sometimes writers take vagueness too far and move into **abstraction**. Most of the time you want to be as **concrete** in your language as possible because you are trying to take ideas from your mind and transfer them intact to your reader's mind; even when you are speaking in generalities, you are thinking in concrete terms.

For example, suppose you come across the sentence, "There is a woman in a red dress." As soon as you read that sentence, you probably pictured a woman wearing a red dress. Was it a red satin dress with a mini skirt and no sleeves? Suppose that description of the red dress is what the writer intended. By speaking in generalities, the writer failed to give you the complete picture, and you made up a red dress of your own.

So avoid expressions like "motor vehicle accident." Talk about a car accident or a truck accident or a motorcycle accident. Those accidents a reader can see. A motor vehicle accident? What is that? Better yet, tell your reader it was an accident involving a blue, 1965 Mustang convertible driven by a woman in a red satin dress with a miniskirt and no sleeves.

Science fiction writer Ray Bradbury summed it up well when he suggested that writers "assault the senses." Readers are sensual beings. Use your reader's senses to transfer the thoughts from your mind to your reader's mind.

Foreign Words

Another common mistake many writers make is to include bits and pieces of foreign languages. That strategy usually doesn't impress your reader. Quite frankly, most readers don't care that you may know Latin or French or even Albanian. If you are writing in English, stick with English. If you are writing in French, stick with French.

Every language, however, adopts words from other languages. For example, this evening you may be eating *crepes* on the *patio* before going to the *rodeo*. But before you use a foreign word or expression, make sure it has legitimately been asssimilated into the language.

The same general rule applies to colloquialisms. Even though most writers aren't formal writers, they can, on occasion, be too informal. Suppose you came across a sentence that read "Buying that carpentry plane for $100 is a rip-off." Certainly, "rip-off" is in common enough usage these days, but who knows how familiar the expression will be a year from now or a decade from now. Also, the expression may be familiar only in particular segments of the population. A perfectly acceptable substitute that can be understood by *all* readers, not just those who are or who have teen-agers, might read "Buying that carpentry plane for $100 is a bad deal."

REVISION #6—GRAMMAR, PUNCTUATION, AND SPELLING

One last revision you need to make is a final proofread for grammar, spelling, and punctuation errors.

While Word can help you with spelling and while there are other computer programs that claim to check your grammar and punctuation, there is no substitute for a careful, slow proofread. You can pass your document through every spell checker, grammar checker, and style checker yet invented, and it will still have mistakes in it. Look at these tools as assistants, not editors.

Since you undoubtedly spotted and marked many of these errors in your previous readings, now is the time to go back and fix them. And you still should read through your document again, word by word, looking for errors.

Style Guides

Grammar, punctuation, and spelling fall into the general category of **usage** or **style**. As with diction, there is one hard and fast rule here: if you have any doubt about word usage, punctuation, or spelling, *look it up.*

Literally dozens of reference works are available that can help you with grammar and usage questions. They are often called **style manuals**. Style manuals answer those pesky questions about word usage (when to use the word "less" and when to use "fewer," the difference between "flout" and "flaunt"), as well as punctuation issues (just when do you use a semicolon?) and even the spelling of tough words. If you are looking for a good style guide, pick up the *Chicago Manual of Style* (13th ed., University of Chicago Press, 1982). Also, the Associated Press and most major newspapers make their internal style guides available to the public for a price.

If you don't have a style guide, get one.

Grammar and Punctuation

The best way to learn grammar and punctuation is through practice and careful proofing; look up every questionable usage.

In general, the proper way to punctuate is by the paragraph and not by the sentence. Paragraphs are the basic unit of thought in English. You must punctuate your paragraph as a unit.

Consider the following paragraph from Jacob Bronowski's book, *The Common Sense of Science* (Harvard Book Press, 1953):

> This brings me to the third failing of eighteenth century science, which I find most interesting. A science which orders its thought too early is stifled. For example, the ideas of the Epicureans about atoms two thousand years ago were quite reasonable; but they did only harm to a physics which could not measure temperature and pressure and learn the simpler laws that relate them. Or again, the hope of the medieval alchemists that the elements might be changed was not as fanciful as we once thought. But it was merely damaging to a chemistry which did not yet understand the composition of water and common salt.

Can you spot what is wrong with the punctuation in that paragraph? Few people can, but if you start to dissect it with Christensen's paragraph analysis system, the problems become obvious.

1.   This brings me to the third failing of eighteenth century science, which I find most interesting.
    2.   A science which orders its thought too early is stifled.
        3.   For example, the ideas of the Epicureans about atoms two thousand years ago were quite reasonable; but
        they did only harm to a physics which could not measure temperature and pressure and learn the simpler laws that relate them.
        3.   Or again, the hope of the medieval alchemists that the elements might be changed was not as fanciful as we once thought.
            4.   But it was merely damaging to a chemistry which did not yet understand the composition of water and common salt.

Look at the two sentences at level 3. Both are examples and both are subject to exceptions introduced by "but"; however, in the first case, Bronowski punctuated with a semicolon and a subordinate clause. In the second case, he punctuated with a period and started a new sentence.

Either punctuation *on its own* is fine; however, they cannot coexist in the same paragraph. One has to change to match the other. He has constructed two *parallel* sentences, and parallel structures require parallel punctuation.

Grammar and Punctuation Programs

Bronowski's mistake is a perfect example of the kind of punctuation or spelling error that will fool a computer program every time. A contextual error such as parallelism is too subtle. In fact, few readers can spot it without help.

You must pursue that kind of excellence in writing, right down to the sometimes ridiculous details, if you want to be a good writer.

Can grammar and punctuation programs help? Certainly, if you use them as you do all computerized writing tools: as assistants, not crutches. Frankly, if you are at all good at writing, you will quickly grow tired of these programs. So, before you invest in a grammar and punctuation program, carefully check it out. When you visit your dealer, bring a disk that contains several typical pieces of your writing. Run those pieces through the program and see what it suggests. You might find it helps; you might find it is only cursory or tedious.

Spelling

Like grammar and punctuation, learning to spell correctly involves time spent looking words up in dictionaries. Keep your dictionary with you as you write. Having several dictionaries nearby is helpful when you're trying to find more obscure words and their meanings.

Remember also that you can have "blind spots" when it comes to spelling. There may be few dozen words you won't be able to spell correctly no matter how hard you try.

Word's Spell Checker

Word's Spell program can be helpful as an *assistant* in your battle to spell words correctly. The Spell program won't make you a better speller, but it can catch typographical errors and those words for which you have blind spots. Chapter 9 discusses Word's Spell program in detail as well as other revision tools available with Word.

CHAPTER 9

WORD'S REVISION TOOLS

When you start revising your document, Word can assist you in the process. It has several abilities that make revision faster and more efficient.

- The **Outliner** can help with structural revision by allowing you to easily and quickly move large blocks of text.

- The **Thesaurus** can help you find just the right word.

- The **Search and Replace** functions can help you easily find problem spots and fix them as fast as you find them.

- The **Spell** program can help you catch misspelled words.

- The **Wordfreq** program (version 3 only) can also help you catch misspellings as well as point out words you may be overusing.

- The **Lookup** and **Wordfind** programs (version 3 only) can also help you with spelling.

WORD'S OUTLINER AS A STRUCTURAL REVISION TOOL

One of the major tasks during structural revision is moving around large blocks of text. While you could certainly use Word's Extend Selection, Delete, Copy, and Insert functions to mark and move blocks of text, it is much easier to use Word's Outliner in the Outline Organize mode.

However, to use the Outliner to move around blocks of text, you must have used the Outliner to organize your document in the first place, or you must have enough headings within your document that can be turned into outline headings.

Turning Headings into Outline Headings

To turn a regular paragraph of text into an outline heading, first switch from document view to outline view. Then place the selection anywhere in the paragraph and press Alt-9. Now you can use Alt-9 and Alt-0 to adjust the level of the heading. To turn a heading into standard text, use Alt-P (Alt-XP if you are using a style sheet). See Chapter 6, "Invention with Word's Integrated Outliner" for details on the Outliner and Chapter 12, "Formatting with Style Sheets," for details on style sheets.

Moving Large Blocks Using the Outliner

When Word is in outline view (Shift-F2) and in Outline Organize mode (Shift-F5), you can easily move large blocks of text. In Outline Organize mode, the minimum size of the selection is a paragraph, and when a heading is selected, it includes *all subordinate headings and text.* So if you select a chapter heading and delete it, you will delete the entire chapter. Select a major section heading and copy it to the scrap, and you will copy the entire section to the scrap.

Tutorial

Enter the following text as it appears in the screen below:

```
──[·········1·········2·········3·········4·········5·········]·········7·····
    Chapter Number 1 — The Speckled Hare¶
    Watson arrives in Brighton¶
    In this section, Watson takes the train down from London and
    checks into his hotel across from the stony beach at
    Brighton.¶
    Watson stumbles across body.¶
    Out for his morning constitutional, Watson literally
    stumbles across a body... or at least a hand sticking up
    from beneath the stones. ¶
    Watson suspected¶
    Watson summons Holmes¶
    With the local police baffled, Watson cables up to London,
    asking his friend Holmes to rush to Brighton to help solve
    the mystery. ¶
    ¶
    ▫
                                                        ──OUTLINE.DOC──
COMMAND: Copy Delete Format Gallery Help Insert Jump Library
         Options Print Quit Replace Search Transfer Undo Window
Key code not defined
Pg1 Li16 Col    {w}              ?              ZM        Microsoft Word
```

Figure 9.1

Now, change some of the body text to headings. Press Shift-F2 to switch to outline view. A "T" should appear at the head of each paragraph. Use Alt-9 to change the chapter title and the four lines that begin with "Watson" into headings. Use Alt-9 and Alt-0 to set those headings' levels so that the chapter title is at the highest level and the first three "Watson" lines are at the next level. Make the last "Watson" line subordinate to "Watson suspected."

For example, to turn the first line into a heading, switch to outline view. The word "Text" should appear in the lower left corner of the screen, and there should be a "T" in front of each paragraph on the screen. Place the cursor anywhere on the first line. Press Alt-9, and the "T" at the beginning of the line should disappear; the line is no longer body text but an outline heading.

Move down to the next line. Press Alt-9 then Alt-0 to turn that line into a second-level heading.

Turn the other lines into headings on your own.

When you are finished, your screen should resemble the following:

```
2—[········1·········2·········3·········4·········5··········]·········7·····]
 |    Chapter Number 1 — The Speckled Hare¶
 |        Watson arrives in Brighton¶
 |T In this section, Watson takes the train down from London and
 |  checks into his hotel across from the stony beach at
 |  Brighton.¶
 |        Watson stumbles across body.¶
 |T Out for his morning constitutional, Watson literally
 |  stumbles across a body... or at least a hand sticking up
 |  from beneath the stones. ¶
 |        Watson suspected¶
 |          Watson summons Holmes¶
 |T With the local police baffled, Watson cables up to London,
 |  asking his friend Holmes to rush to Brighton to help solve
 |  the mystery. ¶
 |T ¶
 |   ◆
 |
 |                                                    —OUTLINE.DOC—
COMMAND: Copy Delete Format Gallery Help Insert Jump Library
         Options Print Quit Replace Search Transfer Undo Window
Edit document or press Esc to use menu
Level 3         {w}               ?              2M      Microsoft Word
```

Figure 9.2

Now press Shift-F10 to select the entire document, and then press Shift-Gray - to collapse all the text into the headings. Your screen should resemble the following:

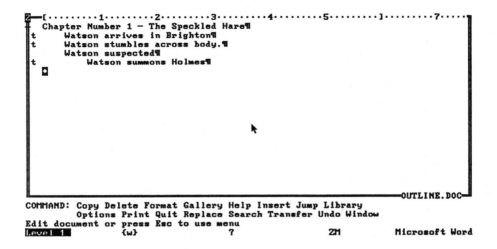

Figure 9.3

Try moving some of the text around with the Outline Organize mode. Switch to Outline Organize by pressing Shift-F5. The message in the lower left corner of the screen will read "ORGANIZE" (or "OUTLINE" in version 3).

Word works differently in Outline Organize mode. Remember that the minimum selection is a paragraph, and if that paragraph is a heading, the selection includes all subordinate headings and text. The arrow keys also work differently. The Up and Down arrow keys move to the next paragraph *at the same level.* If the selection is currently on a level 1 heading, the Up Arrow will take you to the next level one heading up the document; the Down Arrow will take you to the next level one heading down the document. The Left Arrow will take you to the next paragraph up the outline, regardless of level, and the Right Arrow will take you to the next paragraph down the outline.

Try these commands. Use both the Up-Down and Left-Right arrow keys to move around the outline until you get used to those keys.

Now you can revise. Move the selection to the paragraph "Watson suspected." Your screen should resemble the following:

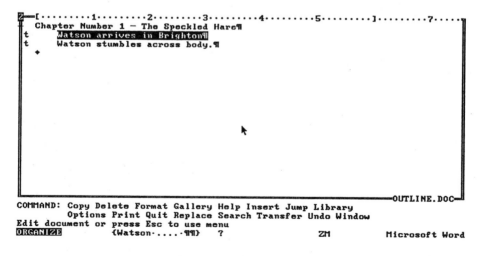

Figure 9.4

Press the Delete key (below the numeric keypad) to delete that heading to the scrap. Note that both the heading and the subheading have disappeared from the screen.

Use the arrow keys to move the selection to the paragraph "Watson Arrives in Brighton." Again, note that the selection encompasses the entire paragraph, but remember that any insert always occurs at the beginning of the selection.

```
2─[·········1·········2·········3·········4·········5·········]·········7·····
¦ Chapter Number 1 — The Speckled Hare¶
t   Watson arrives in Brighton¶
t   Watson stumbles across body.¶
    ◆



                                      ▸




                                                            ─OUTLINE.DOC─
COMMAND: Copy Delete Format Gallery Help Insert Jump Library
         Options Print Quit Replace Search Transfer Undo Window
Edit document or press Esc to use menu
ORGANIZE        {Watson·····¶¶}  ?              ZM        Microsoft Word
```

Figure 9.5

Press Insert (also below the numeric keypad) to insert the contents of the scrap into your document at the beginning of the selection.

```
■—[········1········2········3········4········5········]········7·····■
■  Chapter Number 1 — The Speckled Hare¶
┃      Watson suspected¶
t          Watson summons Holmes¶
t      Watson arrives in Brighton¶
t      Watson stumbles across body.¶
   ◆
                                                      OUTLINE.DOC
COMMAND: Copy Delete Format Gallery Help Insert Jump Library
         Options Print Quit Replace Search Transfer Undo Window
Edit document or press Esc to use menu
ORGANIZE          {Watson·····¶¶}    ?              ZM        Microsoft Word
```

Figure 9.6

Note that both the heading "Watson suspected" and the subheading "Watson summons Holmes" have moved.

Press Shift-F10 to select the entire document again, and then press Shift-Gray + to expand all the text in the document. You will see that you have not only moved the two headings, but you have also moved the text that goes with them.

```
Z━[·········1·········2·········3·········4·········5·········]·········7·····┓
  ┃  Chapter Number 1 — The Speckled Hare¶
  ┃     Watson suspected¶
  ┃        Watson summons Holmes¶
  T With the local police baffled, Watson cables up to London,
  ┃  asking his friend Holmes to rush to Brighton to help solve
  ┃  the mystery. ¶
  T ¶
  ┃        Watson arrives in Brighton¶
  T In this section, Watson takes the train down from London and
  ┃  checks into his hotel across from the stony beach at
  ┃  Brighton.¶
  ┃        Watson stumbles across body.¶
  T Out for his morning constitutional, Watson literally
  ┃  stumbles across a body... or at least a hand sticking up
  ┃  from beneath the stones. ¶
  ┃  ✦
  ┃
  ┃                                                     ━OUTLINE.DOC━
COMMAND: Copy Delete Format Gallery Help Insert Jump Library
         Options Print Quit Replace Search Transfer Undo Window
Edit document or press Esc to use menu
ORGANIZE          {Watson·····¶¶}   ?              ZM       Microsoft Word
```

Figure 9.7

What Can You Do with this Feature?

You can use this new skill to move entire chapters if you want. Just switch to outline view, collapse the text in your document, and rearrange the text using the headings and the Outline Organize mode.

If you plan to use this system of structural revision, you should include plenty of headings in your document when you draft it. When you are revising, you can then move text around easily and in large or small chunks. So don't worry about having too many headings. You can always eliminate some later.

WORD'S THESAURUS

Now that you have some idea of what kinds of word choices to avoid and what words you want to use in their places, Word is ready to provide some assistance. Starting with version 3.1, Word includes a built-in 220,000-word thesaurus. The Thesaurus suggests some alternatives for words you want to replace.

For example, if, as mentioned earlier, "vehicle" is too general a word, you would need to replace it with something more concrete. With Word's Thesaurus, this task is easy. Just place the selection anywhere in the word "vehicle," press Ctrl-F6, and Word opens up a window that contains a list of alternatives. If you are using Word with a floppy disk system, Word may ask you to swap disks and insert the disk containing the Thesaurus file.

If you were working on this particular page of the book, your screen would resemble the following:

```
1 ─┬─[····|····1·········2·········3·········4·········5·········6·········7·]·┐
    │     to replace.¶
    │
 SP │  »      For example, if, as mentioned earlier, "vehicle" is too general a
    │     word, you would need to replace it with something more concrete.  With
    │     Word's Thesaurus, this task is easy.  Just place the selection anywhere
    │     in the word "vehicle," press Ctrl-F6, and Word opens up a window that
    │     contains a list of alternatives. If you are using Word with a floppy
    │     disk system, Word may ask you to swap disks and insert the disk
    │     containing the Thesaurus file.¶
    │
 SP │         If you were working on this particular page of the book, your
    │     screen would resemble the following:  ¶
    ╞═══════════════════════════════ Word Finder  Thesaurus ═══════════════════╡
    │ vehicle:
    │ noun agency, channel, conduit, instrument, mechanism, medium, ministry;
    │      auto, automobile, bus, car, carriage, chariot, coach, jeep, motorcar,
    │      omnibus, sedan, truck, van, wagon;
    │      buggy, carriage, coach, rig, surrey.
    │
    │
    │
    │
    │  ◀─ move left   ─▶ move right   Esc: exit   ◀┘ replace     Ctl-F6: look up
    └──────────────────────────────────────────────────────────────────────────┘
```

Figure 9.8

In Word's Thesaurus there are more than two dozen alternatives for the word "vehicle." Replacing "vehicle" with one of those choices is easy. Just use the arrow keys to move the selection to the word you want for a replacement and press Return.

If none of the choices is appropriate, you can either press Escape to return to your document, or you can move the selection to one of the words on the list that seems close to a replacement and press Ctrl-F6 again.

For example, if you use "vehicle" in a sentence such as, "He was being used as a vehicle to move drugs into Florida," then the meaning of "vehicle" in this context is similar to the meaning of the word "conduit," one of the words suggested by the Thesaurus. If you move the selection to "conduit" and press Ctrl-F6, the Thesaurus will display a new list of words such as the following:

```
[....!...1.........2.........3.........4.........5.........6.........7.].
      to replace.¶

SP »      For example, if, as mentioned earlier, "ve hicle" is too general a
      word, you would need to replace it with something more concrete.  With
      Word's Thesaurus, this task is easy.  Just place the selection anywhere
      in the word "vehicle," press Ctrl-F6, and Word opens up a window that
      contains a list of alternatives. If you are using Word with a floppy
      disk system, Word may ask you to swap disks and insert the disk
      containing the Thesaurus file.¶

SP       If you were working on this particular page of the book, your
      screen would resemble the following:  ¶
╞═══════════════════════════ Word Finder  Thesaurus ═══════════════════════╡
 conduit:
 noun  Agency, channel, instrument, mechanism, medium, ministry, vehicle;
      passageway, pathway, shaft, subway, tube, tunnel;
      canal, channel, crevice, curb, cut, ditch, duct, furrow, gorge,
      groove, gully, gutter, passageway, ravine, rut, trench, trough;
      channel, cylinder, duct, pipe, tube.



 ←- move left    -→ move right   Esc: exit   ↵ replace   Ctl-PgUp: last word
```

Figure 9.9

One of those choices may be just the word you need.

Thesaurus Options for Earlier Versions of Word

If you have Word version 3.0 or earlier, and you don't want to upgrade, you can get exactly the same thesaurus used in Word directly from the company that sold it to Microsoft. The product is called *Word Finder* from Microlytics Incorporated (300 Main Street, East Rochester, NY 14445); however, buying the add-on program will probably cost you more than the upgrade.

The external version of the thesaurus works basically the same way, but it is a memory-resident program; it takes 29k of memory. Also, if you are using Word on an EGA graphics card, you must run the program in character mode. In the end, it might be better to call Microsoft and price out an upgrade to the latest version of Word.

WORD'S SEARCH FEATURE

You can use Word's Search function to search for particular groups of characters that are the marks of bad writing. For example, when you have turned a verb into a noun, that noun will almost always end in "ion." When you are using the passive voice, that sentence will often contain the word "by." Use the Search command to find these marks of bad writing so you can correct them.

To search for a particular string of characters in your document using Word's Search function, select S(earch) from Word's main menu. This command will call up the following set of fields:

```
SEARCH text:
       direction: Up(Down)  case: Yes(No)  whole word: Yes(No)
```

You can enter the text for which you are searching in the *text* field. The *text* field will accept a question mark as a wild card: "?ail" will search for "bail," "fail," "hail," "jail," "mail," "nail," "pail," "rail," "sail," and "tail." The *direction* field lets you search Up, from the selection to the beginning of the document, or Down, from the selection to the end of the document. If you set the *case* field to Yes, Word will match not only the letters you have entered but also the case of those letters. So searching for "pail" would not turn up occurrences of "Pail." If you set the *whole word* field to Yes, Word will only match occurrences of the search string that are words by themselves. For special characters such as the paragraph mark, the new line mark, and others, see the special characters chart that appears later in this chapter.

For example, if you wanted to use the Search feature to find out if you were using any "ion" endings, you would set the search fields as follows:

```
SEARCH text: ion
       direction: Up(Down)  case: Yes(No)  whole word: Yes(No)
```

Presumably, you are searching from the front of the document to the end, so you can leave the search direction as Down. Do not tell Word to match case or you might miss some occurrences of uppercase "ION" in headings. Also, leave the whole word feature set to No. You don't want whole words; you want endings only.

Those search parameters also instruct Word to stop at words such as "*ion*iza-tion," "irrat*ion*al," and "quest*ion*," but it takes you just a second to move on to the next word containing "ion."

Now, press Return and Word will quickly search through your document for the combination of letters "ion." To search for the next occurrence of "ion," just press Shift-F4.

To search for "by," the sign of the passive voice, set the *whole word* field to Yes so Word will only stop when it finds the word "by" and not for "Gab*by*," "*by*pass," or "*by*te."

Word's Replace Feature

Not only can Word search for strings of characters, it can also automatically replace them with others. If you decide that you have used the wrong word somewhere in your document, in one simple operation you can use Word's Replace function to substitute the right word.

Replace works almost exactly as does Search with the addition of a few extra fields. When you select R(eplace) from Word's main menu, the following fields appear:

```
REPLACE text:                          with text:
     confirm:(Yes)No  case: Yes(No)    whole word: Yes(No)
```

As you can see, the Replace fields are almost exactly the same as the Search fields. As in a search, you can enter any string of characters as the Replace *text* field, and you can use a question mark (?) as a wild card. For special characters, such as the paragraph mark, the new line mark, and others, see the special characters chart that appears later in this chapter.

There are two differences between the Search function and the Replace function. In addition to asking for a string to replace, Word asks for the text to put in its place. Also, rather than offering you the option of searching up or down from the selection, Replace always searches down and, instead, offers you a Confirm option. If you leave Confirm set to Yes (the default), Word will stop at each occurrence of the search string and ask if you want to replace it with the replace string. You will have three choices — Y(es), N(o), or Escape — with which to terminate the Search and Replace function. Unless you are *very* sure that you want to replace all occurrences of your search string, you should leave the Confirm option set to Yes.

If the word you are replacing is capitalized, Word will also capitalize the replacement.

Special Characters for Search and Replace

There are several special characters you will occasionally want to use in a Search or Replace function. These characters, such as the Tab character, the new line character, and the division mark, normally cannot be part of the search string because they have special functions; however, you can tell Word to search for these characters by using special symbols shown in the following chart.

<u>Use</u>   <u>To Search For This Character</u>

^p   **End-of-paragraph mark**. You enter an end-of-paragraph mark in your document each time you press the Return key. Be careful of replacing end-of-paragraph marks that contain special formatting. If your replacement string contains a new end-of-paragraph mark, it will not have the old formatting.

^n   **New line mark**. You enter a new line mark in your document every time you press Shift-Return. A new line mark starts a new line without starting a new paragraph. It does not contain any paragraph formatting.

continued...

^d   **New page mark or division mark**. You enter a new page mark into your document each time you press Ctrl-Shift-Return. You enter a division mark into your document with the Format Division command. Use ^d to search for either (or both) of these characters. Remember that division marks contain division formatting, so be careful when replacing them with a new string containing another division mark. That string will not have the same formatting.

^t   **Tab character**. You enter a tab character in your document each time you press the Tab key.

^s   **Nonbreaking space**. You enter a nonbreaking space into your document with the Ctrl-Space Bar combination. Word will not break a line on a nonbreaking space, so you can use ^s to keep words together on the same line.

^w   **All space characters**, which include spaces, nonbreaking spaces, tabs, paragraph marks, new line marks, new page marks, and division marks. Be careful with this command. With the wrong Search and Replace command, you could easily remove all space from your document. If you accidentally do so, don't forget to use the Undo command.

^-   **Optional hyphens**. You enter an optional hyphen with the Ctrl-hyphen combination. Alternatively, Word will enter an optional hyphen into a word when you use the Library Hyphenate command (see Chapter 20, "Sorts, Hyphenation, and Redlining"). An optional hyphen only prints when Word uses it to break a word at the end of a line.

^?   **Question mark**. The search field uses ^? for a question mark because you can use a question mark on its own as a wild card, something that can be matched by any character.

WORD'S SPELL PROGRAM

When you are reviewing your spelling, use the Spell program as your last line of defense. Nothing, however, can beat your own careful proofreading.

The Spell program works by checking each word in your document against a list of words it calls a **dictionary**. If the word in your document is in the the Spell dictionary, Word says that word is spelled correctly. If the word is not in the Spell dictionary, Word asks you to recheck it and gives you an opportunity to correct it, mark it for later correction, or add it to the dictionary.

You can probably see the flaw in this technique. If you misspell a word, but it matches another word in the Spell dictionary, Word will not flag the word. If your finger slips, turning "rail" into "tail," Word will pass by the mistake.

It is best not to rely on Spell. You still need to read through your document word by word, looking for spelling errors. Old hands in the copy-checking business say that best way to check for errors is to read your document backwards. That way, the document has no meaning, and the words stand out on their own; you are more likely to read what is really there instead of what you *expect* to be there.

Starting the Spell Checker

You can run the Spell program three ways: by entering a command from the DOS prompt, by using Word's Library command, or by pressing Alt-F6 (version 4 only).

Starting Spell from the DOS Prompt

To start spell from the DOS prompt, just type the name of the Spell program and the name of the file you want the Spell program to check.

If you are using a floppy disk system, you will probably need to change disks. Also, don't forget to include the complete path name to both the Spell program and the file that needs checking. Your DOS command should look something like the following:

CC:\WORD\SPELL-AM C:\BOOKS\WORD\CHAP09.DOC

If you forget to name the file to proof, Spell will ask you for it.

In version 3, the Spell program is in the file SPELL.EXE; however, in version 4, the Spell program may have a slightly different name, depending on the market for which it was intended. For example, the version for the United States market is in a file called SPELL-AM.EXE. The example command line just shown starts the version 4 Speller for the United States. For version 3, the command line would read as follows:

CC:\WORD\SPELL C:\BOOKS\WORD\CHAP09.DOC

Starting Spell through the Library Command

To start Spell through Word, select L(ibrary) from the main menu, and then S(pell) from the submenu. If necessary, Word will ask you to insert the disk containing the Spell program.

Starting Spell with the Alt-F6 Command

The third way to start Spell is to press Alt-F6. This feature is new with version 4 and will not work with version 3.

Simple Proofing

Whichever way you start Spell, once it is running, it works the same way. Spell's main menu will appear at the bottom of the screen:

```
COMMAND: Dictionary Help Lookup Options Proof Quit
```

Version 3 does not contain the Lookup option.

The default choice from Spell's main menu is Proof, and pressing Return will start the spell check. In version 3, the speller always proofs the entire document. In version 4, if the selection is a single character, the speller will proof the entire document. If the selection is longer than a single character, the speller will proof only the selection.

Just how long the proofing takes will depend on the length of your document and the size of your dictionaries. The larger either of them becomes, the slower the spell check.

In version 4, you can check the spelling of a selected passage, even a single word. Select the passage and press Alt-F6. When the Spell menu appears, press Return to Proof the selection. If the selection is spelled correctly, Spell will display the following message:

```
No incorrect words found.  Press any key to continue.
```

If the selection contains a word not listed in the dictionary, Word will offer you the same choices as it does when it proofs an entire document. Those choices are described in the following sections.

Reviewing an Entire Document

When the program is finished proofing your document (or selection) and has found one or more misspelled words, Spell switches into its review mode. In review mode, it will show you each word it couldn't find in its dictionary. It will show you the context of that word and even look up alternatives for you if you are not sure of the correct spelling.

Spell divides the screen into three windows. The top section is the **context window**, showing the word as it appears in your document. The middle section is the **lookup window** where Spell will list alternative words that are spelled somewhat like your misspelled word. The bottom window is the **correction window**, which shows you the exact word in question.

```
┌─────────────────────────────────────────────────────────────────┐
│┌─────────────────────────────────────────────────────────────────┐│
││                                                                   ││
││    er off, the ball.    Now, admitedly, that is a far out example ││
││                                                                   ││
│├─────────────────────────────────────────────────────────────────┤│
││ ▐ADMITTEDLY▌                                                       ││
││                                                                   ││
││                                                                   ││
││                                 ─                                 ││
││                                                                   ││
││                                                                   ││
│├─────────────────────────────────────────────────────────────────┤│
││ ─> ADMITEDLY                                                      ││
││                                                                   ││
│└─────────────────────────────────────────────────────────────────┘│
└─────────────────────────────────────────────────────────────────┘
 CORRECT: ▐ADMITTEDLY▌                            adjust case: (Yes)No

 Enter correction or select from list
 Total words: 7,605 Unique: 1,354 Unknown: 78    Microsoft Spell: CHAP09.DOC
```

Figure 9.10

When Spell presents you with a word it can't find in its dictionary, it displays several options:

COMMAND: Add Correct Lookup Help Ignore Mark Options Quit
        Resume Next Previous

Version 3 does not contain the Lookup option.

Add allows you to add words to the dictionary. See "Adding Words to the Dictionaries" later in this chapter.

Correct either lets you type in the correct spelling or has Spell look up alternatives for you.

In version 4, Spell automatically looks up the alternative spellings unless you set the *alternatives* field of the Spell Options command to Manual. In version 3, Spell is always set to manual and will not look up the alternatives until you tell it to do so.

In Manual Alternatives mode (and always in version 3), Spell gives you an opportunity to fill in the correct spelling if you know it. Word will then look up your new spelling in the dictionary, and if it cannot find the new work, Word displays the following message:

```
Not in Dictionary; Retype? (Y/N)
```

If you are certain of the spelling, press N for No, but if you are not sure, reach for your printed dictionary and *look it up.*

To get Spell to suggest alternative spellings when in Manual Alternatives mode, press any of the arrow keys (in version 3) or F1 (in version 4), and Spell will look through the dictionary for words starting with the same letter but with another letter missing, added, or transposed. When Word provides you with a list of alternatives, use the arrow keys to move the selection to the correct word on the list and press Return to select it. Word will replace the misspelled word in your document. If the right word is not on the list, press Escape and look it up in a printed dictionary.

The Correct option also contains a field that asks if it should

```
adjust case:(Yes)No
```

The default choice is Yes, which means Spell will tag a misspelled word that begins with an uppercase letter and replace it with the properly spelled word also beginning with an uppercase letter. If the word being replaced is entirely in uppercase, Spell will replace it with a word entirely in uppercase. Select No and Spell will insert your correction exactly as you have typed it.

Lookup is a new feature in version 4. It allows you to quickly check if a particular word is listed in Spell's dictionary. Choose Lookup from the Spell main menu or the Spell Proofing Menu, and type the spelling you want to check. If the word is in the dictionary, Spell will tell you so. If not, Spell will suggest several alternatives.

Help will take you to Word's help system and provide information on how to use Spell.

Ignore is the default choice, which indicates to Word that the word in question is correctly spelled and that Spell can ignore it.

Mark will mark the word with an unusual character such as * or # (you can select which one with the Spell Options command). Use Mark if, even when viewing the word in context, you are not sure how the word should be spelled, and you want to look it up and change it later. Alternatively, you will want to use the Mark command if you have accidentally split a word in two. When Spell is finished, you can use Word's Search function to find all occurrences of that special character and correct the mistakes manually.

Quit will immediately stop the review. It will offer you the opportunity to save the corrections you have already reviewed in your text file (saving the old version with the .BAK extension) or exit without saving changes.

Resume, **Next**, and **Previous** let you move around the list of misspelled words. **Previous** takes you back up the list, allowing you to change your mind about a particular word. **Next** takes you down the list one word at a time to where you first started moving backward. **Resume** jumps straight back to where you were when you first issued the Previous option.

Spell Options

There are two Spell Options commands. One is on the main Spell menu:

```
COMMAND: Dictionary Help Options Proof Quit
```

The other is on Spell's Proofing menu:

```
COMMAND: Add Correct Lookup Help Ignore Mark Options Quit
         Resume Next Previous
```

If you choose Options from the main Spell menu, you will be able to adjust four options:

```
OPTIONS lookup: quick complete          ignore all caps: yes(no)
marking character: #  \  /  %  &( *)+ @  alternatives:(Auto)Manual
```

If you choose Options from Spell's Proofing menu, you will be able to adjust only two options:

```
OPTIONS: lookup: quick complete      alternatives:(Auto)Manual
```

When doing a *quick lookup*, Spell presumes that the first two letters of the misspelled word are correct when it is looking for alternative spellings. A *complete lookup* makes no such presumption. You see more words on your list of alternatives, but the process takes longer.

If you tell Spell to *ignore all caps*, it will ignore words spelled entirely in uppercase letters. Most often those words are acronyms such as USA, UNICEF, or NORAD and not likely to be listed in the dictionary.

The *marking character* is the character Spell uses when you tell it to mark a word during the review phase of proofing.

The *alternatives* field (available only in version 4) lets you determine whether Spell automatically looks up alternatives in the dictionary when you tell it to correct a word, or whether it first gives you time to manually correct the word. Version 3 always operates in manual mode.

Dictionary Management

When Spell checks your document, it actually consults several dictionaries.

The Main Dictionary

Spell treats a set of files as its "main" dictionary. In version 4, Spell always looks in a file called SPELL-AM.LEX, which contains the bulk of the main dictionary. (The name of this file will vary, depending on the country where Word is purchased; for example, in the United Kingdom, the dictionary file will be SPELL-UK.LEX and will contain British spellings rather than American spellings.) In version 3, the equivalent of this file is MAIN-DICT.CMP, which contains most of the words, and a second file called HIGHFREQ.CMP, which contains the words used most often in English. Finally, Spell looks in UPDAT-AM.CMP (UPDICT.CMP in version 3), a standard dictionary that you create. It contains words such as your name, the street where you live, your city, and other words you use often but which would not be in the supplied dictionary files.

Supplemental Dictionaries

In addition, Spell will consult two other dictionaries when proofing a document: a document dictionary and a user dictionary.

The **document dictionary** is attached to a particular document and is always checked each time that document is checked. The document dictionary has the same name as the text document but with the file extension .CMP. So, for example, if you had a document dictionary attached to the file containing this chapter, it would be called CHAP09.CMP.

A **user dictionary** is one you can use with a certain category of documents. For example, if you worked in the computer field, your writing would contain words such as "baud," "byte," and "multiplex." You could enter those words in a user dictionary you might call TECHNICA.CMP, which you would use each time Spell was checking one of your technical documents. You might use another user dictionary for legal writing and a third for those occasions when you're writing about medical subjects. You can create as many user dictionaries as you want.

Specifying the User Dictionary

You don't need to tell Spell to use a document dictionary. When it performs its spell check, it automatically looks for a dictionary file with the same name as the document; however, if you want Spell to use a user dictionary, you must tell it the name of that dictionary.

From Spell's main menu, select D(ictionary). Spell will ask you for the name of the user dictionary you want it to use. If the user dictionary is not in the same subdirectory as your document or the Spell program, you must include the full path name to that dictionary. Spell will continue to use that dictionary as its user dictionary until you change that specification or until you exit from Spell.

If you don't tell Spell to use a particular user dictionary, it will use a user dictionary called SPECIALS.CMP. If there is not a file called SPE-CIALS.CMP in the current directory, Spell will create one.

Adding Words to the Dictionaries

The Add option lets you add words to Spell's dictionaries. When you select Add, Spell will ask you whether it should add the word in question to the standard dictionary (UPDAT-AM.CMP in version 4 or UPDICT.CMP in version 3), the user dictionary (SPECIAL.CMP unless you specified some other name), or the document dictionary (the .CMP file with the same name as the document you are proofing).

Creating Your Own Dictionaries

To create your own user or document dictionaries, just list the words you want in the dictionary in alphabetical order, one word to a line. To make sure the words in your dictionary file are in alphabetical order, use the Autosort command (see Chapter 20, "Sorts, Hyphenation, and Redlining"). Then save the unformatted file with the extension .CMP, and you are finished.

OTHER WORD VERSION 3 REVISION ASSISTANCE

With version 3 of Word, there are three other programs, Wordfind, Lookup, and Wordfreq, that can help you check spelling. Two of these programs, Wordfind and Lookup, are actually used by version 3 Spell to find words in its dictionaries. These programs can help you spell a word correctly before the Spell program has to flag it as misspelled.

Finally, there are two other programs that come with Word version 3. One, WC, counts the number of words in a file, and the other, Anagram, can unscramble word anagrams.

Wordfind

Wordfind is one of the spelling utility programs included with Word version 3. It will look for words that match a certain wild card pattern. For instance, tell Wordfind to look for "*ion" and you will receive a long list of words ending in "ion." "Auto*" will produce "automation," "automobile," "automaton," and many others. "Au?o*" will produce "aurora," "auroral," "auroras," "autobiographer," "autobiographers," "autobiographic," "autobiographical," "autobiographically," "autobiographies," and more than two dozen more words.

You run the Wordfind program either from the DOS prompt or by using Word's Library Run command. Library Run allows you to run other programs without first quitting Word. When the other program is finished, you can quickly return to your current location in Word.

Select L(ibrary) from Word's main menu and R(un) from the Library sub-menu. Word will give you a chance to name the program to run:

```
LIBRARY RUN:
```

Type in "Wordfind" and the ambiguous word name you want Wordfind to look up. For example,

```
LIBRARY RUN: wordfind au?o*
```

Then press Return. If you are using a floppy drive system, Word will give you a chance to insert the Spell disk containing the dictionaries and the Wordfind program; then it will search the dictionaries for you, returning a list of all the words that match that description. If the list is too long, press Ctrl-S or Ctrl-C to interrupt the search. Then reframe your search more specifically and try again.

Lookup

Like Wordfind, Lookup is also used by version 3 Spell to help you spell words correctly. Lookup will let you misspell a word and give you a list of suggested replacements. So, if you tell Lookup to look up "speeling," it will come back with the list "speeding," "spelling," and "steeling." Those are the same three words Spell would have listed had you asked it for help spelling the misspelled word "speeling."

Like Wordfind, you can run Lookup from the DOS prompt or through Word's Library Run command. To run Lookup, you enter the name of the Lookup program and the word you think you are misspelling:

```
LIBRARY RUN: lookup speeling
```

Then press Return and Lookup will search the dictionaries for you, returning a list of all the words spelled somewhat like the word you have listed. If you enter a correctly spelled word, the word itself will appear on the list, and you will know you've spelled it correctly.

Of course, just because Word's dictionary doesn't display a word doesn't mean the word is actually misspelled. Take a moment to look the word up in a printed dictionary.

Wordfreq

The Wordfreq program included with Word has two uses. It can help you avoid overusing a word and can also help you spot a word that has been misspelled as another word.

Most writers on occasion overuse certain words. A perfectly good word can begin to annoy your reader if used too often. Wordfreq counts the occurrences of each word in your document and produces a file listing each word in the document and how many times it is used. You can use this file to quickly see if you are using a word too often. Then you can use the Search command and the Thesaurus to find the word and replace it with another, similar word.

Before you can use Wordfreq, your document must be saved. You can run Wordfreq from the DOS prompt or start it with Word's Library Run command. Choose the L(ibrary) command from the main menu; then choose R(un) from the Library submenu. Library Run will ask for the name of the program to run. Enter "Wordfreq" and the name of the file you want checked. If Wordfreq isn't in the same directory as the one holding the Word program, don't forget to include the path to Wordfreq. Also, include the full path to the file you want to review. The menu command should resemble the following:

```
LIBRARY RUN: wordfreq c:\books\word\chap09.doc
```

Wordfreq produces a list of the words in your document and shows how many times each word is used. The list file has the same name as the document you are checking but with the extension .FRQ, so if you were working on this chapter, the list file would be called CHAP09.FRQ. The list normally starts with the most frequently used word. If you want the list in alphabetical order, include "$a" on the command line:

```
LIBRARY RUN: wordfreq c:\books\word\chap09.doc $a
```

The interesting words are the ones at the top and bottom of a frequency list. The ones at the top are the ones you use most frequently. Look them over to see if there are any you can avoid or change. The ones at the bottom of the list are words you use least often. Survey them for possible misspellings. Often a word that escaped the Spell checker will appear here because it is correctly spelled but is the wrong word choice.

For example, if you are writing about railways, you might misspell "rail" as "tail." Though it will pass through the spell checker without a problem, it may also show up on your word frequency list as being used only once. And why, you would ask yourself, have you used the word "tail" in a document about railways? If you quickly use Word's Search function to find where you have used "tail," you can reassure yourself that it is correct, or correct it if you made a mistake.

WC

The WC program simply counts the words in a file and is useful if you have to write something of a particular length. You must save the document file first. Run WC from the DOS prompt or from the Library Run command, and specify the file you want to count, including the path to that file:

LIBRARY RUN: wc c:\books\word\chap09.doc

If you are using version 4 of Word, you also can receive a count of the words in a file by repaginating the document.

Anagram

The Anagram program is a fun little program that will shuffle around the letters in a word and tell you what other words they will spell. So feed in "eeeflr" and Anagram will give you "feeler." You can also use ? to signify a missing character, and it will give you a list that matches your specification. Feed it "?i?i" and it will come back with "fiji," "ibid," "ibis," "ilia," "iris," "isis," "kiwi," "midi," "mini," and "simi."

Run the Anagram program from the DOS prompt or through Word's Library Run command as follows:

LIBRARY RUN: anagram eeflr

What can you do with the Anagram program? Not much, but it is helpful if you play scrabble and your opponents don't mind you cheating.

PART III

FORM: WORD AS DESKTOP PUBLISHING SOFTWARE

The first half of this book deals with the content of your writing. The remainder of the book covers your writing's form — how it looks on the page.

Word is more than just a word processor; it can also serve as a basic desktop publishing system. Though it is not a dedicated desktop publishing package, Word's superb control of printers allows you to use it as inexpensive desktop publishing software. In particular, by using style sheets (see Chapters 12 and 13), you can perform many stylistic functions with Word that you may have thought possible only with expensive desktop publishing programs.

Part III contains four chapters. In Chapter 10, basic character, paragraph, and division formatting will be reviewed. In Chapter 11, "Multicolumn Formats," you will learn to place two or more columns on a page. Chapter 12, "Formatting with Style Sheets," introduces you to style sheets and how they make formatting — and reformatting — easy. Chapter 13, "Formatting with Style Sheets and the Word Outliner," shows you how to link style sheets and the Outliner, making formatting even easier and faster.

CHAPTER 10

DIRECT FORMATTING

DIRECT FORMATTING VS. STYLE SHEETS

This chapter discusses direct formatting—formatting attached to characters, paragraphs, and divisions. Direct formatting differs from formatting applied with a style sheet. Formats may vary from style sheet to style sheet.

Consider an example. Suppose you have two printers—a laser printer at the office and a daisy wheel at home. The laser printer can perform just about any printing task; the daisy wheel is limited. If you directly format some text as italics, it will print as italics on the office printer; at home, it will print as regular text. The daisy wheel is not capable of italics, so Word ignores the italics command.

Wouldn't it be better if you could at least underline the text at home? Style sheets can help you do just that. Instead of directly formatting the text as italics, you can format it with a style sheet as, for example, character style 2. In the style sheet used with the office printer, you can indicate character style 2 as italics. In another style sheet used at home, you could indicate style 2 as underlined. When you switch style sheets, the formatting is changed.

This versatility applies to all the aspects of formatting. If you format paragraphs with built-in Word paragraph formats, the formats will always apply to those paragraphs. When you use a style sheet format, the formats can vary between style sheets, taking maximum advantage of the capabilities of various printers.

After working with style sheets, you probably won't use direct formats much; however, you'll always have small writing jobs that don't require a style sheet. In these cases, use direct formatting. Also, even when using a style sheet, you will occasionally want to use direct formatting for basic traits or formats that occur only once in a document.

You must also understand basic formatting to develop the formats to be stored in style sheets.

CHARACTER FORMATTING

In Chapter 3, "Editing Basics," you learned the basics of formatting characters in Microsoft Word. You learned two basic ways to format a character or group of characters: using direct character formats and using the Format Character command. Both techniques affect all characters (including spaces) in the selection. Formatted spaces can create surprises if you later delete all recognizable characters and begin writing again on a formatted space. If formatting seems to come from nowhere, just reformat.

Available Formats Depend on the Printer

Just because Word can display a particular character format on the screen doesn't mean it can print the format. Available Word formats depend not on Word but on your printer. For instance, Word cannot force a daisy wheel printer to print in italics if you don't have an italic font wheel.

Experiment to determine which effects are available on your printer. If there are several printer drivers for your printer, experiment with them to see which features are available. (See Chapter 4, "Printing Basics," for information on how to change printer drivers.) Of course, if you are a printer whiz and think your printer can deliver more than any of the available printer drivers, you can always customize your own printer driver. Chapter 22, "Word and Printers," explains more about how printers and Word work together. Chapter 23, "MAKEPRD and How To Use It," explains how to modify and customize printer drivers.

The Format Character Command

When you select the Format Character command, the following set of fields is displayed:

```
FORMAT CHARACTER: bold: Yes(No)   italic: Yes(No)       underline: Yes(No)
     strikethrough: Yes(No)       uppercase: Yes(No)  small caps: Yes(No)
     double underline: Yes(No)    position: (Normal)Superscript Subscript
     font name: Courier           font size: 12            hidden: Yes(No)
```

Eleven character traits can be selected with the Format Character command:

- **Bold characters** are darker and wider than regular characters.

- *Italics characters* slant to the right.

- <u>Underline characters</u> have a single underline.

- ~~Strikethrough characters~~ are useful in showing text that has been removed from a draft.

- UPPERCASE CHARACTERS are all in capital letters.

- SMALL CAPS CHARACTERS replace lowercase characters with uppercase letters from a smaller font.

- <u>Double underline characters</u> have two lines under them. Double underlining appears in financial and accounting statements.

- Normal characters print on the regular print line.

- Superscript characters print above the line.

- Subscript characters print below the line. On some printers, super- script and subscript characters print in a smaller typeface.

- Hidden characters may or may not appear on the screen, depending on the setting of the *show hidden text* field in the Window Options command. In version 3, this setting also controls whether hidden text prints. In version 4, whether hidden text prints depends on the set- ting of the *hidden text* field in the Print Options command.

Why would you want text that doesn't show on the screen or when the docu- ment is printed? You can use such text to annotate a document, and Word uses hidden text to generate indices and tables. (See Chapter 15, "Indexing," and Chapter 16, "Tables.")

Fonts and Typefaces

To typographers, a **typeface** is a particular design of type, including all sizes and variations of that design. For instance, the text on this page is in a Times Roman typeface. It is a classic design with **serifs** (small crossbars at the end of the major lines). The heading of this paragraph in a typeface named Helvetica Condensed, a typeface without serifs. Microsoft calls a typeface a **font name**. When you chose a font name, you are really choosing the name of a typeface.

A **font** is a collection of characters in one typeface, size, style, and weight. Not only is this text in a Times Roman typeface, it is in a 10-point, upright, medium font. *This is a 10-point, italic, medium font, a different font but the same typeface.*

Font Name

Available font names and sizes depend on your printer. Not all fonts may be available in all sizes or with all effects.

To see a list of available fonts, advance the selection to the *font name* field in the Format Character submenu, and press F1 (version 4) or an arrow key (version 3). Word lists fonts available for your printer. As an example, selecting a custom printer driver for the Mannesmann Tally MT910 laser printer might display the following list:

```
Courier (modern a)      Prestige (modern b)
Gothic (modern h)       Roman (roman a)
Optima (modern j)
```

Selecting the standard printer driver included with Word for an Epson FX dot matrix printer provides the following list:

```
Pica (modern a)         Pica D (modern b)
Elite (modern c)        Elite D (modern d)
PS (roman a)
```

Note that each font has two names. When filling in the *font name* field, you may use either the descriptive name (e.g., Courier, Pica) or the generic name (e.g., modern a, roman b).

If you use more than one printer, the generic name is important — it is the name that remains the same from printer to printer. If you format text as Courier (modern a) when using the MT910 printer and then print it on the Epson printer, that text will print as Pica because Pica is the modern "a" font on that printer. Text formatted as Roman (roman a) on the MT910 will print as PS (roman a) text on the Epson.

Font Sizes

Fonts are measured in **points**; there are 72 points in an inch. The size of a font is measured from the baseline of one line of text to the baseline of the next line.

Occasionally, you will see font sizes expressed as 10/12 or 12/14, which indicates 10-point type set on 12-point lines or 12-point type set on 14-point lines. The addition of extra space between the lines is called **leading**.

Available font sizes depend on the chosen font name. Again, this name is a function of the printer driver. If you know the sizes available for that font name, enter the size you want. For a list of available sizes for the chosen font name, move the selection to the *font size* field and press F1 (in version 4) or an arrow key (in version 3). Word lists the available sizes for that font. Select one by moving the highlight and pressing Return.

Built-in Character Formats

As mentioned in Chapter 3, Word comes with nine built-in character formats. Using these formats, you can format characters on the fly, changing character formats as you go. If the format is a single character and you press the command for a built-in format — Alt plus another key — the format will apply to the text you type after that point. If the selection is more than a single character, the format will apply to the characters in the selection. To apply a built-in format to a single character, select it and issue the command twice.

To apply a built-in format when a style sheet is attached to a document, press Alt-X and then the command character (for example, Alt-XB for bold). Following is a list of built-in character formats:

Built-in Character Formats

Character Format	Press Alt and this Key (Alt-X and this key if using a style sheet)
Italic	i
Bold	b
Underline	u
Double Underline	d
Strikethrough	s
Small Caps	k
Superscript	+ or =
Subscript	- (hyphen)
Normal	spacebar
Hidden	e
Uppercase	no built-in format

PARAGRAPH FORMATTING

Direct paragraph formatting is similar to direct character formatting. You can use the Format Paragraph command or apply one of ten built-in paragraph formats.

Paragraph formatting is stored in the paragraph mark at the end of the paragraph. If you delete a paragraph mark and combine two paragraphs, the new paragraph will have the formatting of the second paragraph. If you create a new paragraph by pressing Return, it will have the same format as the paragraph from which it was split.

Format Paragraph Command

The Format paragraph command contains ten fields:

```
FORMAT PARAGRAPH alignment: (Left)Centered Right Justified
      line indent: 0"        first line: 0"        right indent: 0"
      line spacing: 1 li   space before: 0 li      space after: 0 li
      keep together:(Yes)No  keep follow: Yes(No) side by side: Yes(No)
```

The functions of these fields are explained in Chapter 3, "Editing Basics." The last three fields—*keep together*, *keep follow*, and *side by side*—are detailed in Chapter 11, "Multicolumn Formats."

Built-in Paragraph Formats

Word offers ten built-in paragraph formats that cover the majority of paragraph formatting situations.

Built-in Paragraph Formats

Paragraph Format	Press Alt and this Key (Alt-x and this key if using a style sheet)
Italic	i
Justified	j
Left Indent 1/2"	n
Reduce Left Indent 1/2"	m
First Line Indent	f
Flush Left	l
Hanging Indent	t
Flush Right	r
Double-spaced	2
Open Spacing	o
Standard Paragraph	p
Centered (version 4 only)	c

Tabs

Paragraph marks also contain tab formatting.

Tabs are directly set with the Format Tabs command. A paragraph format in a style sheet may also contain tab formatting.

When you issue the Format Tabs command, Word gives you three choices:

```
FORMAT TABS: Set Clear Reset-All
```

Set allows you to set a tab. Word will ask for a tab position and offer you a choice of left, right, centered, decimal, or vertical tabs and a choice of a leader character. The first three tab types are thoroughly covered in Chapter 3. Vertical tabs are available only in version 4 and are explained in Chapter 16, "Tables." Setting any tabs in a paragraph erases default tab stops.

Clear allows you to clear a single tab stop without canceling all tabs in a paragraph.

Reset-All will erase all tab settings for that paragraph and reset the default tabs, which Word sets every 1/2 inch.

The details of tab setting are explained in Chapter 3, "Editing Basics."

Paragraph Borders

A new feature in version 4 of Word is the ability to draw boxes and borders as part of a pargraph's formatting. For example, to leave a note to your editor in the manuscript of a book, put the note in a box so your editor will be sure to catch it. Following is as an example.

This is an example of a paragraph with a border.

To format a paragraph with lines and borders, use the F(ormat) B(orders) command. The following fields will be displayed:

```
FORMAT BORDER type:(None)Box Lines    line style:(Normal)Bold Double
          left: Yes(No)  right: Yes(No)  above: Yes(No)  below : Yes(No)
```

The default *border* type is None. If you want a border around the entire paragraph, simply select a box type and the appropriate line style. If you want lines along fewer than all four sides, select a line type and select from *left*, *right*, *above*, and *below*.

DIVISION FORMATTING

A **division** is a block of text sharing the same basic page layout (margins, column structure, page numbering sequence, etc).

There are four Format Division commands: margins, page-numbers, layout, and line-numbers. The basics of these four commands are explained in Chapter 3. Format Division Margins controls the page margins and the position of running heads. Format Division Page-numbers allows you to start and stop page numbering and to control the numbering system Word uses to number your pages. Format Division Layout lets you control the position of footnotes, the number of newspaper-style columns on the page, and when a new division formatting command takes effect. Columns are covered in Chapter 11, "Multicolumn Formats," and footnotes are explained in detail in Chapter 14, "Footnotes." Format Division line-Numbers, available only in version 4, will number your lines down the left side of the page.

Remember, a division mark appears as a row of colons across the screen at the end of a division.

Running Heads

A major formatting feature is the use of **running heads** — the bits of repeating text that appear at the top and bottom of the page, usually including the page number.

A running head is normal text formatted with the Format Running-head command. To designate a paragraph as a running head, place the selection anywhere in the paragraph and select the F(ormat) R(unning-head) command. You will see the following fields:

```
FORMAT RUNNING-HEAD position:(Top)Bottom
        odd pages:(Yes)No  even pages:(Yes)No  first page: Yes(No)
```

The *position* field determines whether the text in the designated paragraph will appear at the top or bottom of the page.

The *odd* and *even pages* fields determine whether the running head appears on odd or even pages. You can designate different headers and footers for the top and bottom of odd and even pages, for a total of four.

The *first page* field determines whether or not the running head appears on the page that contains the paragraph designating the header or footer.

Running Head Shortcuts

In version 4, two shortcuts exist for formatting running heads.

First, the function key Alt-F2 designates a paragraph as a **footer** (bottom of page), and Ctrl-F2 designates a paragraph as a **header** (top of page). Both of these function keys, however, choose the default running head values; if you want anything different, you must use the Format Running-head command.

Second, version 4 also supports a dedicated paragraph style sheet style for running heads. If you are using the same style of running head through several documents that share a style (such as the chapters of a book), using the dedicated style is the easiest way to designate a running head. See Chapter 12, "Formatting with Style Sheets."

Running Head Margins

Running heads do not obey side margins for a division; they start at the leftmost position on the page instead of the left margin. As a result, you must use the Format Paragraph command to format the left indent and right indent to match the margins in the current division.

Of course, if you want, you can use a running head that starts to the left of the main text and continues to the right of it.

Character Formatting in Running Heads

Characters in a running head print as they are formatted, whether the formatting is direct or from a style sheet.

For example, to specify a 14-point Helvetica bold running head, format the characters as 14-point Helvetica bold (presuming, of course, that your printer can print the font). In other words, a running head is just like any other paragraph, except it prints at the top or bottom of every page.

Page Numbers in Running Heads

To include a page number in a running head, use the built-in Glossary Page command. Type the word "page" in your text. Then, with the selection on the first space after "page," press F3. The text changes on your screen to read "(page)," but it will print with the page number.

Running Head Notes

A running head stays in effect until the end of the division in which it is designated, or until Word encounters another Format Running-head command for the same type of running head (top of odd pages, bottom of even pages, etc.). To stop a running head from printing, either format a new division or designate a blank paragraph (a paragraph mark) as the new running head of the same kind.

A running head must fit within the top or bottom margin. If the head is too large, it won't print. Remember, in the Format Division Margins command, Word gives you a chance to set the running head position from *top* and from *bottom*. These fields set the distance from the top or bottom of the page to the running head. Since most running heads are one line long, the default values of 0.5" are usually fine; however, a running head can be as long as you want, and you can format it in any font (including large fonts). It is easy to create a running head that is larger than the available space. When this happens, use the Format Division Margins command to move the running head or create larger margins.

A running head has a carat (^) character before it on the left side of the screen. If the style bar is showing, there will be a "t" in front of a running head to appear at the top of the page and a "b" in front of a head to print at the bottom.

On the screen, a typical running head will resemble the following:

```
t ^The Power of: Microsoft Word Version 4     Page (page)
```

As with any other paragraph, you can delete a running head by highlighting it and pressing Delete.

CHAPTER 11

MULTICOLUMN FORMATS

TWO KINDS OF COLUMNS

Word can produce multicolumn documents with two different types of column structures: **side-by-side** columns and **newspaper** columns. Use side-by-side columns for tables in which material in one column relates to material in adjoining columns. Use newspaper columns for text that runs from the top to the bottom of one column and continues at the top of the next column.

Side-by-Side Columns

Word produces side-by-side columns using the *keep together*, *keep follow*, and *side-by-side* fields of the Format Paragraph command. If you set all three fields to Yes and adjust the paragraph indents so they don't overlap, Word will print the paragraphs side-by-side on the page. The following chart was produced using side-by-side formatting:

Keep Together　　　When you set the *keep together* field for a paragraph to Yes, Word will always print the paragraph all on one page or in one (newspaper) column. If any part of the paragraph would normally print on the next page (or in the next column), Word will move the entire paragraph.

Keep Follow　　　When you set the *keep follow* field for a paragraph to Yes, Word prints the paragraph on the same page with the following paragraph. Set this field to No for the last paragraph of a side-by-side set.

Side-by-side　　　When you set the *side-by-side* field for two paragraphs both to Yes, Word places those paragraphs side by side on the page as long as the left and right indent settings ensure that the paragraphs don't overlap.

Remember, you must adjust the indents so the paragraphs don't overlap. For example, the print column in this book is 5-1/4" wide. In the table above, the left column has a left indent of 0 and a right indent of 4.25". The right column has a left indent of 1.5" and a right indent of zero. The result is two columns divided by a .5" gutter.

On the screen, Word does not print the columns side by side; instead, each paragraph is formatted into its column, but the paragraphs appear on the screen one after another.

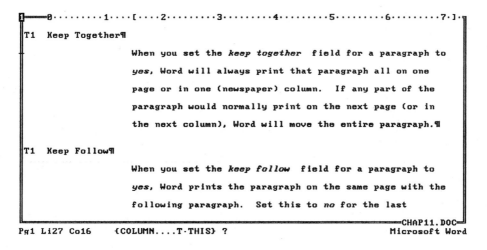

Figure 11.1

Word recognizes side-by-side formatting as a paragraph trait. A newspaper column arrangement, as you will see, is a division trait.

Newspaper Columns

In newspaper columns, text runs down the first column and, if necessary, continues at the top of the next column. Instruct Word to use newspaper-style columns with the F(ormat) D(ivision) L(ayout) command:

```
FORMAT DIVISION LAYOUT footnotes: (Same-page)End
        number of columns: 1          space between columns: 0.5"
            division break:(Page)Continuous Column Even Odd
```

Set the *number of columns* field to the number of columns you want, and set the *space between columns* field to the desired value.

Finally, with the *division break* field, instruct Word where you want the new column format to start. In this field, selecting "Page" instructs the new formatting to start immediately and on a new page. Setting the *division break* field to "column" instructs Word to start a new column immediately and may also result in Word starting a new page. The last two settings — "even" and "odd" — are similar to the Page command, but they instruct Word to immediately start the new formatting on a new even or odd-numbered page, leaving a blank page if necessary.

Division Break Bug

The last *division break* setting — "continuous" — does not work as Word documentation indicates. According to the documentation for version 3, at least two books from Microsoft Press, and a letter from the Product Support Division of Microsoft, you should be able to use a continuous division break to instruct Word to automatically start new column formatting when it moves to a new page. For example, you might use it if the front page of a newsletter is to have two columns, the interior pages are to have three columns, and you don't really care where in the text the change takes place. Microsoft, in the above sources, claims that if you set the division break to "continuous" for the first of the two divisions involved and to "page" for the second division, Word fills out the last page of the first division with text from the second division and starts the new format on the next page. It does not.

After additional investigation by Microsoft Product Support personnel, the company claimed that if you set the division break to "continuous" for both divisions involved, the command will work as documented. It still does not.

Version 4 documentation claims that a continous division break's new formatting "takes effect immediately without performing a page break." That may be so if all you are changing between the divisions is the right margin, but if you try anything more fancy, it still doesn't work.

You might want to experiment with the command to determine whether it can be of any use to you.

Microsoft is aware of the problem; they claim to be working on a solution, and perhaps the command will work properly in version 4.1.

Same Width

Word newspaper columns in a single document must all be of the same width. There is no way, for example, to have a 2" left column and a 4" right column.

You can, however, cheat a bit to produce asymmetry on the page. For example, set the division to two columns with no dividing gutter. Then, adjust the right indent of the paragraphs in the left column. The result will be a thinner left column with a gap between the columns. This solution is not elegant, but it works.

MIXING ONE- AND TWO-COLUMN TEXT

Word is not particularly adept at combining multicolumn text with single-column text, but there are ways to fool Word and combine single- and multi-column text on the same page.

The first method is to use running heads. Remember, running heads ignore page formatting commands, and you must format them with the Format Paragraph command. Also, you can extend a paragraph by using the new line character (press Shift-Return). By using new lines instead of paragraph ends, you can place several paragraphs of information at the top of a page, format it all as a running head, and then adjust the top margin to make sure there is enough room for it. In practice, this method is more useful if you want to place a title across a two-column page.

The second method is to use side-by-side columns and hand-format the text, which means you must carefully count lines and again use new line characters to introduce breaks between the paragraphs.

CHAPTER 12

FORMATTING WITH
STYLE SHEETS

This chapter discusses **style sheets**, which format text indirectly by associating a preformatted style with a group of characters, a paragraph, or a division. A style sheet is a collection of styles. Use the Gallery command on Word's main menu to create style sheets and manipulate stored styles.

NORMAL.STY

Even if you haven't noticed, you have already been working with a style sheet; it is named NORMAL.STY and is stored on your Word program disk or in the Word directory of your hard disk. When you first start Word, the program searches for this style sheet. Word 3.0 or earlier searches the Word program diskette or in the Word subdirectory of your hard disk. Beginning with version 3.1, Word first searches for NORMAL.STY on the default disk drive or in the default directory. If it can't locate NORMAL.STY, it searches the program disk or the Word subdirectory. If it cannot find NORMAL.STY, Word creates an empty style sheet and names it NORMAL.STY.

Until now, NORMAL.STY has been empty, but you will soon create styles and save them as part of NORMAL.STY.

STYLE BY EXAMPLE WITH 4.0

Starting with Word 4.0, you can instruct Word to use a new style by creating the formatting you want, naming the style, and saving it. (Version 3 does not offer style by example; you must use the Gallery command to create new styles.)

Consider an example. Suppose you want your standard paragraph to be indented 0.5" on the first line, single-spaced, and with a single line of blank space ahead of it. To perform this task, place the selection anywhere in a paragraph, choose the Format Paragraph command, and set the fields as follows:

```
FORMAT PARAGRAPH alignment: Left Centered Right Justified
      left indent: 0"          first line: .5"        right indent: 0"
      line spacing: 1 li       space before: 1 li     space after: 0 li
      keep together: Yes(No)   keep follow: Yes(No)   side by side: Yes(No)
```

Alternatively, you can use the built-in commands Alt-O (Open spacing) and Alt-F (First line indent).

Recording the Style

To record a style, press Alt-F10 or use the F(ormat) S(tyle) S(heet) R(ecord) command. Word will display the following fields:

```
FORMAT STYLESHEET RECORD key code:        usage: Character Paragraph Division
                variant:                  remark:
```

The Key Code

Word identifies each format in a style sheet with a one- or two-character key code used to format characters, paragraphs, and divisions in the same way you use Word's built-in formats. Press and hold the Alt key and simultaneously press the key code for a particular format. Word applies the format to the selected text.

To define a new Standard Paragraph, enter a key code of "SP."

Rules for Key Codes

You can use any one or two keys as a key code; however, there are points to consider when giving key codes to styles.

You are better off using two-key combinations. You will need the extra combinations, particularly when assigning key codes to paragraph styles, because 72 paragraph styles are available.

Also, select the same second character for division and the same second character for character styles. For example, all division styles might end with the letter D. Another appropriate second character might be /, the mathematical symbol for division.

There's one more important rule: *never* use an X as the first letter of a key code; doing so will prevent you from using Word's built-in styles. These styles are still available when using a style sheet by pressing Alt-X and the normal one-character code. For example, the code for built-in italics characters becomes Alternate-XI; however, if you define a style that has a key code starting with X, Word will not allow you to use the built-in styles.

Usage

The type of format defined is called the **usage**. Three kinds of formats can be defined with style sheets — character formats, paragraph formats, and division formats. Since you are formatting a paragraph style, choose Paragraph by pressing "P" or pressing the Space Bar to advance the high-light to "Paragraph." Then, press the Tab key to accept the choice and move on to the variant field.

Variant

Word allows a limited number of styles in each usage; the individual styles are called **variants**. Advance the selection to the *variant* field with the Tab key, and press F1 for a list of the variants available for paragraphs.

```
Standard           Footnote           Running Head       Heading level 1
Heading level 2    Heading level 3    Heading level 4    Heading level 5
Heading level 6    Heading level 7    Index level 1      Index level 2
Index level 3      Index level 4      Table level 1      Table level 2
Table level 3      Table level 4      1                  2
3                  4                  5                  6
7                  8                  9                  10
11                 12                 13                 14
15                 16                 17                 18
19                 20                 21                 22
23                 24                 25                 26
27                 28                 29                 30
31                 32                 33                 34
35                 36                 37                 38
39                 40                 41                 42
43                 44                 45                 46
47                 48                 49                 50
51                 52                 53                 54
55                 56

INSERT key code: {}                      usage: Character(Paragraph)Division
        variant: Standard                remark:
Enter variant or press F1 to select from list
GALLERY         {}                ?                      Microsoft Word
```

Figure 12.1

The list contains 72 variants, including the Standard variant currently needed, one for footnotes, another for running heads, seven for outline headings, four for index entries, four for table entries, and 54 numbered variants. The Standard variant is reserved by Word to replace default paragraph parameters. Press the Tab key to accept this choice and move to the *remark* field.

The Remark

With the *remark* field, Word allows you to give a name in "plain English" to each format in a style sheet. Type in STANDARD PARAGRAPH. It is suggested that you use uppercase letters, which will make styles much easier to find.

Any Style Sheet May Be Recorded

You can record any style using the Format Style Sheet Record command or the Alt-F10 key combination. If you choose "character" as the usage, Word will record the format of the characters contained in the selection. If you choose "paragraph," Word records the format of the paragraph containing the selection. If you choose "division," Word records the format of the division containing the selection.

If the selection text is in more than one format, Word will select the common elements of those formats and record them. For example, if you select two words, one of which is in Times Roman, 10-point italic type and the other in Times Roman, 10-point bold, when you record the character style of that selection, Word will record a format of Times Roman, 10-point and ignore the conflicting italic and bold traits.

ATTACHING A STYLE SHEET TO A DOCUMENT

When you first create a new document, it will automatically have the NORMAL.STY style sheet attached to it. If you want to attach another style sheet to a document, you must use the F(ormat) S(tyle) S(heet) A(ttach) command (F(ormat) S(tyle) S(heet) in version 3). Word requests the name of the style sheet to be attached to the document. Enter the style sheet name. If it is not on the current drive or in the current directory of a hard disk, you must specify the path to that style sheet. For example, to attach the style sheet called WORDBOOK.STY (from the \WORD subdirectory of the \BOOKS directory) to a manuscript, enter the name of the style sheet as follows:

FORMAT STYLE SHEET ATTACH: C:\BOOKS\WORD\WORDBOOK

Once a style sheet has been attached to a document, Word automatically loads the style sheet as it loads the document; the two remain linked until a new style sheet is specified for the document.

No Style Sheet

To remove all style sheets from a document, proceed as if attaching a style sheet. Instead of typing a new style sheet name, press Delete and then Return.

USING A STYLE SHEET TO FORMAT TEXT

Once a style sheet is attached to a document, there are two ways to apply a particular style to selected text. The first method is to use the key codes; the other method is with the Format Style Sheet command (Format Style in version 3).

Key Codes

To apply a particular style to selected text, press and hold the Alternate key and simultaneously press the key code for that style.

If you are applying a character style, it will apply to all text within a selection that is two or more characters long. If the selection includes only one character, enter the key code twice.

When applying a paragraph style, simply place the selection anywhere within the paragraph and issue the key code. If the selection extends across one or more paragraph boundaries, the new paragraph style will apply to all paragraphs containing part of the selection.

If you are applying a new division style, the new style will apply to all divisions containing part of the selection.

Format Style Sheet Command

The second way to apply a style to the selection is with the Format Style Sheet command (Format Style in version 3). When you choose Format Style Sheet, Word will offer you four choices:

```
FORMAT STYLESHEET: Attach Character Paragraph Division Record
```

In version 3, the submenu is a bit different:

```
FORMAT STYLE: Character Paragraph Character Sheet
```

As previously mentioned, you can use the Format Style Sheet Attach command (Format Style Sheet in version 3) to attach a style sheet to a document. Format Style Sheet Record (version 4 only) records a style and is the same as Alt-F10.

If you select any of the other three commands, Word will request the name of the style to be applied to the selected text. Word will suggest the standard style for that usage (Division Standard, Paragraph Standard, or Character Standard). If you want, enter the name of another style for that usage.

For example, to format a word in italics, select the word and choose Format Style Character. Word will suggest the Character Standard for the word:

```
FORMAT STYLESHEET CHARACTER: Character Standard
```

The result is not satisfactory, so press F1 (in version 4) or one of the arrow keys (in version 3) to see a list of the character styles available for the style sheet. The list will resemble the following:

```
 Character Standard               OP Character 5 (OPTIMA - SMALL CAPS -)
FN Character Footnote reference (FOOTN) GO Character 1 (GOTHIC CHARACTERS)
IC Character 2 (ITALIC CHARACTERS)      UC Character 3 (UNDERLINED CHARACTERS)
BC Character 4 (BOLD CHARACTERS)
```

```
FORMAT STYLESHEET CHARACTER: Character Standard

Enter character style or press F1 to select from list
Pg1 Li181 Co29   {command.}          ?                    CHAP12.DOC
```

Figure 12.2

As you can see, one of the styles is Character 2, italic characters. Use the arrow keys to move the selection to Character 2, and press Return to implement the choice.

Choose paragraph and division formats in a similar manner.

THE GALLERY COMMAND

There is another way to create style sheet formats: using the Gallery command. In version 3, the Gallery command is the only way to create style sheet formats.

Choose the Gallery command from the main menu. The screen will change to display all styles in the style sheet currently attached to your document.

The word GALLERY that appears at the bottom left of the display identifies Word's Gallery screen. The Gallery screen is organized much like the edit screen, and, in many ways, it functions similarly. Just as on the edit screen, the Gallery screen contains a text area and a command area with a menu, a message line, and a status line. The Gallery screen, however, exists solely to create and edit style sheets.

Examine the bottom right border of the screen. On the edit screen, this area lists the file currently being edited. On the Gallery screen, the name of the style sheet loaded for editing is listed — in this case, NORMAL.STY. If you have created a Standard Paragraph format with the Record Style command, it will appear in the gallery and should resemble the following:

```
■─[····│····1·········2·········3·········4·········5·········6·········7·]···■
  1    SP Paragraph Standard                        STANDARD PARAGRAPH
       Courier (modern a) 12. Flush left (first line indent 0.5"), space
       before 1 li.
  ◆
          ▶



                                                         ═NORMAL.STY═
COMMAND: Copy Delete Exit Format Help
         Insert Name Print Transfer Undo
Select style or press ESC to use menu
GALLERY            {}                    ?              CL             Microsoft Word
```

Figure 12.3

By choosing commands from the Gallery menu, you can add new styles to the style sheet and apply them to text.

DIVISION STYLES

Word allows you to define frequently used division formats and save them in style sheets. For example, if you edit a newsletter that uses both two- and three-column formats, you can define two division styles to include those formats. You can also define one division that prints page numbers at the top left corner of the page and another that prints page numbers in the bottom center of the page. Anything that can be done to a division with direct formatting can be done with a style sheet format. With a style sheet, however, you need only define the format once instead of every time it is used.

The Standard Division

One of the first things many Word users must do is change default page margins. Because a laser printer cannot print within 1/4" of the paper's edge, the actual paper size is 10.5" ×8". To properly position text, Word must be informed of this difference.

Each Word style sheet can contain a format called the Standard Division. If no Standard Division is defined for a style sheet, Word uses the default division parameters. A new Standard Division for NORMAL.STY must be defined, thus redefining Word's default margins.

The Gallery Insert Command

To create the Standard Division, you must insert a new format into the style sheet. Select the Insert command from Word's Gallery menu. In the command area, Word displays the following fields:

```
INSERT key code: {}            usage:(Character)Paragraph Division
          variant:              remark:
```

These fields are identical to those used to record a style. Enter a key code such as SD (for Standard Division). The usage is Division. The variant is Standard. Use F1 (in version 4) or the arrow keys (version 3) to display a list of available division formats. Type the words STANDARD DIVISION in the *remark* field.

When you press Return, Word inserts a new division format named Standard Division into the Gallery; it will now resemble the following:

```
⌐─[········1········2········3········4········5········6········7·]····⌐
│ 1    SD Division Standard                    STANDARD DIVISION
│      Page break. Page length 11"; width 8.5". Page # format Arabic. Top
│      margin 1"; bottom 1"; left 1.5"; right 1.5". Top running head at
│      0.5". Bottom running head at 0.5". Footnotes on same page.
│ 2    SP Paragraph Standard                   STANDARD PARAGRAPH
│      Courier (modern a) 12. Flush left (first line indent 0.5"), space
│      before 1 li.
│ ◆
│
│
│
│
│
│
│                                                        ─NORMAL.STY─
COMMAND: Copy Delete Exit Format Help
         Insert Name Print Transfer Undo
Key code not defined
GALLERY              {Division Stan...} ?         CL            Microsoft Word
```

Figure 12.4

The Gallery Format Command

The Standard Division — as Word first defines it — is the same as Word's default division formatting. To change it, select it and use the Format command on Word's Gallery menu.

Word recognizes that you have selected a division format, so it offers you the same choices as if you had chosen the Format Division command from the main menu:

FORMAT DIVISION: Margins Page-numbers Layout line-Numbers

Select the Margins option and Word will present you with the standard Format Division Margins fields:

FORMAT DIVISION MARGINS top: 1" bottom: 1"   left: 1.25" right: 1.25"
                page length: 11"   width: 8.5" gutter margin: 0"
            running head position from top: 0.5" from bottom: 0.5"

This screen should look familiar; it is the same as the Format Division Margins screen you examined in Chapter 3, "Editing Basics."

To correct the laser printer's inability to print near the edge of the page, you must adjust the values in the Format Division Margin fields as follows:

```
FORMAT DIVISION MARGINS top: 1"    bottom: 1"    left: 1"  right: 1"
              page length: 10.5"    width: 8"  gutter margin: 0"
          running head position from top: 0.5"  from bottom: 0.5"
```

Pressing Return then formats a new Standard Division with a paper size of 10.5" × 8" inches and margins set at 1" around the entire edge, resulting in real margins of 1.25" (due to the 1/4" unprintable area around the edge of the page).

When you are finished, the Gallery should resemble the following:

```
▐─[·········1·········2·········3·········4·········5·········6·········7·]···▌
  1    SD Division Standard                      STANDARD DIVISION
           Page break. Page length 10.5"; width 8". Page # format Arabic. Top
           margin 1"; bottom 1"; left 1"; right 1". Top running head at 0.5".
           Bottom running head at 0.5". Footnotes on same page.
  2    SP Paragraph Standard                      STANDARD PARAGRAPH
           Courier (modern a) 12. Flush left (first line indent 0.5"), space
           before 1 li.
  ♦

                                 ▸

                                                            ─NORMAL.STY─
COMMAND: Copy Delete Exit Format Help
         Insert Name Print Transfer Undo
Select style or press ESC to use menu
GALLERY              {}              ?                    Microsoft Word
```

Figure 12.5

Note that in the description of the Division Standard on the screen, the left and right margins are now changed to 1", and the paper size is 10.5" × 8".

Formatting Other Divisions

Just as you changed the Standard Division style, you can store other division styles in a style sheet. In these styles, you can change more than the margins; you can create styles with any division parameter you can adjust with direct division formatting commands.

For example, create a second division style for a two-column format. In doing so, you will learn more about the Gallery's Insert command and how to use the Gallery Copy and Delete commands.

The Gallery Copy Command

Begin by copying the existing Standard Division format. You will soon modify it.

If you are not already at the Gallery screen, select the Gallery command from Word's main menu. If the Standard Division is not already selected, use the arrow keys to select it.

Choose the Copy command from the Gallery menu. This command copies the selected style (or styles) into the Gallery scrap. The Gallery scrap is separate from the edit screen's scrap, so you needn't worry about overwriting material in the edit scrap.

The Gallery Delete Command

The Gallery's Delete command will also copy selected styles into the Gallery scrap. As on Word's edit screen, the difference between Copy and Delete is that Copy copies the selection to scrap while leaving it in the style sheet or document. Delete copies the selection to the scrap but also removes it from the style sheet or document.

The Gallery Insert Command

When the Gallery scrap is empty, the Gallery Insert command creates a new style. You've already used the Gallery Insert command to create the new Standard Division.

When there *is* something in the Gallery scrap, you can also use the Gallery Insert command to copy the contents of the scrap into the style sheet rather than create a new style.

Select the Insert command from the Gallery menu:

```
INSERT key code: {}          usage:(Character)Paragraph Division
          variant: 1         remark:
```

If you want to create a new style, enter a new key code in place of the curly brackets. If you want to copy the style contained in the Gallery scrap into the style sheet, just press Return.

For this exercise, press Return, which writes a second copy of the Standard Division back into the style sheet. The screen should now dispay two copies of the Standard Division format.

Use the arrow keys to select either of the two identical formats. Choose Format and then Layout. You'll receive the standard Format Division Layout fields:

```
FORMAT DIVISION LAYOUT footnotes:(Same-page)End
         number of columns: 1        space between columns: 0.5"
              division break:(Page)Continuous Column Even Odd
```

Use the Tab key to advance the selection to the *number of columns* field, and change it to 2. Press Return to return to the Gallery screen. You will see that the version of the selected division has changed to reflect the selected two-column style.

The Gallery Name Command

You can now use the Gallery's Name command to rename this new division format. Select the Name command; Word allows you to change the *key code*, *variant*, and *remark* fields of this style. Before the change, the command area of your screen will resemble the following:

```
NAME key code: SD                    variant: Standard
          remark: STANDARD DIVISION
```

After the change, it might resemble the following:

```
NAME key code: 2D                    variant: 1
        remark: 2-COL STANDARD DIVISION
```

You can choose the key code and remark. The variant can be any variant not already in use. For a list of available variants, advance the selection to the *variant* field and press F1 (in version 4) or an arrow key (in version 3).

When you make the changes and press Return, the Gallery screen listing will reflect the new names.

```
□─[········1········2········3········4········5········6········7·]···□
│ 1   SD Division Standard                    STANDARD DIVISION
│         Page break. Page length 10.5"; width 8". Page # format Arabic. Top
│         margin 1"; bottom 1"; left 1"; right 1". Top running head at 0.5".
│         Bottom running head at 0.5". Footnotes on same page.
│ 2   2D Division 1                         2-COL STANDARD DIVISION
│         Page break. Page length 10.5"; width 8". Page # format Arabic. Top
│         margin 1"; bottom 1"; left 1"; right 1". Top running head at 0.5".
│         Bottom running head at 0.5". 2 columns; spacing 0.5". Footnotes on
│         same page.
│ 3   SP Paragraph Standard                    STANDARD PARAGRAPH
│         Courier (modern a) 12. Flush left (first line indent 0.5"), space
│         before 1 li.                ▶
│ ◆
│
│                                                         ─NORMAL.STY─
COMMAND: Copy Delete Exit Format Help
         Insert Name Print Transfer Undo
Select style or press ESC to use menu
GALLERY            {Division Stan...} ?        CL            Microsoft Word
```

Figure 12.6

As many as 22 division styles can be included in each style sheet.

The Gallery Transfer Save Command

Before continuing, save the style sheet by selecting the Transfer Save command from the Gallery menu. Word presumes a file extension of .STY and saves the style sheet with the name and in the directory you specify. If you don't specify a drive or directory, Word will save the style sheet on the drive or in the directory specified by the Transfer Options (or Gallery Transfer Options) command.

Save the style sheet as TEST.STY:

`TRANSFER SAVE style sheet name: TEST`

Other Gallery Transfer commands will be discussed later in this chapter.

PARAGRAPH STYLES

Word contains 10 built-in paragraph styles, as discussed in Chapters 3 and 10; however, by using style sheets, you can add another 74 paragraph styles, including styles for footnotes, headings, indices, and tables.

The Standard Paragraph

Word's built-in standard paragraph isn't of much use. It is flush left, ragged right, single-spaced, and contains no spacing before or after the paragraph. There are no indents in the paragraph's format, so it is hard to tell where one paragraph ends and another begins, which is why, along with a new Standard Division style, one of the first things you did in this chapter was create a new Standard Paragraph style by using the Format Style Sheet Record command in version 4. To create the same standard paragraph through the Gallery, select the Gallery Insert command again. The screen will appear as follows:

```
INSERT key code: {}          usage:(Character)Paragraph Division
         variant: 1          remark:
```

Enter a key code of SP (for Standard Paragraph). Select "Paragraph" for usage. The *variant* field should read "Standard." Press F1 (in version 4) or one of the arrow keys (in version 3) to display a list of available paragraph styles.

```
Standard (SP)        Footnote             Running Head          Heading level 1
Heading level 2      Heading level 3      Heading level 4       Heading level 5
Heading level 6      Heading level 7      Index level 1         Index level 2
Index level 3        Index level 4        Table level 1         Table level 2
Table level 3        Table level 4        1                     2
3                    4                    5                     6
7                    8                    9                     10
11                   12                   13                    14
15                   16                   17                    18
19                   20                   21                    22
23                   24                   25                    26
27                   28                   29                    30
31                   32                   33                    34
35            ▶      36                   37                    38
39                   40                   41                    42
43                   44                   45                    46
47                   48                   49                    50
51                   52                   53                    54
55                   56

NAME key code: SP                  variant: Standard
       remark: STANDARD PARAGRAPH
Enter variant or press F1 to select from list
GALLERY           {}                     ?                 Microsoft Word
```

Figure 12.7

The selection should be on "Standard." Press the Tab key to accept the choice and move the selection back to the *remark* field in the command area of the screen. Type STANDARD PARAGRAPH.

Next, press Return, and Word adds the Standard Paragraph to the style sheet.

```
├─[····!····1·········2·········3·········4·········5·········6·········7·]···┐
│  1   SD Division Standard                        STANDARD DIVISION
│         Page break. Page length 10.5"; width 8". Page # format Arabic. Top
│         margin 1"; bottom 1"; left 1"; right 1". Top running head at 0.5".
│         Bottom running head at 0.5". Footnotes on same page.
│  2   2D Division 1                               2-COL STANDARD DIVISION
│         Page break. Page length 10.5"; width 8". Page # format Arabic. Top
│         margin 1"; bottom 1"; left 1"; right 1". Top running head at 0.5".
│         Bottom running head at 0.5". 2 columns; spacing 0.5". Footnotes on
│         same page.
│  3   SP Paragraph Standard                       STANDARD PARAGRAPH
│         Courier (modern a) 12. Flush left (first line indent 0.5"), space
│         before 1 li.
│  ◆      ▶

                                                               ─NORMAL.STY─┘
COMMAND: Copy Delete Exit Format Help
         Insert Name Print Transfer Undo
Select style or press ESC to use menu
GALLERY           {}                     ?                 Microsoft Word
```

Figure 12.8

Modifying the Standard Paragraph

When you created the Standard Paragraph using the Record Style function, the paragraph was already formatted, but the Standard Paragraph just created in the Gallery is not. You can, however, use the Gallery Format command to adjust all parameters of the new Standard Paragraph. Only now can you adjust paragraph spacing (alignment, indents, line spacing, space before, and space after); you can also adjust the tab settings and characters to be used for your Standard Paragraph.

A useful Standard Paragraph might contain the following nonstandard traits:

- Times Roman 10-point font
- 0.5" first-line indent
- 1 line of spacing before

By selecting the Standard Paragraph style and choosing the Gallery Format command, you can change both the font and the spacing used in the Standard Paragraph. Note that the Gallery Format command takes you directly to the Format Paragraph screen. Because you have selected a paragraph style on the Gallery edit screen, you are only allowed to adjust paragraph format features.

Formatting Other Paragraphs

The power of style sheets becomes apparent when you work with paragraph styles. For example, a style sheet used to write a book may include many different paragraph styles. In addition to a Standard Paragraph, there may be styles for tables, outline heading styles, long quotes, and screen displays. Changing the look of a manuscript requires only a few quick keystrokes.

Other Dedicated Variants

In addition to the dedicated Standard Paragraph, Word also reserves other paragraph styles for particular purposes.

The Footnote Style

One variant is reserved for footnotes. To print footnotes at the bottom of the page, you normally define the style as a smaller version of your normal font, if the smaller font is available. If the footnotes will appear at the document's end, you can format the footnote style with an indent so each note will stand out.

The Running Head Style

The task of formatting running heads can become tedious if you must do it for each chapter file of a book; however, if you use the running head dedicated paragraph format, you can quickly and easily create running heads for documents.

The dedicated format for running heads is only available in version 4.

Heading Levels

Word also dedicates seven paragraph styles to outline heading levels. These styles are extremely powerful tools for formatting manuscript headings. The next chapter, "Formatting with Style Sheets and the Word Outliner," fully discusses this feature.

Index and Table Levels

Word also reserves special paragraph formats for index and table entries. In Chapters 15 and 16, you will learn how to automatically generate indices or tables for documents and how to use these styles to produce dynamic indices and tables.

Numbered Variants

The majority of Word paragraph styles are numbered. When you instruct the Gallery to insert a new paragraph style, it suggests the next available numbered style as the variant. Most of the time, the choice will be adequate. These styles can be used for formatting any paragraph style you want.

CHARACTER STYLES

As you might expect, you can use character styles to format the characters in the selection. Once defined, the styles work much like Word's built-in character styles; you select the text to be formatted, press and hold the Alt key, and simultaneously press the key code.

Variants

Word offers 28 possible character styles. Two of the styles — page number and footnote reference — are dedicated. The other 26 styles are available for other formats.

Note that there is no Standard Character. Word uses the character defined for the Standard Paragraph as its standard character.

Page Number

The page number style applies only to page numbers created with the Format Division Page-number command. Page numbers created with the built-in Glossary command (page) carry the same formatting as the paragraph containing them.

Footnote Reference

Word also dedicates a character style to footnote reference marks. Don't confuse this style with the footnote paragraph style, which attaches to the footnote text. Usually, the style for footnote reference marks is defined as superscript text. Footnotes are covered in detail in Chapter 14, "Footnotes."

REORGANIZING A STYLE SHEET

Often, if you develop a style sheet as you work on a document and add new styles as needed, you will end up with a disorganized style sheet combining character, paragraph, and division styles. By using the Gallery commands, however, it is easy to quickly rearrange styles in a style sheet because you can delete and insert styles as simply as you can delete and insert text.

If you want to move a style to another position in a style sheet, just select it, delete it to the scrap, and insert it in the new position.

You are better off keeping styles of various kinds together in the style sheet. For instance, keep all character styles at the beginning of the style sheet, all paragraph styles in the middle of the style sheet, and all division styles at the end of the style sheet. Also organize styles within the categories. You might want to keep outline heading styles together, index styles together, and so on.

THE RELATIONSHIP BETWEEN STYLE SHEETS

Why should you bother to define a style for italic characters when Word already has a built-in italic character style? The answer involves the way different style sheets relate to one another.

When you examined direct character formatting, you saw that each typeface has both a proper name and a generic name. As mentioned, the generic name is important because it is used by Word to transport formatting between printers. In the example, the "roman a" font on a Mannesmann Tally laser printer was a Roman typeface, and the "roman a" font on an Epson FX printer was Pica. If a document created on the first printer was printed on an Epson printer, text formatted for Roman on the first printer would print as Pica on the Epson. The link is the generic name of the font.

Linked by Variants

Style sheets are linked in a similar way — by the style variants; thus, if you format text in one style sheet with Paragraph 1 and then change to another style sheet, you will find that text formatted by the new style sheet's instructions for Paragraph 1.

For example, if you are using different printers (perhaps a laser printer at work and a daisy wheel at home), you might design a style sheet to take advantage of the formatting power of the laser printer while considering the limitations of the daisy wheel. If Character 2 is defined as italics on the laser printer, it might be defined as underlined on the daisy wheel.

DIRECT FORMATTING WITH AN ATTACHED STYLE SHEET

When you format text with direct formatting commands, the direct formatting overrides style sheet formatting. Consider an example.

Suppose you are debating whether to use 10-point or 12-point type as the standard character in a style sheet named LETTER.STY used for correspondence. You have occasionally changed the type fonts in the style sheet's various definitions to compare the appearance of both sizes.

Suppose you wrote a letter yesterday in a style sheet that specified 12-point type. In the letter, you directly formatted some text as italics using the Alternate-XI command. Later, you decided to use 10-point type and made the changes in the style sheet by selecting all the character and paragraph styles and specifying 10-point Roman type. When you print the letter, however, the text that had been formatted as italics in 12-point type still prints as 12-point italics. The direct formatting, originally installed when 12-point was the selected font, overrides the new definitions in the style sheet. Had you been using the style sheet definition for italics, the font size would have changed with the style sheet.

THE REMAINING GALLERY COMMANDS

Gallery Transfer

The Gallery Transfer commands work much like the Transfer commands on Word's main menu, but they can only be used to manipulate style sheets.

Gallery Transfer Save

You have learned to save a style sheet using the Gallery Transfer Save command. Remember, unless you specify otherwise, the style sheet will be stored on the drive or in the directory specified with the Transfer Options command (or the Gallery Transfer Options command).

Gallery Transfer Load

You may use the Gallery Transfer Load command to load a style sheet into the Gallery for editing. If the style sheet's Gallery contains unsaved changes, Word will allow you to save them before loading the new style sheet for editing.

Loading a style sheet into the Gallery does not attach that style sheet to the current document. You may edit it, save it, and edit another style sheet without affecting the document being edited when the Gallery command was issued.

In version 4, when you exit from the Gallery, Word allows you to attach the style sheet in the Gallery to the current document.

Gallery Transfer Clear

The Gallery Transfer Clear command clears the Gallery screen and provides a blank style sheet with which you can work; however, if unsaved changes exist in the style sheet on the screen, Word first allows you to save them.

Gallery Transfer Delete

The Gallery Transfer Delete command can be used to delete files from disk. This command presumes a file extension of .STY unless you specify otherwise.

Gallery Transfer Merge

Use this command to merge two style sheets. The style sheet you name will be added to the style sheet already in the Gallery.

If there are any conflicting styles — two styles defined as the same variant or two styles using the same key code — you must use the Gallery Name command to assign a new variant to one of the styles before you can save the combined style sheet.

Gallery Transfer Options

The Gallery Transfer Options command is the same as the main menu Transfer Options command. If you use either command to change the default drive or directory, change it for both style sheets and documents.

Gallery Name

The Gallery Name command allows you to change the key code, variant, or remark attached to a style:

```
NAME key code: UC                    variant: 1
        remark: UNDERLINED CHARACTERS
```

Change any of the three fields by advancing the selection to the field (with the Tab key or, in version 4, the arrow keys), and then enter the new information. To display a list of available variants, press F1 (version 4) or one of the arrow keys (version 3) when the selection is on the *variant* field.

Gallery Print

The Gallery Print command prints a hard copy of the Gallery listing for reference.

Gallery Undo

The Gallery Undo command works much like the Undo command on the main menu; it reverses your last editing decision. Remember, you can also undo an Undo command.

Gallery Exit

The Gallery Exit command indicates that you are finished working with style sheets and want to return to editing. If you have modified a style sheet other than the style sheet attached to the current document, you will be allowed to save any changes before returning to the edit screen. In version 4, you will also be allowed to attach the style sheet to the current document. If you have edited the style sheet already attached to the current document, you needn't save the changes at this point. Word allows you to save the style sheet when you finish editing.

Gallery Help

The Gallery Help command starts Word's help function.

SEARCHING FOR STYLES

Starting with Word 4.0, you can also search through a document for particular styles. Use the Format sEarch command. The following fields will be displayed:

```
FORMAT SEARCH:(Character)Paragraph Style
```

Searching for Character Formats

If you select "Character," Word displays the following choices:

```
FORMAT SEARCH CHARACTER direction: Up Down
         bold: Yes No           italic: Yes No        underline: Yes No
         strikethrough: Yes No  uppercase: Yes No    small caps: Yes No
         double underline: Yes No  position: Normal Superscript Subscript
         font name:             font size:            hidden: Yes No
```

Fill in a the direction in which you want Word to search and a description of the character format you want to find. You needn't fill in all fields. For example, if you want to find all occurrences of Prestige type, regardless of their style, just fill in the font name field with "Prestige." Press Return when the character format is described to your satisfaction; Word will find the first occurrence of the format.

As with a regular search, press Shift-F4 to repeat the search.

Searching for Paragraph Formats

When you select Format sEarch Paragraph, the following fields are displayed:

```
FORMAT SEARCH PARAGRAPH direction: Up Down
      alignment: Left Centered Right Justified
      left indent:            first line:          right indent:
      line spacing:           space before:        space after:
      keep together: Yes No   keep follow: Yes No  side by side: Yes No
```

As with a character search, fill in the direction of the search and a description of the paragraph format you want to find. Then press Return. To repeat the search, press Shift-F4.

Searching for Style Sheet Styles

Searching for a style sheet style is even easier; just specify the key code of the style you want Word to find, indicate the direction of the search, and press Return.

```
FORMAT SEARCH STYLE key code:          direction: Up(Down)
```

Again, to repeat the search, press Shift-F4.

CHAPTER 13

FORMATTING WITH STYLE SHEETS AND THE WORD OUTLINER

As you learned in the last chapter, Word dedicates seven paragraph formats to outline headings. By using these styles, you can simultaneously increase outlining speed and neatly format your document.

The first thing you need is an outline to work with. Start Word, make sure you have a clear screen, and then switch to outline view and enter the following outline. Remember, use Alt-9 and Alt-0 to set outline heading levels, Alt-9 to change text into a heading, and Alt-P to change a heading back to text.

```
▯─────[·········1·········2·········3·········4·········5·········]·········7···▯
* ▪   Invention¶
* ▪ +     Starting Off¶
* ▪       Focusing and Negative Invention¶
* ▪       Positive Invention¶
* ▪           Hueristics¶
* ▪           Outlining¶
* ▪       Goals of Invention¶
* ▪   Drafting¶
* ▪       Red Queen School of Writing¶
* ▪   Revision¶
* ▪       Truth and Accuracy¶
* ▪       Structure¶
* ▪           Beginning, Middle and End?¶
* ▪       Paragraphs¶
* ▪           Christensen Analysis¶
* ▪               General to Specific¶
* ▪ +   Sentences¶
* ▪   Diction¶
* ▪           The Right Meaning¶
* ▪           Foreign Words¶
* ▪       Grammar, Spelling and Punctuation¶
```

Key code not defined

Figure 13.1

You must attach a style sheet to this outline. Choose Format Stylesheet Attach from the main menu (Format Style Sheet in version 3). Word requests the name of the style sheet to attach to this document. Type OUTLINE and press Return.

If the OUTLINE.STY style sheet included with Word is on the Word program disk or in the Word subdirectory of your hard disk, Word will attach that style sheet to this document. If that style sheet is not available, don't panic. Word will display the following:

```
Enter Y to create style sheet
```

Enter Y and proceed.

Choose Gallery from Word's main menu. If OUTLINE.STY is on your disk, you'll see a full Gallery screen. You must modify the styles for Paragraph Heading Level 1 through Level 7 and the Standard Paragraph according to the following table. If OUTLINE.STY is not on your disk, the Gallery screen will be empty. In such a case, you must create the eight styles. Either method requires approximately the same amount of work.

Paragraph	Paragraph Parameters
Heading Level 1	**BOLD, UNDERLINED, UPPERCASE** characters. Centered, 1.5 lines of spacing before. Key code Alt-1.
Heading Level 2	**Bold, underlined, mixed-case** characters. Flush left, 1 line of spacing before. Key code Alt-2.
Heading Level 3	**Bold** characters. Flush left, 1 line of spacing before. Key code Alt-3.
Heading Level 4	UNDERLINED, UPPERCASE characters. Flush left, 1 line of spacing before. Key code Alt-4.
Heading Level 5	Underlined, mixed-case characters. Flush left, 1 line of spacing before. Key code Alt-5.
Heading Level 6	UPPERCASE characters. Flush left, 1 line of spacing before. Key code Alt-6.
Heading Level 7	Mixed-case characters. Flush left, 1 line of spacing before. Key code Alt-7.
Standard Paragraph	Mixed-case characters. Flush left, 1 line of spacing before. Key code SP.

When you are finished, the Gallery screen should resemble the following. Your font choices may differ depending on your printer.

```
1[·······1·········2········3·······4·······5·······]····7·····
 1    1  Paragraph Heading level 1            ALT-1 HEADING LEVEL 1
         Roman (roman a) 10/12 Bold Underlined Uppercase. Centered, space
         before 1.5 li (keep with following paragraph).
 2    2  Paragraph Heading level 2            ALT-2 HEADING LEVEL 2
         Roman (roman a) 10/12 Bold Underlined. Flush left, space before 1
         li (keep with following paragraph).
 3    3  Paragraph Heading level 3            ALT-3 HEADING LEVEL 3
         Roman (roman a) 10/12 Bold. Flush left, space before 1 li (keep
         with following paragraph).
 4    4  Paragraph Heading level 4            ALT-4 HEADING LEVEL 4
         Roman (roman a) 10/12 Underlined Uppercase. Flush left, space
         before 1 li (keep with following paragraph).
 5    5  Paragraph Heading level 5            ALT-5 HEADING LEVEL 5
         Roman (roman a) 10/12 Underlined. Flush left, space before 1 li
         (keep with following paragraph).
 6    6  Paragraph Heading level 6            ALT-6 HEADING LEVEL 6
         Roman (roman a) 10/12 Uppercase. Flush left, space before 1 li
         (keep with following paragraph).
 7    7  Paragraph Heading level 7            ALT-7 HEADING LEVEL 7

COMMAND: Copy Delete Exit Format Help
         Insert Name Print Transfer Undo
         e sheet or choose Exit to see document
GALLERY  {}                          ?         NL Microsoft Word: OUTLINE.STY
```

Figure 13.2

Exit from the Gallery and return to Word's edit screen. The outline will have changed.

```
1——0···1···[·········2········3·······4·······5·······]·······7···
1   INVENTION¶
2 +   Starting Off¶
2     Focusing and Negative Invention¶
2     Positive Invention¶
3        Hueristics¶
3        Outlining¶
2     Goals of Invention¶
1   DRAFTING¶
2     Red Queen School of Writing¶
1   REVISION¶
2     Truth and Accuracy¶
2     Structure¶
3        Beginning, Middle and End?¶
2     Paragraphs¶
3        Christensen Analysis¶
4           GENERAL TO SPECIFIC¶
2 +   Sentences¶
2     Diction¶
3        The Right Meaning¶
3        Foreign Words¶
2     Grammar, Spelling and Punctuation¶
T1       ◆

Level 2 {¶}                       ?         Microsoft Word:
```

Figure 13.3

Note that character formatting defined in the Gallery has attached itself to your headings. First-level headings are **<u>BOLD, UNDERLINED, AND UP-PERCASE</u>**; second-level headings are **<u>Bold, underlined, and mixed-case</u>**; third-level headings are **Bold**, and so on. This definition provides another clue as to a heading's level.

Paragraph formatting, however, is not applied in outline view. Note that the level 1 heading is flush left, not centered as specified by the style definition. In outline view, the outline hierarchy takes precedence over formatting such as paragraph alignment, paragraph indents, and space before and after the paragraph.

CHANGING HEADING LEVELS

You can still use Alt-9 and Alt-0 to change heading levels in your outline. Now, however, when you change a heading's level, you also change its style.

You can also apply a new style to change heading levels. Furthermore, when you use heading level styles to set a heading level, you can violate the hierarchy and skip outline levels.

To skip levels, position the selection on the line that reads "Red Queen School of Writing." Press Alt-9 to raise the heading to level 1; its format changes from underlined bold to underlined bold uppercase. Next, press Alt-0 twice to attempt to lower it to level 3. Word will accept one Alt-0 and lower the heading to level 2, but when you try to force the heading down to level 3, Word just beeps. The program won't allow you to use Alt-0 to move a heading because this violates the hierarchy.

Try pressing Alt-3, the key code for a level 3 heading. The line switches to level 3 without an intervening level 2.

```
┌─────0·········!····[····2·········3····!····4·········5·········]·········7···┐
│1    INVENTION¶                                                                │
│2  + Starting Off¶                                                             │
│2    Focusing and Negative Invention¶                                          │
│2    Positive Invention¶                                                       │
│3        Hueristics¶                                                           │
│3        Outlining¶                                                            │
│2    Goals of Invention¶                                                       │
│1    DRAFTING¶                                                                 │
│3        Red Queen School of Writing¶                                          │
│1    REVISION¶                                                                 │
│2    Truth and Accuracy¶                                                       │
│2    Structure¶                                                                │
│3        Beginning, Middle and End?¶                                           │
│2    Paragraphs¶                                                               │
│3        Christensen Analysis¶                                                 │
│4            GENERAL TO SPECIFIC¶                                              │
│2  + Sentences¶                                                                │
│2    Diction¶                                                                  │
│3        The Right Meaning¶                                                    │
│3        Foreign Words¶                                                        │
│2    Grammar, Spelling and Punctuation¶                                        │
│T1       ◆                                                                     │
└──────────────────────────────────────────────────────────────────────────────┘
```
`Level 3` `{¶}`   ?   Microsoft Word:

Figure 13.4

In other words, style takes priority over heading levels.

OUT OF OUTLINE VIEW

When you leave Word's outline view, you will find that all formatting assigned to the headings comes into play. In text view, major headings are centered and the spacing before and after paragraphs makes them stand out. A few paragraphs of text have been added with Standard Paragraph formatting to make the contrast clearer.

```
┌─────[····!····1·········2·········3·········4·········5·········]·········7···┐
│1                        DRAFTING¶                                            │
│SP       This a paragraph of text under the major heading                      │
│     "Drafting."  It is here just to fill space on the screen. ¶               │
│3    Red Queen School of Writing¶                                              │
│SP       This paragraph is under the third level heading "Red                   │
│     Queen School of Writing."  Notice that there is no second                  │
│     level heading between the first level "Drafting" and the                   │
│     third level "Red Queen School of Writing." ¶                              │
│SP       It's not needed because I used a style sheet to format                 │
│     the headings, not the Alt-9 and Alt-0 commands.  Alt-9 and                 │
│     Alt-0 do not allow you to skip outline levels.  Style sheets               │
│     do.¶                                                                       │
│SP       In addition, style sheets attach formatted styles to                  │
│     the headings making them easier to distinguish on the screen               │
│     as well as on the page. ▯                                                 │
└──────────────────────────────────────────────────────────────────────────────┘
```
Key code not defined

Figure 13.5

USES OF STYLE SHEET OUTLINING

It is possible to outline almost exclusively by applying styles rather than using Alt-9 and Alt-0. The style sheet for a book manuscript, for example, might use all seven outline heading styles. The highest level might use a key code of "PT" for Part Title. The next level down might be Chapter Title ("CT") followed by A-Heading ("AH") through E-Heading ("EH"). For this type of project, such names make more sense than levels 1 through 7.

A Problem with Style Sheet Outlining

Because using styles to outline allows you to violate the outline hierarchy, it may sometimes appear that the Outliner isn't working correctly.

For example, suppose you have an outline with a heading preceded by a + sign to indicate that it contains subheadings. When you try to expand it with the Gray + key, however, nothing happens because the Gray + key only expands headings one level below the selected heading. If your outline skips a level (for example, jumps from a level 1 to a level 3), pressing the Gray + key while the level 1 heading is selected might not do anything.

Use the Gray * key to expand all subheadings at all levels; this will expand your recalcitrant level 3 heading.

PART IV

WORD AND THE ACADEMIC

CHAPTER 14

FOOTNOTES

One of the most difficult tasks of preparing an academic or scientific paper is adding and formatting footnotes. Do you put the footnotes at the bottom of the page or at the end of chapters? How many lines do you leave for the footnotes at the bottom of the page? What format do they take? Do you number them sequentially, or are there so few that you can indicate them with an an occasional asterisk or dagger?

Formatting footnotes is a complex task, but a task that is sometimes necessary. Fortunately, Word makes formatting footnotes almost tolerable.

FOOTNOTE PRINT POSITION

Whether footnotes print at the bottom of the page or at the end of the division depends on the setting of the F(ormat) D(ivision) L(ayout) command:

```
FORMAT DIVISION LAYOUT footnotes:(Same-Page)End
        number of columns: 1        space between columns: 0.5"
            division break:(Page)Continuous Column Even Odd
```

Examine the first field, which controls the location of footnotes in this division.

FOOTNOTE ACTUAL POSITION

Footnotes are actually stored in a document at the end of each division. If a document has more than one division, each will have its own footnotes and footnote numbering sequence.

ENTERING THE FOOTNOTE REFERENCE MARK

The first step to adding a footnote to a Word document is to place a footnote reference mark in the document. Use the Format Footnote command, which produces a single field for you to fill in:

```
FORMAT FOOTNOTE reference mark:
```

In version 3, the field reads as follows:

FORMAT FOOTNOTE:

When you choose the Format Footnote command, Word allows you to enter anything you want as the footnote reference mark.

You will usually want sequentially numbered footnotes. For numbered footnote reference marks, just press Return. Word automatically supplies the correct footnote number.

If you rarely use footnotes, use an asterisk or other single character. Type the asterisk and press Return.

More intricate footnotes are just as easy. For example, the citation standards of the American Psychological Association call for the author's name and year of publication in parentheses, e.g., (Perrin, 1987).

ENTERING THE FOOTNOTE ITSELF

As soon as you press Return for the Format Footnote command, Word enters the footnote reference and jumps the selection to the end of your document. Actually, the selection jumps to a position beyond the end of the text in the document. You will see that the selection follows a duplicate of your footnote reference and the end-of-file marker.

Type the content of the footnote.

Don't worry yet about formatting the footnote; this process will be discussed later in the chapter.

THE JUMP FOOTNOTE COMMAND

To return to your text, use the J(ump) F(ootnote) command. Word will return you to the footnote reference mark in the main text.

The previous method is just one use of the Jump Footnote command. Depending on the location of the selection, the Jump Footnote command will have one of several effects:

- When the selection is in a footnote, the Jump Footnote command will take you to the corresponding footnote reference mark.

- If the selection is on a footnote reference mark, the Jump Footnote command will jump you to the corresponding footnote.

- If you are in the middle of text, the Jump Footnote command will jump toward the end of the document, stopping at the next footnote reference mark. If there are no more footnote references in the document, Word will give you the message "No more footnote references."

- If an extended selection (such as an entire paragraph) contains a footnote reference, the Jump Footnote command will jump you to the included reference.

- If a selection contains more than one footnote reference, Word will jump to the first reference.

THE FOOTNOTE WINDOW

Word takes care of all navigating while jumping between footnote references and footnotes, but you can't see them both on the screen at the same time until you open a **footnote window**. A footnote window stretches across the bottom of the window containing the document. When a footnote reference mark is visible in the main window, Word places the corresponding footnote in the window.

```
┌┤────────────────────────────────────────────────────────────────┐
│1                                                                 │
│ AH   The Footnote Window¶                                        │
│                                                                  │
│ SP        Word takes care of all navigating while jumping between footnote │
│      references and footnotes, but you can't see them both on the screen at │
│      the same time until you open a footnote window.  A footnote window │
│      stretches across the bottom of the window containing the document.  When │
│      a footnote reference mark is visible in the main window, Word places the │
│      corresponding footnote in the window.¹ ¶                     │
│                                                                  │
│                                                                  │
│ FH                          Figure 14▪1 here¶                    │
│                                                                  │
│                                                                  │
│2─────────────────────────────────────────────────────────────── │
│ FS        ¹This footnote is just to demonstrate the use of a footnote window, │
│      showing both main text and the footnote on the screen at the same time.¶ │
│                                                      ─CHAP14.DOC─ │
└──────────────────────────────────────────────────────────────────┘
COMMAND: Copy Delete Format Gallery Help Insert Jump Library
         Options Print Quit Replace Search Transfer Undo Window
Edit document or press Esc to use menu
Pg3 Co38          {n}                    ?                  Microsoft Word
```

Figure 14.1

Opening a Footnote Window

There are two ways to open a footnote window.

The W(indow) S(plit) F(ootnote) command works just as it would for a regular window:

WINDOW SPLIT FOOTNOTE: at line 12

Word suggests the line containing the selection as the split site. In the example, this is line 12. You can change the site to any line you want by entering the new value and then pressing Return.

You can also use a mouse to open a footnote window. Position the mouse pointer along the right border of the window from which you want to split the footnote window. Press a Shift key and either mouse button. If you are too near the top or bottom of the main window, Word will beep and refuse to open the window. Move farther in from the top or bottom border, and try again.

When a footnote window opens, it is distinguished from the main window with a row of hyphens. If the main window has a visible ruler, the row of hyphens will also contain the ruler.

Like a regular window, a footnote window has a number in its upper left corner.

How Big Should the Window Be?

In a document with many footnotes, it is often useful to keep a small footnote window open at the bottom of the screen as you scroll through the main document. When a footnote reference appears on the screen, the corresponding footnote appears in the window.

Make sure the footnote window contains at least two lines. If you format footnotes with one line of space before them, all that will show in a one-line footnote window is the empty space.

Closing a Footnote Window

A footnote window is closed in much the same way as a regular window. Use the W(indow) C(lose) command and refer to the window by number. With a mouse, place the mouse pointer on the right footnote window margin and click both mouse buttons. Unlike closing a regular window, you cannot close a footnote window by clicking both mouse buttons on the top window border.

If you close the main window, a subordinate footnote window will close with it.

When you close a footnote window, footnotes are not affected; they remain at the end of the document. You have only given up the window used to view them.

No Clearing a Footnote Window

While you may close a footnote window, you cannot clear it with the Transfer Window Clear command. If you try, Word beeps and refuses to execute the command.

Resizing a Footnote Window

Footnote windows are resized in much the same way as regular windows. Use the W(indow) M(ove) command to adjust the lower right corner of the window or its neighbors, or use the mouse to drag the lower right corner of the footnote window or one of its neighbors.

Moving In and Out of a Footnote Window

There are three ways to move the selection into a footnote window. The first method is to use the Jump Footnote command to jump from a footnote reference to the corresponding footnote. The second method is to use the F1 key to move into the footnote window as you would into any other window. The third method is to position the mouse pointer anywhere inside the footnote window and press either button. You can move out of the footnote window with the same techniques.

Working in a Footnote Window

Though you can create a footnote window before there are any footnote references in your document, or use F1 or the mouse to move the selection into the footnote window, Word will not allow you to write directly into a footnote window until there is a footnote reference mark in the main document.

EDITING FOOTNOTES

Once a division has one or more attached footnotes, those footnotes act much like regular text. You can edit the footnotes just as you would edit the main text. Footnotes can be several paragraphs long, and they can combine direct and style sheet formatting. You can move freely around the footnote section of the document just as you do in the main section of the document, and you can also move between body text and the footnote section.

Invalid Actions with Footnotes

There are invalid footnote actions, however. If you attempt these actions, Word will beep and display the following message:

```
Not a valid action for footnotes.
```

Deleting a Footnote

You cannot delete the paragraph mark at the end of a footnote, which is similar to deleting the footnote, and the only way to delete a footnote is to delete the footnote reference mark.

A deleted footnote reference mark accompanies its associated footnote to the scrap and may be inserted elsewhere in the document. If it is an automatically numbered reference, Word will renumber it and the other references and insert the footnote back into the footnote section at the end of the division (but in a new position corresponding to the position of its footnote reference mark).

Other Invalid Actions

You will also receive the invalid message if you attempt any of the following:

- placing a footnote on a footnote

- starting a new division on a footnote

- clearing a footnote window (though you may close it)

- writing in a footnote window before there are any footnote references in the document

- loading a document into a footnote window.

Disaster Recovery

If you delete the footnote reference mark at the beginning of the footnote itself (in the footnote window), use the built-in Glossary entry "footnote" to restore it. Type FOOTNOTE and press F3. The footnote reference is restored.

This trick works only for the footnote reference mark on the footnote itself. You cannot recover a deleted footnote reference mark in the body text. If you accidentally erase a body footnote reference, try the Undo command.

THE STYLE OF YOUR FOOTNOTES

Word also allows you to format your footnotes as you want. You can use direct formatting or style sheets to format footnotes and footnote references.

Style Sheets

The easiest way to format footnotes is, as might be expected, with style sheets. Word dedicates two style sheet styles to footnotes: a footnote reference style and a footnote style.

Footnote Reference Style

The Footnote Reference style is a character style; it applies to the footnote reference mark in the body of your text.

When using standard, numbered footnotes, you will probably want to make the footnote reference style a superscript version of the standard character, but this style is not mandatory. For example, a footnote reference at the end of a sentence might be not only superscript but also of a smaller font. In this sentence, the reference is superscripted, underlined, and followed by a slash as some kinds of writing require.[*] (This type of formatting requires that you add and directly superscript the slash; the footnote reference style only applies to the reference itself.)

Footnote Style

A footnote style is a paragraph style; it applies to the text of footnotes, whether printed at the bottom of the page or collected as endnotes. Like all paragraph styles, the footnote style allows you to adjust the paragraph alignment, indents, internal spacing, and space before and after the text, as well as the standard character for that paragraph.

The footnote reference mark at the beginning of each footnote takes the footnote reference style.

Direct Formatting

Neither the footnote reference style nor the footnote style is absolute; either may be overridden with direct formatting, or you can ignore them and do all formatting directly. The decision is yours.

LIMITATIONS ON FOOTNOTES

There are two other important limitations on footnotes.

First, Word automatically renumbers footnotes in each division. To carry a continuous numbering scheme through several divisions, you must manually renumber the footnote references in all but the first division. Use the Jump Footnote command, or search for the footnote reference style to advance from one footnote reference to the next. Renumbering the reference in the text will, of course, automatically renumber the reference number of the footnote itself.

Second, remember that footnotes are stored at the end of each division. If a document has more than one division and you want to collect all your footnotes in one place as endnotes, you must manually collect and combine them.

CHAPTER 15

INDEXING

Including a good index in your document is one of the greatest favors you can do for your reader. Creating an index is also one of the most tedious jobs you can assign to yourself.

With the assistance of Word, creating a good index is still hard work, just not as hard as it used to be. Before computerized indexing, you had to write each index entry on an index card (hence the name) and then alphabetize those entries manually. No wonder many students once worked their way through college preparing indices for faculty members; no academic professional with any brains wanted to do an index.

THINKING ABOUT INDICES

Before you start indexing, you should spend a few moments thinking about indices: what are they for and how can you make them useful? In this chapter, some issues are raised about indices that you may not have considered. Before you actually tackle an indexing project, however, you should read the section on indices in a good style guide.

What is an Index and What Does It Do?

The *Canadian Style Guide* (Department of the Secretary of State, Canada) defines an index as "a systematic guide to significant items or concepts mentioned or discussed in a work or works; the items and concepts are represented by a series of entries arranged in a known or searchable order, with a locator, which is an indication of the place(s) in the work(s) where reference to each item or concept may be found."

Notice that the definition says nothing about an alphabetical listing. It says the items must be arranged in a "known or searchable order." Most of the time, that order is alphabetical, but not always.

For example, chemicals, patents, or highways might best be indexed by number. Historical items might best be indexed both alphabetically (Waterloo, battle of) and by year (1815, Battle of Waterloo).

So spend some time thinking of the best arrangement for your index before you start creating it.

Kinds of Alphabetical Arrangements

There are two kinds of alphabetical arrangements for indices: word-by-word and letter-by-letter. In a word-by-word arrangement, all entries beginning with the same word are alphabetized together, i.e., spaces break the alphabetical sequence. In letter-by-letter arrangements, spaces are ignored.

Word-by-Word	Letter-by-Letter
van Denberg	Vancouver
van Santen	van Denberg
Vancouver	Vandenberg
Vandenberg	van Santen

In constructing indices, Word uses a word-by-word arrangement. If you want letter-by-letter alphabetization, delete all the spaces from your index entries, and then add the spaces again after the index is generated.

How Long Should an Index Be?

You may have heard the story about the man who was considering purchasing a dachshund. "His legs are awfully short, aren't they?" he commented to the pet store clerk. "How long do you want them to be?" she asked. "They reach all the way from his body to the floor."

A good index is long enough but not too long. Some guides say an index should be no more than five percent of the length of the document being indexed. That may be a guideline, but it is hardly absolute. A book could contain a fifteen-page index for 200 pages of text, and some readers and reviewers would comment favorably that the manual was "meticulously indexed."

What Should Be Indexed?

Many writers' pursuits of a complete index probably lead them to construct longer indices than necessary unless they happen to have readers who need that extra information.

You may need to pretend you don't know anything about the subject of your document. Some or even many readers may not know the terminology of a particular field, so you need to provide them with common terms for technical ideas. In other words, make your indices as complete as you possibly can. If an index is more than five percent of the length of the document, the index might be long but necessary. As the writer, you need to consider your readers, not the authors of style guides.

Do remember to index not only the body text but the introduction, preface, afterword, appendices, addenda, and substantive notes. Include references to tables and illustrations if they carry information not found in the text. You can skip the title page, table of contents, abstracts of articles, and synopses at the beginning of chapters.

Five Levels Allowed

Word's indexing capabilities can handle indices with five levels of headings (the main heading and four subheadings). The first four levels have dedicated paragraph styles in style sheets.

CREATING AN INDEX

There are two steps involved in creating an index. First, you must code your text with hidden index marks. Second, you must use the Library Index command to read the document, find the index marks, extract the index entries, and alphabetize them.

The Index Marks

There are three special index marks:

.i.   Starts an index entry. This set of three characters must be in hidden text.

;   Terminates an index entry. A paragraph mark will also terminate an index entry. These characters may be in hidden text.

:   Creates a subheading or suppresses the page number for a cross-reference. This character may be in hidden text.

For example, a typical index entry might look like the following:

.i.hidden text :use in index coding;

This entry would create a two-level index listing:

Hidden text
  use in index coding

If you want to include spaces in your entries for readability, enter them just ahead of a colon or semicolon, which will place blank space at the end of a line in an index listing, not at the beginning where it might look a bit unusual.

Hidden Text

Remember that the .i. that begins an index entry must be hidden text in order for it to be recognized as starting an index entry. Colons and semicolons in index entries may be hidden text. In fact, the entire index entry may be hidden text.

Hidden text is text for which the hidden attribute has been set to Yes. You can mark existing text to be hidden by selecting it and then either pressing Alt-e (Alt-Xe if using a style sheet) or using the Format Character command. Remember, to hide a single character, you need to press Alt-e twice.

Following is an example of an index entry created with hidden text. This paragraph you are reading right now contains an index entry for hidden text. You can't see it on the page but look at Figure 15.1, which replicates the screen as the text was entered.

```
█══[····¦····1········2········3········4········5········6·····7·]·█
  SP      Following is an example of an index entry created with hidden text.
       This paragraph you are reading right now contains an index entry for
       ··¦··hidden text;.  You can't see it on the page but look at Figure 15.1,
       ⌐which replicates the screen as the text was entered. █


  FH                        Figure 15-1 here¶


  SP      The mouse pointer is pointing at the hidden text.  See the .i.
       before the words hidden text and the ; after.  Notice that both the .i.
       and the ; have little dots under them which are the indicators for
       hidden text.  (If you are running Word in character mode, hidden text
       will be underlined, a different color or on a different background.)
       You can only see hidden text when the show hidden text field of the
       Window Options command is set to Yes.  ¶
  SP      Now, look at the next illustration.¶
                                                              ┌CHAP15.DOC┐
  Pg4 Li4 Co54      {is·}                ?               Microsoft Word
```

Figure 15.1

The mouse pointer is pointing at the hidden text. See the .i. before the words
"hidden text" and the ; after. Notice that both the .i. and the ; have little
dots under them, which are the indicators for hidden text. (If you are running Word in character mode, hidden text will be underlined, in a different
color, or on a different background.) You can only see hidden text when the
show hidden text field of the Window Options command is set to Yes.

Now, look at the next illustration.

```
█══[····¦····1········2········3········4········5········6·····7·]·█
  SP      Following is an example of an index entry created with hidden text.
       This paragraph you are reading right now contains an index entry for
       ◄hidden text►.  You can't see it on the page but look at Figure 15.1,
       ⌐which replicates the screen as the text was entered. █


  FH                        Figure 15-1 here¶


  SP      The mouse pointer is pointing at the hidden text.  See the .i.
       before the words hidden text and the ; after.  Notice that both the .i.
       and the ; have little dots under them which are the indicators for
       hidden text.  (If you are running Word in character mode, hidden text
       will be underlined, a different color or on a different background.)
       You can only see hidden text when the show hidden text field of the
       Window Options command is set to Yes.  ¶
  SP      Now, look at the next illustration.¶
                                                              ┌CHAP15.DOC┐
  Pg4 Li4 Co54      {is·}                ?               Microsoft Word
```

Figure 15.2

The mouse pointer is still pointing to the hidden text, but the .i. and ; have been replaced with double-headed arrows; here, the Window Options command was used to change the parameters for the screen window to set the *show hidden text* field to No, and the *visible* field of the Options command is set to Partial or Complete.

If the *visible* field in the Options command is set to None, and the *show hidden text* field of the Window Options command is set to No, hidden text is truly hidden and won't appear on your screen.

Following is a table showing the various field combinations and their effects:

Options *visible*	Window Options *show hidden text*	
	Yes	*No*
None	visible	hidden
Partial	visible	arrowheads
Complete	visible	arrowheads

Embedded Characters

If your index entry includes colons, semicolons, or quotation marks, you need to take special care. Word would normally interpret those characters as commands to either create a subheading or end the index listing. To include those characters as part of the listing itself, you must enclose the index listing in hidden quotation marks.

For example, say you wanted to index the book *The Works of Timothy Perrin: A Literary Appreciation*. Normally, Word would interpret the colon as a command to create a subheading and would create an index listing such as the following:

The Works of Timothy Perrin, 45
  A Literary Appreciation, 45

Figure 15.3 shows how you can use hidden quotation marks to let Word know that the entire expression should be treated as a unit.

```
▯──┌·········1·········2·········3·········4·········5·········6·········7·]·▮
  │BH  ▮EMBEDDED CHARACTERS▮
  │SP       If your index entry includes colons, semicolons or quotation marks,
  │     you need to take special care.  Word would normally interpret those
  │     characters as commands to either create a subheading or end the index
  │     listing.  To include those characters as part of the listing itself, you
  │     must enclose the index listing in hidden quotation marks.  ▮
  │SP       For example, let's say you wanted to index the book ..i.."The Works
  │     of Timothy Perrin: A Literary Appreciation".;.  Normally Word would
  │     interpret the colon as a command to create a subheading and would create
  │     an index listing such as the following:▮
  │S4  ▮
  │S4  ▮
  │S4  The Works of Timothy Perrin, 45▮
  │S4    A Literary Appreciation, 45▮
  │S4  ▮
  │SP       Figure 15.3 shows how you can use hidden quotation marks to let
  │     Word know that the entire expression should be treated as a unit.  ▮
  │                                                      ──CHAP15.DOC──
  Pg5 Li6 Co1     {you·}          ?                      Microsoft Word
```

Figure 15.3

Notice how the quotation marks are hidden so they won't print, but Word can still see them.

If your index entry itself contains quotation marks, then you must enclose the entry in hidden quotes and enclose the quotation marks themselves in hidden quotes. It makes for a lot of quotation marks, but the strategy works.

WHAT CAN BE AN INDEX ENTRY?

Word looks at the words between the .i. and the ; (or paragraph mark) to see what should be in an index entry. It can be a single word, or it can be an entire paragraph. The entry cannot be more than a paragraph because a paragraph mark, like a semicolon, ends an index entry.

An Entirely Hidden Index Entry

The entire index entry can also be hidden, which means that when you talk about the Battle of Waterloo without the phrase "Battle of Waterloo" appearing on the page, you can include an index entry under that name as hidden text. You can even include multiple entries in one batch of hidden text. The only requirement is that each entry start with a hidden .i. and end with a hidden semicolon.

```
┌──[········1·········2·········3·········4·········5·········6·········7·]·┐
│CH  AN ENTIRELY HIDDEN INDEX ENTRY¶
│
│SP       The entire index entry can also be hidden,.i.index.entries.:hidden:.
│    which means that when you talk about the Battle of Waterloo without the
│    phrase Battle of Waterloo appearing on the page, you can include an
│    index entry under that name as hidden text.  You can even include
│    multiple entries in one batch of hidden text.  The only requirement is
│    that each start with a hidden .i. and end with a hidden semicolon.
│    ..i.Waterloo:battle of:.i.Battle of Waterloo:.  ¶
│                                          ▲
│
│FH                         Figure 15-4 ⌐
│
│
│CH  A MIX OF HIDDEN AND VISIBLE TEXT¶
│
│SP       An index entry can also be a combination of hidden and visible
│    text.  For example, an index for this book will need an entry for
│                                                    ┌CHAP15.DOC┐
│ Pg6 Li9 Co42      {hat·}            ?              Microsoft Word
```

Figure 15.4

A Mix of Hidden and Visible Text

An index entry can also be a combination of hidden and visible text. For example, an index for this book will need an entry for the words "hidden text" that appear on this page, but that entry will need the subheading combined with visible text, and the entry might itself be a subheading of "index." If you look at Figure 15.5, you will see how the entry is done.

```
┌──[········1·········2·········3·········4·········5·········6·········7·]·┐
│CH  A MIX OF HIDDEN AND VISIBLE TEXT¶
│
│SP       An index entry can also be a combination of hidden and visible
│    text.  For example, an index for this book will need an entry for
│    "..i.index:hidden text:combined with visible text:" that appear on this
│  ⌐page but that entry will need the subheading "combined with visible
│    text" and the entry might itself be a subheading of "index."  If you
│    look at the illustration, you'll see how it's done.  ¶
│
│FH                         Figure 15-5 here⌐
│
│
│SP       Only the words "hidden text" are visible on the page but the rest
│    of the index entry surrounds it in hidden text. ¶
│
│CH  AN ASSIST FROM THE GLOSSARY¶
│                                                    ┌CHAP15.DOC┐
│ Pg6 Li17 Co45      {hat·}            ?             Microsoft Word
```

Figure 15.5

Only the words "hidden text" are visible on the page, but the rest of the index entry surrounds it in hidden text.

An Assist from the Glossary

To ease the job of entering hidden characters, you might want to dedicate two glossary entries to a hidden .i. and ;. The glossary allows you to store sections of text, which you can enter into your document with "shorthand."

To store a hidden .i. in the glossary, first create it conventionally. Type .i. and then select it and press Alt-e (or Alt-Xe if you are using a style sheet). Now, while the entry is still highlighted, choose the Copy command from Word's main menu.

```
COPY to: {}
Enter glossary name or select from list
```

Word proposes that you copy the selected text to the scrap. But note the message on the message line. Word will let you copy the selected text to a glossary entry. Type i as the name of the glossary entry and press Return.

```
COPY to: i
```

Now, type i in your text. With the selection on the space just after the i, press F3. Word will look in the glossary and place a hidden .i. in place of the i.

You can save a hidden semicolon in the glossary in the same way. Create a hidden text semicolon, and copy it to the glossary name of ;. Then, when you type a semicolon to end an index entry, you can simply press F3 to turn it into a hidden semicolon. One rule may give you some problems. The glossary name must be preceded by a space, so if you type ".i.index entry;" and press F3, nothing will happen. Try typing ".i.index entry ;" and pressing F3. The space before the semicolon is critical.

CROSS-REFERENCES

In any index, you will need a number of cross-references, entries that refer the reader to another entry. It is best to limit the number of cross-references; give the reader specific references. Instead of saying "Bosnia, See Austro-Hungarian Empire," you can simply list the pages that cover Bosnia. That said, a certain amount of cross-referencing is probably unavoidable.

Coding a Cross-Reference

To code a cross-reference, enter the text of the cross-reference and use a hidden colon to suppress the page number at the end of the entry. For example,

.i.Bosnia. *See* **Austro-Hungarian Empire:;**

Separate a cross-reference from the index listing with a period. The cross-referencing word or words should be in italics unless the item being cross-referenced is in italics:

Tonto. *See* **Silverheels, Jay**
Talese, Gay, 234-35. See also *New York Times*

Kinds of Cross-References

There are five kinds of cross-references.

Use a *See* reference when you want to refer the reader to another term used for the indexed item. These references do not contain page numbers.

Baker, Norma Jean. *See* **Monroe, Marilyn**
War of 1812-1814. *See* **Invasion of Canada**

Use *See Also* to refer the reader to additional information on the subject.

Monroe, Marilyn, 152. *See Also* Hollywood

Use *See Under* if the reader has gone directly to a subentry, and you want to refer him or her to the main entry. This type of reference should have no page numbers.

Tonto. *See under* Native Actors

Use *See also under* when you want to refer a reader to a subentry for additional information.

Tonto, 165, 178. *See also under* Native Actors

Finally, use *q.v.* to indicate that a particular word or expression used in an entry is an entry in its own right.

Dutch
settlement of New Amsterdam (now New York, *q.v.*), 154

WHEN TO CODE FOR AN INDEX

Depending on the size of your document and the way the final version is to be produced, there are two ways to code a document for index generation. One way is to code as you go, entering index entries hidden in your document. The other way is to wait until the final, printed version of the document is prepared and to then read it through, preparing a separate document that consists of nothing but index entries. On the first page of the document you are using to generate the index, make the index entries for the first page of your real document. Then use a forced page break (Ctrl-Shift-Return) to move to the next page, and make the index entries for the second page, and so on.

The second method tends to be easier. If you try to write and make index entries at the same time, you may not do particularly well at either, but if you concentrate on one job at a time, you might do better at both. Also, if you try to hide index entries in your main text after it is written, you might find that you spend a lot of time moving around with the mouse or cursor keys. In other words, the process is more tedious than it need be.

COMPILING THE INDEX

Whichever way you produce the code for the index, when you are ready to compile it, use the Library Index command to actually generate the index.

Hide Hidden Text

In version 3, make sure that you hide the hidden text in your document by setting the *show hidden text* field of the Window Options command to No. If you forget, the hidden text of your index entries could throw off the pagination of your document.

In version 4, Word ignores hidden text when it is printing unless the *hidden text* field of the Print Options command is set to Yes.

Library Index Command

When you choose L(ibrary) I(ndex) from Word's main menu, Word will present you with four fields:

```
LIBRARY INDEX entry/page # separated by:     cap main entries:(Yes)No
              indent each level: 0.2"         use style sheet: Yes(No)
```

The individual fields are as follows:

- *Entry/page # separated by.* This field specifies what character(s) is to go between the entry and the page number in the finished index. Word proposes blanks. Some style guides say the character should be a comma and a space. If that is the style you want to use, just enter a comma and a space, and then use the Tab key to advance to the next field.

- *Cap main entries.* When you set this field to Yes, the first letter of each index entry will be in uppercase regardless of whether or not the word being indexed is capitalized. Generally you will want this field set to Yes, but you will have to do an edit of the index for such anomalies as the names "van Santen" and "ffolkes."

- *Indent each level.* Use this field to specify the size of the indent for subheadings. Word suggests 0.2", which is fine for most indices.

- *Use style sheet.* When this field is set to No, the default setting, Word will ignore the styles established for index headings in the style sheet attached to the document; however, Word will use the character formatting specified for the Standard Paragraph in that style sheet. If you set this field to Yes, Word will ignore the value in the *indent each level* field and format the index entries in accordance with the formats in the style sheet. Remember that the style sheet can only format the top four levels of an index. The fifth level will have the Standard Paragraph format. Also, any index entries for which the format is undefined will take the formatting of the Standard Paragraph.

When you finish filling in the fields, press Return, and Word will begin to generate the index. It may take a while depending on the speed of your computer, the speed of the disk drives, and just how much of an index you are trying to put together.

INDEXING LARGE DOCUMENTS

When indexing very large documents like books, you may run out of memory. Indexing is a very intensive task that takes all of a computer's capabilities and memory. Most of the time, indexing won't pose any problem, but if you receive the message "Insufficient Memory," you will need to juggle things around for Word to finish the indexing job.

Adding More Memory

If you are using Word on a computer with anything less than the maximum 640K of memory installed, your best solution is to add more memory to your computer. Word version 3 requires 256K of memory. Version 4 needs 320K; however, both versions perform better with more memory.

Reclaiming Memory

Of course, if you must generate the index today, adding more memory to your computer isn't really an option. Following are some other suggestions that will reclaim memory for Word.

First, while still in Word, perform the following steps:

- Use the Print Option command to change to Word's generic print driver, PLAIN.PRD. It is smaller and takes less memory.

- Close all windows other than the one you are using.

- Save the file you are working on. As you work, Word keeps more and more of the file in memory. When you save the file, Word reloads only a minimal amount of the file back into memory until it needs other parts.

- If there is a style sheet attached to the document, remove it. Choose F(ormat) S(tyle) A(ttach) from the main menu. When Word asks for a style sheet name, press the Delete key and then the Return key.

Now, try to generate your index again. If you still don't have enough memory, quit Word and remove all memory-resident programs from memory. Examples of memory-resident programs are Sidekick, Superkey, Prokey, Lotus Metro, Poly Windows, and most print spoolers and RAM disk programs. Memory-resident programs take memory away from an application program like Word. When generating an index, Word needs all the memory it can get.

Stripping Text from File

If Word still doesn't have enough memory, it is time to reconsider your index coding. If your index code is in a separate file by itself, you've done what you can do. If it is not, you might consider stripping the text out of your document and leaving only the index code. This process takes several steps.

1.   Save your document under a different name, such as
       INDEXGEN.DOC.

2.   Use the P(rint) R(epaginate) command to ensure that the page
       breaks are where they belong. Now, search (manually) through
       the document for the page breaks, and enter hard page breaks with
       the Ctrl-Shift-Return key combination in place of each page break
       entered by Word.

3.   Set the *show hidden text* field of the Window Options command to
       Yes to make sure your index entries are showing.

4.   Move to the very top of your document (Ctrl-PgUp), and press F6
       to turn on the Extend Selection.

5.   Use Word's search capabilities to search for .i. Since the Extend
       Selection feature is on, the selection will extend to the .i. Press the left
       arrow three times to move the end of the selection back to exclude
       the .i. Now press the Delete key to delete the text up to the end of
       that index entry.

6.   Move to the end of that index entry, turn on Extend Selection again
       (F6), and repeat the search (F4), again deleting the text between
       the first index entry and the next.

When you arrive at the end of your document, only index entries will be left; however, your original document will be intact under the original name, and the original page breaks will be in place because you entered hard page breaks to replace the soft breaks Word had entered.

Indexing Separately and then Combining

The final solution to indexing large documents, and one that you may have to use for book-length manuscripts, is to index each chapter separately, and then use Word's Library Autosort command to sort the entries together into a single index.

This technique is discussed in detail as an example of a difficult sorting job in Chapter 20, "Sorts, Hyphenation, and Redlining."

THE COMPLETED INDEX

Presuming that you have not run into near fatal memory problems, Word should have produced an index for you when you pressed Return after filling in the fields for the Library Index command.

In a New Division

The first thing to notice about this index is that it is in a new division. You can see the division maker (a row of colons) across the screen just above the beginning of the index.

A new division is created because Word expects you will want to format your index differently than the rest of your document, often in two columns. If you have a predefined index format in your style sheet, you can now apply it to the index division.

Reformatting the Old Division

You should also check the formatting of the old division. In some versions of Word, when it creates the new division to hold the index, it formats the old division with Word's built-in division parameters. If you are using a style sheet, you will want to explicitly apply your Standard Division style to the main text.

If there are two division markers between the text and the index, you can delete the second one. The first holds formatting you applied directly to the division; the second was added by Word when it created the index, so it can be deleted.

Beginning and End Markers

If you set your screen to show hidden text again, you will see that Word has put beginning and end markers on the index. At its start is *.Begin Index.* and at the end is *.End Index.* If, for some reason, you want to compile a second index and don't want to lose the first, remove those markers from the index, or Word will write the new index over the old one, but only after asking for confirmation that you do want to destroy the old index.

EDITING YOUR INDEX

Even when your index is generated, your work is not yet finished. You must still edit the index.

Indented vs. Run-in

Your first choice is whether to stick with the indented style or to convert to a run-in index format. Following is an example of an indented index entry.

Indexes, 929-952
  alphabetizing of entries, 939-40, 942, 944, 947
  capitalization in, 941
  cross-references, 938, 949
  format of entries in, 935

Now consider the same entry in run-in style:

Indexes, 929-952: alphabetizing of entries, 939-40, 942, 944, 947; capitalization in, 941; cross-references, 938, 949; format of entries in, 935

To convert from the indented style used by Word to a run-in style, you will need to do a lot of editing by hand; however, you can use Word macros (see Chapter 18) or a macro program like Superkey or Prokey to automate at least part of the task.

Basically, you need to jump to the end of each line, add a semicolon, delete the end-of-paragraph marker, and then delete any extra spaces. The following macro performs those functions:

<end>;<del> <F6> <F8> <del> <space>

Plurals and Singulars

You also need to scan your index for a mixture of singulars and plurals. For example, in one index entry you might have used a main heading of "index," in another "indexes," and in a third "indices." The only way to find those references is to hunt for them and pull together the various headings by hand.

Contiguous Page Problems

One problem with Word's indexing is its inability to deal properly with groups of contiguous pages. If a reference occurs on a series of pages, say, 15, 16, and 17, the index entry will read

Index entry, 15, 16, 17

You must edit those kinds of entries so they read

Index entry, 15-17

Capitalization

With the *cap main entries* field of the Library Index command, you can tell Word whether or not to capitalize all main entries in your index. As a rule, leave this field set to Yes, but remember that there are some entries that should not start with a capital letter.

Among the most common exceptions to the capitalization rule are names in foreign languages like "van Santen," "de la Madrid," "ffolkes," and others. Also, many standard terms such as "pH" and chemical terms that begin with italics characters such as "*p*-Aminobenzoic acid" should be listed in your index with a leading lowercase letter.

More on Names

You should index names beginning with "Mc," "Mac," and "M'" together as if they all begin with "Mac." Alphabetize Irish names like "O'Doherty" as if they did not have the apostrophe. For compound names like "de la Madrid," alphabetize the name according to the form used by the person in question. For example, you would enter "Balzac, Honore de" but "La Fontaine, Jean de."

Dangling Entries

Never leave just the first line of a multiline entry at the bottom of a column. If necessary, add a blank paragraph or two to force an entry to start at the top of the next column.

Blind or Circular References

Also, as you are editing, watch for circular references as in

Circular references. *See* **References, circular**
References, circular. *See* **Circular references**

You will need to go back through your document, find the pages that mention circular references, and add them to the index.

Numbers in an Index

Some indices require that you index numbers. Word can handle numbers in index entries as well as it can handle letters; however, Word will sort the numbers into alphanumeric rather than numerical order. As a result, 125 will be ahead of 13 because 2 is less than 3. Use Word's Library Autosort command to sort them into numerical order if that is what you need. See Chapter 20 for details on using the Autosort command.

FORMATTING WITH A STYLE SHEET

Formatting of your index is controlled by either the Library Index command or by a style sheet. Remember that there are only four styles for index entries, so if your index has five levels, those fifth-level entries will take the Standard Paragraph format, and you will need to format them by hand.

A FINAL WORD

As was said at the beginning of this chapter, preparing an index, even with assistance from Word, is a lot of work. But most books not only need a good index, they are almost useless without one. Preparing an index takes time, but your readers will thank you for it.

CHAPTER 16

TABLES

TWO KINDS OF TABLES

This chapter discusses tables and how to produce them using Microsoft Word. The first part of this chapter covers **compiled tables**, which are tables that Word produces for you much like it produces indices. Compiled tables can be tables of contents, tables of figures, tables of illustrations, or the like. Word can handle them all, quickly and easily. The second part of this chapter covers **formatted tables**, which are tables you create using tabs and paragraph formatting.

COMPILED TABLES

There are two types of compiled tables. In version 4, you can easily generate a table of contents using your outline headings. In both versions 3 and 4, you can use special hidden text coding to tell Word which text to put in other kinds of tables such as a table of illustrations. In version 3, you must also use this system to generate tables of contents.

Table of Contents from Headings

In version 4, you can compile a table of contents from outline headings. If you are using style sheets and outlines in your writing, you will find this method the easiest way to compile a table of contents for your document.

This feature is only available in version 4. In version 3, you must code for the table of contents just as you would for any other table. See "Fully Compiled Tables" later in this chapter.

To generate a table of contents based on your outline headings, select the ·L(ibrary) T(able) command. Word will present you with a set of six fields:

```
LIBRARY TABLE from:(Outline)Codes   index code: C
           page numbers:(Yes)No     entry/page number separated by: ^t
           indent each level: 0.4"  use style sheet: Yes(No)
```

Following are explanations of each field:

- *From.* When this field is set to Outline, Word will compile the table from the outline headings. When it is set to Codes, Word will compile the table using the hidden text coding detailed in the next section of this chapter.

- *Index code.* You use this field only if you are creating a table compiled from hidden codes. (See the next section of this chapter.)

- *Page numbers.* Set this field to No if you want to generate a table that lists the headings but does not give their page numbers.

- *Entry/page # separated by.* This field specifies what character(s) is to go between the entry and the page number in the finished table. Word suggests a tab character (ˆt). For simple tables, the tab character is usually adequate; however, for more complex tables, you will often want to vary this character. Later in this chapter, you will see how you can use two tabs and style sheets to produce impressive tables.

- *Indent each level.* Use this field to specify the size of the indent for lower level table entries. Word suggests 0.4", which is fine for most tables.

- *Use style sheet.* When this field is set to No, Word will ignore the styles established for table headings in the style sheet attached to the document; however, Word will use the character formatting specified for the Standard Paragraph in that style sheet. If you set this field to Yes, Word will ignore the value in the *indent each level* field and format the table entries in accordance with the formats in the style sheet. Style sheets can only format four levels of a table. Any table entries for which the table format is undefined will take the formatting of the Standard Paragraph.

Normally, you will want to leave these entries set to their defaults and just press Return. Word will automatically generate a table of contents for each division in your document and place the table at the end of each division.

See "Executing the Library Table Command" later in this chapter for more details on using that command and for solutions to possible problems.

Fully Compiled Tables

There are two steps in creating a fully compiled table. First, you must code your text with hidden table marks. Second, you must use the Library Table command to read the document, find the table marks, extract the table entries, and create the table. This process may sound familiar because indexing with Word operates in the same way. If you read Chapter 15, you should feel right at home here.

If you are using Word version 3, you must use this technique for generating all tables, including a table of contents.

Table Marks

There are three special table marks:

.c.   Starts a table entry. This set of three characters must be in hidden text. Actually, any letter set between periods (except i) can be used to head a table entry. The default is .c.

;   Terminates a table entry. A paragraph mark also terminates a table entry. When working with tables, you will terminate most entries with a paragraph mark. These characters may be in hidden text.

:   Creates a subordinate table listing. This character need not be in hidden text, but it almost always will be.

For example, a typical table entry might resemble the following:

.c.Chapter 16 - Tables
.c.:Two Kinds of Tables

This entry would create two table listings:

Chapter 16 - Tables   25
Two Kinds of Tables   25

Note how the colon in the second entry formatted the entry as a subentry, which is how the colons work:

.c.   creates a top-level entry.
.c.:   creates a second-level entry.
.c.::   creates a third-level entry
.c.:::   creates a fourth-level entry.

Four Levels

Word will create tables up to four levels deep, which is probably as much as you will need. If you go deeper, you risk creating a table that has too much detail to be useful.

Other Characters in Table Marks

The table mark need not be *.c.* You can use any letter but *i* in your table marks. The *i* is reserved for indices. Each set of table marks sharing the same letter is used to compile a single table. So, for example, you could use *.c.* for the table of contents (in version 3), *.f.* for a table of figures, *.p.* for a table of photos, *.t.* for a table of tables. But remember that you cannot use *.i.* for a table of illustrations because *.i.* is reserved for indices.

Each table must be compiled separately. Before you start to compile a second table, you must remove the hidden *.Begin Table.* and *.End Table.* commands Word inserts into the previously compiled table, or the new table will over-write the old table.

Terminating a Table Entry

While you may use a semicolon to terminate a table entry, you will rarely need to do so. Since most table entries are on lines by themselves, the paragraph mark at the end of the line is usually sufficient.

Hidden Text

Remember that the table mark that begins a table entry must be hidden text in order for Word to recognize it as starting a table entry. Colons and semicolons in table entries may be hidden text. In fact, the entire table entry may be hidden text, but that case would be most rare.

Hidden text is text for which the hidden attribute has been set to Yes. You can mark existing text to be hidden by selecting it and then either pressing Alt-E (Alt-XE if using a style sheet) or using the Format Character command. Remember, to hide a single character, you need to press Alt-E twice.

Embedded Characters

If your table entry includes colons, semicolons, or quotation marks, you need to take special care. Word will interpret those characters as commands to either create a subheading or end the table listing. To include those characters as part of the listing itself, you must enclose the table listing in hidden quotation marks.

For example, say you wanted an entry in the table of contents for "Chapter 1: The Mystery Begins." That embedded colon after the number 1 would normally create a two-level heading such as the following:

Chapter 1   25
The Mystery Begins   25

To list the chapter title as one table entry, you need to put hidden quotation marks around it. Figure 16.1 shows how the entry should look on the screen.

Note how the quotation marks are hidden so they don't print but so Word can still see them.

If your table entry itself contains quotation marks, then you must enclose the entry in hidden quotes and enclose the quotation marks themselves in hidden quotes.

```
▯━━[····|····1·········2·········3·········4·········5·········6·········7·]·▯
 SP        For example, let's say you wanted an entry in the table of contents
     for .c."Chapter 1: The Mystery Begins".   That embeded colon would
     normally create a two level heading ▯ike this:¶
 S3  ¶
 S3  ¶                                          ▸
 S4        Chapter 1 25↓
              The Mystery Begins     25¶
 S3  ¶
 S3  ¶

 SP        To list the chapter title as one table entry, you need to put
     hidden quotation marks around it.   See the illustration to see how it
     looks on the screen.   ¶


 FH                          Figure 16-1 here¶


                                                        ━━━CHAP16.DOC━
 Microsoft Word Version 4.0          (S/N 034899-400-xxxxxxx)
```

Figure 16.1

An Assist from the Glossary

To ease the job of entering hidden table marks, dedicate a set of glossary entries to them. The glossary allows you to store sections of text that you can enter into your document with "shorthand."

To store a hidden .c. in the glossary, first create it conventionally. Type .c. and then select it and press Alt-E (or Alt-XE if you are using a style sheet). Now, while the text is still selected, choose the Copy command from Word's main menu:

COPY to: {}

Enter glossary name or select from list

Word proposes that you copy the selected text to the scrap, indicated by the curly brackets ({}). But note the message on the message line. Word will let you copy the selected text to a glossary entry. Type 1 as the name of the glossary entry:

COPY to: 1

and press Return.

Now, type 1 in your text. With the selection on the space just after the 1, press F3. Word will look in the glossary and put a hidden .c. in place of the 1.

You can save .c.:, .c.::, and .c.::: to other glossary entries, logically 2, 3, and 4.

When to Code for a Table

Depending on the size of your document and the way the final version is to be produced, you can use several ways to code a document for table generation.

First, you can code as you go, entering hidden table marks in your document as you write.

Second, if you are coding for a table of contents in version 3, since the headings you want in your table of contents are often also headings in your outline, you will find it easier to code for the table of contents in outline view after the document is complete.

Finally, if the document is going to be printed on a different printer, which might change the pagination, wait until the final, printed version of the document is prepared, and then read it through, preparing a separate document that consists of nothing but table entries or only table and index entries. This technique is outlined in Chapter 15.

Compiling for a Table

Whichever way you produce the code for a table, when you are ready to compile it, use the Library Table command to actually generate the table.

Hide Hidden Text

Before you choose the Library Table command in version 4, make sure that the *hidden text* field of the Print command is set to No. In version 3, make sure the hidden text in your document doesn't print. Set the *show hidden text* field of the Window Options command to No. If you forget to set either of those fields to No, the hidden text of table and index entries could throw off the pagination of your document.

The Library Table Command

When you choose L(ibrary) T(able) from Word's main menu, Word will present you with six fields:

```
LIBRARY TABLE from: Outline Codes   index code: C
        page numbers:(Yes)No        entry/page number separated by: ^t
        indent each level: 0.4"     use style sheet: Yes(No)
```

In version 3, four fields appear:

```
LIBRARY TABLE index on: C       entry/page # separated by: ^t
        indent each level: 0.4"          use style sheet: Yes(No)
```

Following are explanations of each field:

- *From.* In version 4, when this field is set to Outline, Word will compile the table from the outline headings. When it is set to Codes, Word will compile the table using the hidden text coding you have entered into your document.

- *Index code* (*Index on* in version 3). You use this field only if you are creating a fully compiled table. In this field you specify the character you have used in the table mark for this table. The default is C.

- *Page numbers.* Set this field to No if you want to generate a table that lists the headings but does not give their page numbers. This feature is not available in version 3.

- *Entry/page # separated by.* This field specifies what character(s) is to go between the entry and the page number in the finished table. Word suggests a tab character (^t). For simple tables, the tab character is usually adequate; however, for more complex tables, you will often want to vary this character. Later in this chapter, you will see how you can use two tabs and style sheets to produce very impressive tables.

- *Indent each level.* Use this field to specify the size of the indent for lower level table entries. Word suggests 0.4", which is fine for most tables.

- *Use style sheet.* When this field is set to No, Word will ignore the styles established for table headings in the style sheet attached to the document; however, Word will use the character formatting specified for the Standard Paragraph in that style sheet. If you set this field to Yes, Word will ignore the value in the *indent each level* field and format the table entries in accordance with the formats in the style sheet. Style sheets can only format four levels of a table. Any table entries for which the table format is undefined will take the formatting of the Standard Paragraph.

Executing the Library Table Command

When you finish filling in the fields, press Return, and Word will begin to process the table. It may take a while depending on the speed of your computer, the speed of the disk drives, and just how much of a table you are trying to put together.

Tables for Large Documents

When creating tables for very large documents, such as books, you may receive the message "Insufficient Memory," which means that Word needs more memory to finish compiling the table. See "Indexing Large Documents" in Chapter 15 for some suggestions on how to deal with this problem.

The Completed Table

Presuming that you have not run into near fatal memory problems, Word should have produced a table for you when you pressed Return after filling in the fields for the Library Table command. After executing the Library Table command, Word moves the selection to the beginning of the table.

In a New Division

The first thing to notice about this table is that it is in a new division. You can see the division maker (a row of colons) across the screen just above the beginning of the table because Word expects you will want to format your table differently than the rest of your document. If you have a predefined table format in your style sheet, you may now apply it to the table division.

Reformatting the Old Division

You should also check the formatting of the old division. In some versions of Word, when the program creates the new division to hold the table, it formats the old division with Word's built-in division parameters. If you are using a style sheet, you will want to explicitly apply your Standard Division style to the main text.

If there are two division markers between the text and the table, you can delete the second one. The first holds formatting you had applied directly to the division; the second was added by Word when it created the table, so you can delete it.

Beginning and End Markers

If you set your screen to show hidden text again, you will see that Word has put beginning and end markers on the table. At the table's start is *.Begin Table.* and at the end is *.End Table.* If you want to compile a second table, perhaps a table of figures, remove those markers from the existing table, or Word will write the new table over the old, but only after asking for confirmation that you really want to destroy the old table.

Formatting with a Style Sheet

Formatting of your table is controlled by either the Library Table command or by a style sheet. You will probably want to use the style sheet formats dedicated to table entries. They give you a real opportunity to make your tables shine.

Using Two Tabs for Formatting

As mentioned earlier in this chapter, if you used two tabs (ˆtˆt) in the *entry/page # separated by* field of the Library Table command, you could then use a style sheet to make very impressive tables. Following is an example:

Introduction

PART I - Word Fundamentals

Note how the two tabs were used. The first is set about half an inch from the left margin with the fill character set to periods. The second is set to be flush right and at the right margin.

Figure 16.2 shows the styles (numbers 1-4) used to create the table of contents.

```
█─0····[····1·········2·········_L·········4·········5·········]·······7·····█
│  1    TP Paragraph Table level 1              TABLE – PART NAME
        Roman (roman a) 12 Bold. Centered, space before 3 li, space after 1
        li.
   2    TC Paragraph Table level 2              TABLE – CHAPTER TITLE
        Roman (roman a) 10/12 Bold. Flush left, Left indent 0.2" (first
        line indent -0.2"), space before 1 li, space after 0.5 li. Tabs at:
        5.6" (left flush, leader dots), 6" (right flush).
   3    TA Paragraph Table level 3              TABLE – A LEVEL
        Roman (roman a) 10/12. Flush left, Left indent 0.6" (first line
        indent -0.2"), space before 4 pt. Tabs at: 5.6" (left flush, leader
        dots), 6" (right flush).
   4    TB Paragraph Table level 4              TABLE – B LEVEL
        Roman (roman a) 10/12 Italic. Flush left, Left indent 1" (first
        line indent -0.2"). Tabs at: 5.6" (left flush, leader dots), 6"
        (right flush).
   5    D1 Paragraph 15                         DEMO TABLE – 1
        Helvetica (modern i) 10/12 Underlined. Flush left, Left indent
        0.5", space before 1 li (keep in one column, keep with following
        paragraph). Tabs at: 3" (left flush, leader underscore).
─────────────────────────────────────────────────────────────────────────────
COMMAND: Copy Delete Exit Format Help
         Insert Name Print Transfer Undo
Edit style sheet or choose Exit to see document
GALLERY  {Paragraph Table level 1 } ?            Microsoft Word: WIDE.STY
```

Figure 16.2

Remember that the table styles and the outline heading styles are not the same, even though headings and tables often contain the same text.

By using style sheets, you can experiment with other formats and produce the best tables that your printer is capable of printing. For example, if you are using a standard printer without a lot of font variation, you can still use it to produce a table like the following:

INTRODUCTION

What this Book Covers 1
How This Book is Different 1
Form vs. Content 2
Printers 5
Complex But Not Difficult 5

continued...

...from previous page

Feel free to experiment with the table styles to get just the table you want.

FORMATTED TABLES

Formatted tables are tables you produce using tabs and paragraph formatting. Most of the tables in this book have been produced with this method.

Using Tabs

To produce a table using tabs, you need to see things clearly, including the exact location and effect of all your tab characters and tab stops. So configure Word according to the following table.

Option	Setting
Options *visible*	*Complete*
Options *printer display*	*Yes*
Window Options *ruler*	*Yes*

What those settings do is illustrated in Figure 16.3. First, you can see your tabs on the screen as little arrows facing right. Second, you can see spaces you have entered into the text by pressing the Space Bar. Third, when the selection is in a paragraph, you can see the tab settings in the ruler. In Figure 16.3, the two Cs on the ruler show that the paragraph containing the selection has two tab stops set, both centered, one at 2" and the other at 4". The line below the heading was created using the Format Border command, which will be explained later in this chapter.

```
⌐──────0·········[·········C·········3·········C·········]·········6·········7···⌐
|        →      Option→           Setting⍰
|                                         ─────────────────────────────
|        →      Options·visible→          Complete¶
|        →   Options·printer·display→     Yes¶
|        →     Window·Options·ruler→      Yes¶
|SP        What·those·settings·do·is·illustrated·below.··First,·
|          you·can·see·your·tabs·on·the·screen·as·little·arrows·facing·
|          right.··Second,·you·can·see·spacebar·spaces·you·have·entered·
|          into·the·text·by·pressing·the·spacebar.··Third,·when·the·
|          selection·is·in·a·paragraph,·you·can·see·the·tab·settings·in·
|          the·ruler.··In·the·illustration,·the·two·Cs·on·the·ruler·
|          show·that·the·paragraph·containing·the·selection·has·two·tab·────CHAP16.DOC─
Key code not defined
```

Figure 16.3

Setting Your Own Tabs

When you are trying to set up tables using tabs, it is best to format the tabs explicitly rather than rely on Word's built-in tabs. That way, you can be sure that columns line up exactly where you want them. Use the *Leader char.* field to specify the character that is to fill the space from the end of text to the next tab stop. You can use the leader character to draw horizontal lines, as you will see later.

Better yet, use style sheets to handle the formatting.

Tabs vs. Spaces

The reason you should set the Options *visible* field to Complete is so you can see the difference between spaces and tabs. The difference here relates to the difference between the way characters appear on the screen and how they print. On the screen, every character takes up the same amount of space; however, in many type fonts, some characters such as "w" and "m" are wider on the page than thin characters such as "i" or "l." This difference is called **proportional spacing**. As a result, two words that have the same number of letters and appear the same length on the screen may be widely different widths on the printed page. Following is an example:

Wham
ills

Both words contain four letters, yet one is twice as wide as the other.

Now, if you try to create a table by using spaces (with the Space Bar) to align a second column on the screen, the table will not line up correctly on the page. In this example, both "Wham" and "ills" are followed by twenty spaces:

Wham   second column
ills   second column

Tabs, on the other hand, control both content and form. A tab character is a single character, and Word deals with it that way when editing; however, its function is one of form: it advances the print position to the next tab stop.

Tab stops are stored as absolute positions. For example, once you set a tab stop three inches from the left margin, Word is smart enough to always position text three inches from the left margin, regardless of the size of the characters in the font you are using.

So if a tab character is used to set up your column layout, the columns will be aligned. If spaces are used, you may be in trouble. Following is an example. Tabs were used in the first two lines, and spaces were used in the last two lines. Both of these examples are lined up on the screen (see Figure 16.4) but not, as you can see, on the page.

```
▯━━[·········1·········2·········3·········4·········5·········6·········7·]·▯
│DZ      ¶
│DZ      Wham→                   second·column↓
│        ills→                   second·column¶
│DZ      Wham···················second·column↓
│        ills···················second·column¶
│                        ▸
│FH                              ▯igure·16—4·here¶
│
│SP      Unless·the·Options·visible·field·is·set·to·Complete,·you·won't·be·
│        able·to·see·the·little·arrows·that·mean·tabs·and·the·little·dots·that·
├        mean·spaces·and·you·may·find·yourself·reprinting·a·lot·of·your·tables,·
│        trying·to·get·them·aligned.··¶
│
│CH      Keep·Together¶
│                                                          ━CHAP16.DOC━
 Pg14 Li18 Co29    {→}                ?              Microsoft Word
```

Figure 16.4

Following is how they would look when printed:

Wham   **second column**
ills   **second column**

Wham   **second column**
ills   **second column**

Unless the Options *visible* field is set to Complete, you won't be able to see the little arrows that mean tabs and the little dots that mean spaces, and you may find yourself reprinting a lot of your tables, trying to get them aligned.

Keep Together

It is important that tables appear all in one piece. There are several ways you can ensure that they are kept together.

One way is to set the *keep follow* field of the Format Paragraph command to Yes for all but the last paragraph. You can skip the last paragraph because it doesn't matter if there is a page break at the end of the table.

Alternatively, you can set the *keep together* field of the Format Paragraph command to Yes, and then make the entire table one large paragraph by using new line characters to start new lines. New line characters start new lines without starting new paragraphs. You enter new line characters in your text by pressing Shift-Return. If the Options *visible* field is set to Partial or Complete, new line characters will appear on your screen as arrows pointing down and left. For an example, see Figure 16.4.

The problem with this technique is that, because the table is a single paragraph, you cannot vary the tab stops. If you need to make changes in tabs within a table, you will need to use more than one paragraph.

Finally, if you are sure your document is completely finished, you can use the Print Repaginate command to position the page breaks, and then use Ctrl-Shift-Return to insert hard page breaks ahead of tables if necessary.

DRAWING LINES

Often, as you have seen, you will want to use a line to break up text in a table (or elsewhere). Word version 4 can draw both horizontal and vertical lines. Version 3, unfortunately, will let you create horizontal lines but not vertical lines.

Version 4

Starting in Word version 4, Microsoft has added some very useful line drawing capabilities to Word. Word can draw borders as part of a paragraph's format. You can use vertical tabs to draw vertical lines, and you can draw lines directly on the screen with Word's line drawing mode.

And, of course, all the line drawing techniques that are available in version 3 are also available in version 4.

Format Border Command

In version 4, the command F(ormat) B(order) lets you draw lines above, below, beside, or around paragraphs. These borders are part of the paragraph formatting.

You can use paragraph borders to set off a table or simply separate the headings from the entries. When you choose this command, Word will present you with six fields:

```
FORMAT BORDER type:(None)Box Lines    line style:(Normal)Bold Double
          left: Yes(No)  right: Yes(No)  above: Yes(No)  below: Yes(No)
```

Following are explanations of the two major fields:

- *Border type.* The default border type is None because you won't normally want borders on paragraphs. Set the type to Box, and Word will draw a box all the way around the paragraph. When you set the type to Lines, you must specify the positions in which you want lines. A box is the same as choosing a border type of Line and then setting the *left*, *right*, *above*, and *below* fields all to Yes.

- *Line style.* Set the line type to Normal (single), Bold, or Double. Not all printers are capable of printing all three types of line styles. You will need to experiment with your printer to find out which ones work for you.

Vertical Tabs

Version 4 offers another way of drawing lines, in this case, vertical lines. You can use the vertical tab setting. You set a vertical tab the same way you set any other kind of tab: with the F(ormat) T(ab) S(et) command.

```
FORMAT TAB SET position:
          alignment:(Left)Center Right Decimal Vertical    leader char:(Blank). - _
```

The difference between vertical tabs and others is that a vertical tab does not align text. Instead, it draws a vertical line at the tab stop. The line stretches the entire height of that paragraph.

For example, following is the simple table you saw earlier in this chapter.

Option	Setting
Options *visible*	*Complete*
Options *printer display*	*Yes*
Window Options *ruler*	*Yes*

Look at the formatting of that table so you can see how it was put together. Then look at variations of that style so you can see how you can use paragraph borders and vertical tabs to create professional-looking tables in your documents.

In the original table, the first line is a separate paragraph. Its *left indent* is set to one inch, and its *right indent* is also set to one inch. The paragraph has two *centered tabs* for the column headings. These tabs are set at 2" and 3.5". The line spacing is set to 1.5 lines. The *keep follow* field is set to Yes so that this paragraph is certain to stay with the rest of the table. Finally, the Format Border command was used to create the line underneath the headings. Because the left and right indents affect the border as well as the text, the line is also indented from the margins.

Each of the other lines in the table is part of a single paragraph formatted with centered tabs at 2" and 3.5" so that the text lines up with the column headings. The line spacing is set to 1.5 lines, and the separate lines are created using the new line command (Shift-Return). This paragraph has the *keep together* field set to Yes to ensure that it all stays on one page.

Adding Vertical Lines

Now, add a vertical tab to that table to create a vertical line dividing the two columns.

Option	Setting
Options *visible*	*Complete*
Options *printer display*	*Yes*
Window Options *ruler*	*Yes*

The vertical tab is set at 3.5", which is just a guess, but it seems to be about right, so leave it set as is.

Boxing the Table

Finally, you can put the entire table in a box.

Option	Setting
Options *visible*	*Complete*
Options *printer display*	*Yes*
Window Options *ruler*	*Yes*

Creating the box is a bit trickier. First, there are actually two boxes here, one around the paragraph containing the column headings and one around the paragraph containing the table's contents. You will find that those two boxes will separate if the line spacing in the two paragraphs is not the same, in this case, 1.5 lines with no space before or after.

Also, when you get the text into boxes, notice that the right column might look off-center. In the open table design used earlier, that lack of perfect alignment didn't matter much, but in the box it is quite pronounced. So you can adjust the right centered tab and move it over from 4 to 4.2".

Alternative to Boxes

Sometimes you cannot make all the elements of your table parts of a single paragraph, but that doesn't mean you still cannot box the table. The following table looks exactly like the last one, but it is really completely different. Each line in the table is a separate paragraph but with different settings for the Format Border command. The heading line still has a box around it, but the first line of table information has a line above and lines on the left and right. The second line of table information has lines on the left and right, while the bottom line has lines on the left, right, and below. The result, as you can see, looks just fine:

Option	Setting
Options *visible*	*Complete*
Options *printer display*	*Yes*
Window Options *ruler*	*Yes*

Experimentation

The key to fully understanding and being able to use the Format Border command and Vertical Tabs in your tables is practice and experimentation. Soon, you will be using borders like a pro.

Line Draw

If you just need some quick lines on the screen, or if you want something other than the single, bold, and double lines offered by Word's Format Border command and vertical tabs, then try version 4's line draw mode. In line draw mode, you can use the arrow keys on your keyboard to draw lines on the screen in several different character sets.

When using Word's line draw mode, you first need to choose which set of line-drawing characters you want to use. The *linedraw character* field of the Options command lets you make this choice. Choose O(ptions) from the Word main menu; then move the highlight to the *linedraw character* field and press F1. Word will offer you a dozen different sets of characters you can use for line drawing on the screen.

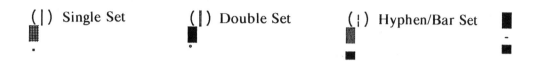

(|) Single Set   (|) Double Set   (¦) Hyphen/Bar Set

Use the arrow keys to move the highlight to the character set you want to use and press Return.

By creatively mixing the character sets, you can create some interesting effects. For example, consider the following:

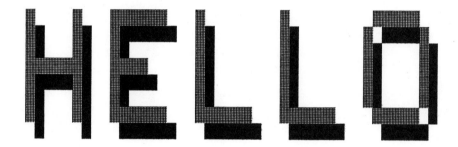

The best way to learn about Word's line-drawing capabilities is to experiment. Not all line-drawing characters may be available on your printer, so you will need to try each of them out to see which work and which do not.

Version 3

Version 3 offers only a few line-drawing capabilities, at least when compared to version 4 of Word, but you can use horizontal tabs with leader characters to draw horizontal lines.

Horizontal Tab Leader Characters

To draw a horizontal line, use the Tab Set command and specify an underline leader character. For example, to draw a line .5" in from the left margin to .5" in from the right margin (on a five-inch-wide print column), set a left tab at .5" with no leader character. Then set a second left tab at 4.5", but this time specify the underline character as the leader character. Now, put two tab characters on the line and the result will look like the following:

_____

Line Styles

It doesn't take a lot of imagination to see that you can define a group of paragraph styles that draw horizontal lines. You can have one, say, L1, that has a left indent of .5" and a tab set .5" from the left margin to draw a line similar to the one above. Another, say, L2, can draw two shorter lines. Leave the indent at .5", and then set one tab at 2" with an underline leader character. Set another tab with no leader character at 3" and a third one with a leader at 4.5". The result should look like the following:

_____   _____

Using Two Tabs to Control Leaders

When you were looking at compiled tables earlier in this chapter, you saw the technique of using two tabs, one with leader characters, the other without, to control the look of column material. That trick works as well in formatted tables as it does in compiled tables.

Vertical Lines in Version 3

It is a lot of work, but you can use the vertical bar character (|) to draw some vertical lines in Word version 3; however, the process will take a lot of playing around, and the result won't look all that good. On most printers, the line will look like a series of vertical dashes.

Polaris Print Merge

There is one way to get real vertical lines using Word version 3, but it requires that you buy a second program and that you use a Hewlett-Packard LaserJet+ or compatible printer.

The additional program is called Polaris RAM-Resident Print Merge (Polaris Software, 613 West Valley Parkway, Suite 323, Escondido, CA 92025). Print Merge lets you embed in Word documents instructions to the printer. Not only will the program draw vertical lines, but you can also use it to draw boxes, shade parts of the page, change fonts, or issue any other command that the LaserJet accepts. Print Merge is a good solid program, but it requires that you use your imagination since you won't see its effects on the screen. Before you lay out good money for Print Merge, check the cost of an upgrade for your copy of Word. It may be cheaper just to move up from version 3 to version 4.

COLUMNS

By its nature, information in tables is in columns. Starting with Word 3.0, Microsoft has added a Column Select mode that makes it possible to move columns of text. (In later chapters, you will also learn how to use Column Select to control the sorting of material and to perform mathematical functions on screen.)

Column Moves

To move a column of text, press Shift-F6 to turn on the Column Select mode. In this mode, Word will select a rectangular area starting at the position of the selection and extending in a rectangle.

Following is an example of a listing of the populations and population densities of several countries.

Country	Population	Density
Spain	38,234,000	193
Sri Lanka	15,300,000	582
Sudan	20,539,000	19
Suriname	363,000	6
Swaziland	632,000	82
Sweden	8,331,000	48
Switzerland	6,463,000	398
Syria	9,700,00	126

If you look at Figure 16.5, you can see the formatting of the table. Each paragraph has three tab stops, one at 1", one at 3.5", and one at 5" (see the ruler line in Figure 16.5). The first tab stop is left-aligned; the other two are right-aligned, hence the "L" and two "R"s in the ruler line.

```
1     0····[····1·········L·········3····R····4·········R·········6·········7·····
      populations·and·population·densities·of·several·countries.¶

      Country·→        →    Population→        Density¶

      Spain→           →    38,234,000→        193¶
      Sri·Lanka→       →    15,300,000→        582¶
      Sudan→           →    20,539,000→        19¶
      Suriname→        →       363,000→        6¶
      Swaziland→       →       632,000→        82¶
      Sweden→          →     8,331,000→        48¶
      Switzerland→     →     6,463,000→        398¶
      Syria→           →     9,700,000→        126¶
      ¶
                                              ▸
SP        If·you·look·at·Figure·16-5,·you·can·see·the·formatting·

      of·the·table.···Each·paragraph·has·three·tab·stops,·one·at·

      1",·one·at·3.5",·and·one·at·5"·(see·the·ruller·line·in·

      Figure·16.5).···The·first·tab·stop·is·left—aligned;·the·other·

      two·are·right—aligned,·hence·the·"L"·and·two·"R"s·in·the·
Key code not defined
```

Figure 16.5

Set up such a table for yourself. Make sure that the Options *visible* field is set to Complete so you can see the tab marks on the screen.

Now, perform a column move. Position the selection on the tab mark (the right arrow) just after the word "Population" in the top row. The selection will extend across the gap between the words. Now press Shift-F6 to turn on the Column Select mode. The letters "CS" will appear at the bottom of the screen, and the selection will shrink to just one character.

```
▌     0····[····1·········L········3····R····4·········R·········6·········7·····
      populations·and·population·densities·of·several·countries.¶

         Country·→        →    Population→      Density¶

         Spain→           →    38,234,000→          193¶
         Sri·Lanka→       →    15,300,000→          582¶
         Sudan→           →    20,539,000→           19¶
         Suriname→        →       363,000→            6¶
         Swaziland→       →       632,000→           82¶
         Sweden→          →     8,331,000→           48¶
         Switzerland→     →     6,463,000→          398¶
         Syria→           →     9,700,000→          126¶
         ¶
                                              ▶
SP          If·you·look·at·Figure·16-5,·you·can·see·the·formatting·

         of·the·table.···Each·paragraph·has·three·tab·stops,·one·at·

         1",·one·at·3.5",·and·one·at·5"·(see·the·ruller·line·in·

         Figure·16.5).···The·first·tab·stop·is·left—aligned;·the·other·

         two·are·right—aligned,·hence·the·"L"·and·two·"R"s·in·the·
Pg25 Li8 Co36      {}                  ?                    CS        CHAP16.DOC
```

Figure 16.6

Whenever you turn on the Column Select mode, Word reduces the selection to a single character.

Now, use the arrow keys to extend the selection to cover all of that column. Do not include the paragraph marks. You can also use the mouse to extend the selection by pointing to where you want the selection to end and clicking either mouse button.

```
1    0····[····1·········L·········3····R····4·······R········6········7·····
     populations·and·population·densities·of·several·countries.¶

          Country·→        →       Population→███████Density¶

          Spain→           →       38,234,000→███████193¶
          Sri·Lanka→       →       15,300,000→███████582¶
          Sudan→           →       20,539,000→███████19¶
          Suriname→        →          363,000→███████6¶
          Swaziland→       →          632,000→███████82¶
          Sweden→          →        8,331,000→███████48¶
          Switzerland→     →        6,463,000→███████398¶
          Syria→           →        9,700,000→███████126¶
          ¶
                                             ▶
SP        If·you·look·at·Figure·16-5,·you·can·see·the·formatting·

     of·the·table.··Each·paragraph·has·three·tab·stops,·one·at·

     1",·one·at·3.5",·and·one·at·5"·(see·the·ruller·line·in·

     Figure·16.5).··The·first·tab·stop·is·left-aligned;·the·other·

     two·are·right-aligned,·hence·the·"L"·and·two·"R"s·in·the·
Pg25 Li16 Co50   {}                      ?                  CS      CHAP16.DOC
```

Figure 16.7

Press Delete and the selected text will be deleted to the scrap. You can tell that the text in the scrap comes from a column deletion because it has small squares in it, which is how Word marks the end of a line in a column that has been deleted or copied to the scrap.

Next, move the selection to the second tab stop on the first line.

```
1    0····[····1·········L·········3····R····4·······R········6········7·····
     populations·and·population·densities·of·several·countries.¶

          Country·→        →███████Population¶
                         ─────────────────────────────────────────────────
          Spain→           →       38,234,000¶
          Sri·Lanka→       →       15,300,000¶
          Sudan→           →       20,539,000¶
          Suriname→        →          363,000¶
          Swaziland→       →          632,000¶
          Sweden→          →        8,331,000¶
          Switzerland→     →        6,463,000¶
          Syria→           →        9,700,000¶
          ¶
                                             ▶
SP        If·you·look·at·Figure·16-5,·you·can·see·the·formatting·

     of·the·table.··Each·paragraph·has·three·tab·stops,·one·at·

     1",·one·at·3.5",·and·one·at·5"·(see·the·ruller·line·in·

     Figure·16.5).··The·first·tab·stop·is·left-aligned;·the·other·

     two·are·right-aligned,·hence·the·"L"·and·two·"R"s·in·the·
Pg25 Li8 Co21    {→Densit...→126■}  ?                      CHAP16.DOC
```

Figure 16.8

If you press the Insert key or choose I(nsert) from the main menu, Word will transplant the deleted column into its new position.

```
▯    0····[····1········L·······3···R···4········R·······6········7·····
     populations·and·population·densities·of·several·countries.¶

        Country·→        ▮      Density→    Population¶
        ─────────────────────────────────────────────
        Spain→          →         193→     38,234,000¶
        Sri·Lanka→      →         582→     15,300,000¶
        Sudan→          →          19→     20,539,000¶
        Suriname→       →           6→        363,000¶
        Swaziland→      →          82→        632,000¶
        Sweden→         →          48→      8,331,000¶
        Switzerland→    →         398→      6,463,000¶
        Syria→          →         126→      9,700,000¶
        ¶                                   ▲
SP      If·you·look·at·Figure·16-5,·you·can·see·the·formatting·

        of·the·table.···Each·paragraph·has·three·tab·stops,·one·at·

        1",·one·at·3.5",·and·one·at·5"·(see·the·ruller·line·in·

        Figure·16.5).···The·first·tab·stop·is·left—aligned;·the·other·

        two·are·right—aligned,·hence·the·"L"·and·two·"R"s·in·the·
Pg25 Li8 Co21    {→Densit...→126▮}   ?                    CHAP16.DOC
```

Figure 16.9

SIDE-BY-SIDE PARAGRAPHS

The final way to produce tables is by using side-by-side paragraphs. This technique is covered in Chapter 3, "Editing Basics," and in Chapter 11, "Multicolumn Formats."

PART V

WORD AND THE OFFICE

CHAPTER 17

MERGE AND FORMS

Suppose you had to send out more than 150 virtually identical letters to prospective donors for a project on which you were working. Back in the days before you used a computer, you would probably have typed a single copy of the letter and sent each recipient a photocopy; however, by using Word's merge abilities, you are now able to send each person an individually addressed letter in less time than you would have spent a few years ago just hanging around the photocopier.

But a mass mailing is not the only merging job Word can accomplish. You can also use it to produce individual copies of a document that you prepare frequently but not always in big batches. For example, a lawyer could use Word's merge feature to produce individual copies of a standard agreement for the sale of a home. She may produce only one of these agreements a week, but, over a year, the total would be more than 50 copies. No one wants to waste time making 50 copies of basically the same document.

Finally, in version 4, you can use Word to create and fill in standard forms, such as employment applications, expense sheets, telephone logs, and others. Version 4 also provides an alternative method of preparing those standard agreements and letters you use often.

FORM LETTERS

Preparing individually addressed yet mass-produced letters (or a standard contract) is a two-step project. First, you must write the master letter or contract. In doing so, you must tell Word where to insert names, dates, terms, and conditions. Second, you must tell Word just what those names, dates, terms, and conditions are.

First Step—Writing the Master Document

The first step in preparing any merge document is writing the master document. For an example, prepare a fund-raising letter to be sent to members of a computer user's group.

Variables

The difference between a document to be used for merging and a regular document is that a merge document contains **variables**. A variable is a specially marked word in your master document that tells Word to substitute another word or phrase in its place.

In Word merge documents, variables are marked with double angle brackets (« »). You get the angle brackets by pressing the Control key (usually marked Ctrl and next to the A at the left side of the keyboard) and one of the square bracket keys, [or].

For example, to tell Word to insert a particular name in a letter, you might create a variable called «YOURNAME». Wherever the variable «YOURNAME» appeared in the master document, Word would substitute the value assigned to that variable. Variables may be more than one word long and may contain letters in uppercase, lowercase, or mixed case.

For example, following is a typical example of a form letter that uses several variables.

«DATE»

«TITLE» «FIRST» « LAST»
«ADDRESS1»
«ADDRESS2»
«ADDRESS3»

Dear «TITLE» «LAST»,

As you may know, the Vancouver PC User's Group is trying to raise money to sponsor an exhibit of personal computing technology for the British Columbia Arts, Science and Technology Center. We can't do it without your help. Please send what you can afford today.

Sincerely,

Tim Perrin

Second Step—Collecting Data

Of course, you can't send a form letter that says "Dear «TITLE» «LAST»."
Somehow, you must let Word know what the values of those variables are.
Like many situations in life, the easiest way to get the answer to a question
is to simply ask another question.

ASK and SET

Word provides two simple ways of providing values for merge variables. One
way is the keyword **SET** and the other is the keyword **ASK**. These terms are
called keywords because Word has assigned them special tasks. You cannot
use them as variables in a Word merge document. Instead, when Word comes
across one of these keywords, it stops and asks you for the value of a particular variable.

For example, to get Word to ask you for the date, you would enter this line
at the beginning of your letter:

«SET DATE=? What is today's date?

When Word comes to that line in preparing to merge and print the letter, it
will stop and, at the bottom of the screen, ask for the date:

```
RESPONSE: _

What is today's date?
```

In version 3, Word uses the word VALUE in place of RESPONSE.

For each of the other variables, you need to include a similar line:

«ASK TITLE = ? Mr., Ms., Mrs.
«ASK FIRST = ? First name and initial
«ASK LAST = ? Last Name
«ASK ADDRESS1 = ? First line of address
«ASK ADDRESS2 = ? Second line of address
«ASK ADDRESS3 = ? Third line of address

Each SET and ASK statement has three parts: the keyword SET or ASK, a variable name set equal to a question mark, and a prompt. The prompt is the text Word uses to ask you for the value to be assigned to this variable.

A SET or ASK statement does not require a prompt. For example, you could simply put this line in your document.

«SET DATE = ?»

If you do not include a prompt line in the SET or ASK statement, Word will prompt you with the words "Enter text. Press Enter when done." (Version 3 just displays the words "Enter text.") Since that message is not much assistance when you are preparing merge letters, be sure to include a specific prompt in all your SET and ASK statements.

The Difference between ASK and SET

When Word encounters the keyword SET, it asks for the value of that variable and then applies it to every copy of the document printed in that session. In other words, you are only asked for the DATE once.

With the keyword ASK, Word stops and asks for that value every time it merge prints the document. Presumably, if you prepare several copies of this document at one sitting, you will want each one to go to a different person, so you use the ASK keyword to get Word to ask for those variables each time the letter is merge printed.

Terminators

Notice that the » character was not used to end all of the ASK or SET lines. They are omitted because a paragraph mark also ends an ASK or SET statement. If you use both characters to end a line, Word will interpret the » as ending the ASK or SET statement, and then it will print the paragraph end mark, adding unwanted line spaces to the top of your document.

THE PRINT MERGE COMMAND

Now you can pull all of this information together. If you haven't done so already, prepare a master letter similar to the one developed earlier. Following is the complete example for you to copy:

«SET DATE = ? Enter the date
«ASK TITLE = ? Mr., Ms., Mrs.
«ASK FIRST = ? First name and initial
«ASK LAST = ? Last Name
«ASK ADDRESS1 = ? First line of address
«ASK ADDRESS2 = ? Second line of address
«ASK ADDRESS3 = ? Third line of address

«DATE»

«TITLE» «FIRST» «LAST»
«ADDRESS1»
«ADDRESS2»
«ADDRESS3»

Dear «TITLE» «LAST»,

As you may know, the Vancouver PC User's Group is trying to raise money to sponsor an exhibit of personal computing technology for the British Columbia Arts, Science and Technology Center. We can't do it without your help. Please send what you can afford today.

Sincerely,

Tim Perrin

Now choose the P(rint) M(erge) command from the Word main menu. In version 3, Word will move directly to printing. There is no submenu, and Print Merge is the same as Print Merge Printer in version 4 (discussed in the next section).

In version 4, Word will present you with this submenu:

```
PRINT MERGE: Printer Document Options
```

Print Merge Printer Command

The Print Merge Printer command in version 4 is the same as Print Merge in version 3. Word will ask you for each variable, prompting you with the text after the question mark. Press Return after entering the text you want assigned to each variable. When you have answered each prompt, Word will print a copy of the letter addressed as you instructed. Then it will go back to the top of the list and ASK you for the TITLE of the next person to receive a copy of your letter. If you want to stop, just press the Escape key.

Print Merge Document Command

The Print Merge Document command sends the output of the merge to a new document. When you issue this command, Word will ask you for the name of the file into which it is to put the results of the merging operation:

```
PRINT MERGE DOCUMENT filename:
```

The resulting document contains all the merged data. For example, if you prepared 15 copies of the sample letter using Print Merge Document, the resulting document would contain 15 letters, each correctly addressed. If you want a hard copy, you then print that merged file.

This command does not exist in version 3.

Print Merge Options Command

The Print Merge Options command allows you to conduct a merge operation for a portion of the data stored in a separate data file. The next section explains data files, following which will be a detailed discussion of the Print Merge Options command.

This command does not exist in version 3.

DATA FILES

Using ASK and SET statements is not a bad way to prepare form letters, but this method has its limits. What if you need to prepare 150 letters? You hardly want to sit there individually typing names and addresses and then waiting for each one to print before you can proceed.

Instead, Word will let you enter your entire mailing list into a second file called the **merge data file**. Word then reads the merge data file and uses the values in it to fill in the variables in your main letter.

For this example, call the merge data file MAILLIST.DOC.

The Header Paragraph

The first paragraph in MAILLIST.DOC, or in any merge data file, must be a **header** that sets out which variables are being supplied by this data file. In the previous example letter, the header line would read

TITLE,FIRST,LAST,ADDRESS1,ADDRESS2,ADDRESS3

Fields and Records

The balance of a merge data file consists of a group of **records**. There should be one record for each letter you are going to prepare. Each record ends with a paragraph mark.

Each record consists of several **fields.** Each field contains the text to assign to a single variable. Each field ends with a comma or tab character. (If you have chosen the comma as your decimal character in the *decimal character* field in the Options command, then just use tabs or semicolons to separate fields.)

Following is an example of three records for the example letter asking for money for a computer display:

Mr.,John,Jones,123 Any Street,"Vancouver, BC",
Ms.,Martha,Smith,Smith's Bar and Grill,457 W. Pender St.,"Seattle, WA"
Dr.,"Michael ""the Knife""",Doe,1457 - 185th Ave.,"Surrey, BC"

Embedded Commas, Tabs, and Quotation Marks

Note how quotation marks have been entered around the city and province or city and state. Without the quotes, Word would interpret the comma after each city name as terminating the field. The quotation marks tell Word that everything between the quotes is a single field. You also need to place quotes around fields containing tab characters.

If a field contains either single or double quotation marks, enclose the entire field in quotation marks and double the quotes within the field. An example is the entry for *"Michael ""the Knife"""* The triple quotes at the end consist of two sets around *the Knife* and one set to balance the quotation marks at the beginning of the line.

Blank Fields

Sometimes, no information will exist for a particular field. For example, the address may have only two lines. When a field is empty, you must mark it with a comma to create a blank field. For example, the entry,

Mr.,John,Jones,123 Any Street,"Vancouver, BC",

ends with a comma, creating a blank field for the third line of the address. If, strangely, Mr. Jones had no first name, the entry would look like the following:

Mr.,,Jones,123 Any Street,"Vancouver, BC",

The DATA Statement

The next step in using a merge data file is to let Word know the name of the merge data file. You do so with a DATA statement at the beginning of your letter. This statement *must* be at the *beginning* of your file. You cannot even enter a blank line or space ahead of it.

For the example merge, the DATA statement would read

«DATA MAILLIST.DOC»

The DATA statement should include the disk drive and path to the merge data file if that file is not in the currently logged directory, for example,

«DATA B:\SUBDIR\MAILLIST.DOC»

You can also place the header paragraph in a separate file, in which case Word would expect you to list two file names separated by a comma. The first should be the file containing the header paragraph; the second should be the file containing the mailing list itself:

«DATA HEADER.FIL,MAILLIST.DOC»

Finally, if you do not want the line feed at the end of the line containing your DATA statement to print in your letters, then leave off the trailing » and let the paragraph end serve as terminator for the DATA statement, for example,

«DATA MAILLIST.DOC

The master letter now should resemble the following:

«DATA MAILLIST.DOC
«SET DATE = ? Enter the date

«DATE»

«TITLE» «FIRST» «LAST»
«ADDRESS1»
«ADDRESS2»
«ADDRESS3»

Dear «TITLE» «LAST»,

As you may know, the Vancouver PC User's Group is trying to raise money to sponsor an exhibit of personal computing technology for the British Columbia Arts, Science and Technology Center. We can't do it without your help. Please send what you can afford today.

Sincerely,

Tim Perrin

Note that the «SET DATE = ? statement is retained because you still need to set the date for these letters.

Print Merge Options Command Explanation

As promised, here are the details on how to use the Print Merge Options command to produce form letters for only part of your file. When you select the command P(rint) M(erge) O(ptions), Word asks you for two pieces of information:

```
PRINT MERGE OPTIONS range:(All)Records         record numbers:
```

Normally, you will want to merge all the records in your data file; however, occasionally, you may want to merge only a few of them. Use this command to select the records you want to merge. Set the *range* field to Records. Then, list the record numbers. List contiguous record numbers separated by a hyphen, for example, 1-10. For noncontiguous numbers, separate them by commas, for example, 1, 3, 9, 12, 14. You may combine both types of lists as in 1-10, 14, 22, 35.

After you select the range of records to merge, use the Print Merge Printer or Print Merge Document command to perform the actual merging.

CONDITIONAL MERGE

So far, merge printing has been interesting but not spectacular. Where the real power of merge printing comes to the forefront is when you use **conditional merges**. These types of merges allow you to include certain parts of your text only when certain conditions are met.

IF . . . ELSE . . . ENDIF

The key to conditional merging is the IF . . . ELSE . . . ENDIF statement, which says, "IF a certain condition is met, do this, or ELSE do this."

For example, if you know that one of the people to whom you are writing is also a member of the Friends of the Arts, Science and Technology Center, you could include another line saying, "I know that you, as a long-time supporter of the Center, will help us." The central paragraph of that letter would read as follows:

As you may know, the Vancouver PC User's Group is trying to raise money to sponsor an exhibit of personal computing technology for the British Columbia Arts, Science and Technology Center. We can't do it without your help. «IF CENTER = "Y"»I know that you, as a long-time supporter of the Center, will help us. «ENDIF»Please send what you can afford today.

That paragraph says that IF a field called CENTER contains the letter Y (for Yes), then print the text up to the ENDIF. So when CENTER = "Y" the paragraph will read:

As you may know, the Vancouver PC User's Group is trying to raise money to sponsor an exhibit of personal computing technology for the British Columbia Arts, Science and Technology Center. We can't do it without your help. I know that you, as a long-time supporter of the Center, will   help us. Please send what you can afford today.

Making this merge a bit more complex, you can add the ELSE part of the statement this way:

As you may know, the Vancouver PC User's Group is trying to raise money to sponsor an exhibit of personal computing technology for the British Columbia Arts, Science and Technology Center. We can't do it without your help. «IF CENTER = "Y"»I know that you, as a long-time supporter of the Center, will help us. «ELSE»The Center needs all the new supporters it can get. Won't you become one? «ENDIF»Please send what you can afford today.

That paragraph says that IF the field called CENTER contains the letter Y, then print the text up to ELSE; otherwise, print the text between ELSE and ENDIF. So now, when CENTER is Y, the paragraph will read as follows:

As you may know, the Vancouver PC User's Group is trying to raise money to sponsor an exhibit of personal computing technology for the British Columbia Arts, Science and Technology Center. We can't do it without your help. I know that you, as a long-time supporter of the Center, will help us. Please send what you can afford today.

When CENTER is anything other than Y, the paragraph will read as follows:

As you may know, the Vancouver PC User's Group is trying to raise money to sponsor an exhibit of personal computing technology for the British Columbia Arts, Science and Technology Center. We can't do it without your help. The Center needs all the new supporters it can get. Won't you become one? Please send what you can afford today.

Kinds of Comparisons

Word can use the IF. . .ELSE. . .ENDIF structure to check whether a variable is equal to (=), greater than (>), less than (<), or not equal to a number or a string of characters. It can also simply check to see if the variable has any value at all.

IF NUMBER

To check whether a variable is equal to a number, use the form «IF VARIABLE = 000». Substitute any variable name for VARIABLE. Substitute any number for 000. For example:

«IF SALARY = 25000 > »

The number must be an integer; no decimal values are allowed. The number must also be positive but with no plus sign. And no commas are allowed either, just digits.

You may, of course, also use > and < as comparators.

IF STRING

You can use «IF VARIABLE = "match text"» to see whether a variable is the same as a particular string of text. You might use this statement, for example, to send one letter to people living in California («IF STATE = "CA"») and another to residents of Washington («IF STATE = "WA"»).

Note the quotation marks around the text to be matched. You must use the quotation marks; otherwise, Word expects a number.

IF ANYTHING

A final form of the IF statement is «IF VARIABLE» without any comparison. This statement just asks if there is anything assigned to VARIABLE.

By using this statement, you avoid blanks in your form letters when there is no value assigned to a variable. For example, in two of the three sample addresses listed earlier in this chapter, there was nothing assigned to the variable ADDRESS3. These addresses were discussed under the heading "Blank Fields," which is why they ended in commas—to create that blank field:

Mr.,John,Jones,123 Any Street,"Vancouver, BC",
Dr.,"Michael ""the Knife""",Doe,1457 - 185th Ave.,"Surrey, BC",

If you left the address block of the master letter as it is, for each of those letters, Word would insert a blank line in each letter where it was supposed to print the variable ADDRESS3; however, if you change the address block of the letter a bit, you can make Word skip that blank line:

«DATA MAILLIST.DOC
«SET DATE =? Enter the date

«DATE»

«TITLE» «FIRST» «LAST»
«ADDRESS1»
«ADDRESS2»
«IF ADDRESS3»«ADDRESS3»
«ENDIF»
Dear «TITLE» «LAST»,

When you enter the IF statement in the ADDRESS3 field, Word first tests to see if anything at all has been assigned to ADDRESS3. If so, it prints the text between the IF statement and the ENDIF statements – which, in this case, is the variable ADDRESS3 – and the end of the paragraph. If there is nothing assigned to ADDRESS3, Word skips ahead to the ENDIF.

Not Equal To

You can use IF statements to see if a variable is equal to (=), greater than (>), or less than (<) a certain value; however, if you want to see if a variable is not equal to something, use the equal comparator followed immediately by the ELSE statement:

«IF SALARY =25000»«ELSE» Your salary is not $25,000.«ENDIF»

If SALARY is equal to 25,000, Word is supposed to print the text immediately following, but, since there is no text, it prints nothing. If SALARY is not equal to 25,000, Word jumps to ELSE and prints the text that follows it. The effect is to ask if SALARY is not equal to 25,000.

Nesting

You can nest IF statements in the form of a simple program. **Nested** conditions are conditions on conditions. For example, IF someone's salary is greater than $25,000 and IF that person works in the accounting department, then tell him/her that he/she is entitled to a 50% raise; however, IF he/she works in any other department, tell him/her that he/she must take a 50% pay cut. But IF that person's salary is less than $25,001, tell that person he/she is fired. In a Word document such a paragraph would look like the following.

```
«IF SALARY>25000»«IF DEPARTMENT="ACCOUNTING"»  This letter is
to offer you a 50% raise.  «ELSE»This letter is to inform you
that we are cutting all salaries by 50%.  «ENDIF»«ELSE»This
letter is to inform you that you are fired.  «ENDIF»
```

If you look at the following structured version of the paragraph where each IF is linked to its ENDIF, you can better see how nesting works.

```
«IF SALARY>2500»
|    «IF DEPARTMENT="ACCOUNTING"»
|    |    50% raise
|    «ELSE»
|    |    50% cut
|    «ENDIF»
«ELSE»
|    Fired
«ENDIF»
```

The IF . . . ELSE . . . ENDIF sequence farther to the right is nested in the other.

NEXT STATEMENTS

If you want to print side-by-side mailing labels, you will need to know how to use NEXT statements.

Normally, Word produces one document per record; however, when Word finds «NEXT» in a merge master document, it reads another record from the merge data file and applies the variables that record contains to the current document rather than to the next document.

For example, if you wanted to make up mailing labels for the addresses in a mailing list, you could design a document such as the following:

«DATA MAILLIST.DOC»«TITLE» «FIRST» «LAST»
«ADDRESS1»
«ADDRESS2»
«ADDRESS3»
«NEXT»
«TITLE FIRST LAST»
«ADDRESS1»
«ADDRESS2»
«ADDRESS3»
«NEXT»
«TITLE FIRST LAST»
«ADDRESS1»
«ADDRESS2»
«ADDRESS3»
«NEXT»

The NEXT statements tell Word to continue working in this document but to read the next set of data from MAILLIST.DOC.

To get these labels to print three across, use the Format Division Margin command to set the margins to 0 all the way around, the page size to the width of three labels, and the page height to a height of four lines (because there are four lines on each label). Then use the Format Division Layout command to tell Word that there are three columns on the page.

Word will print the first label and, because of the NEXT statement, read another record from MAILLIST.DOC and prepare to print a second label; however, because the page length has been set to four lines, Word will move to the top of the second column for the second label and then to the top of the third column for the third label.

INCLUDE STATEMENTS

The INCLUDE statement is another powerful merging tool. It lets you merge entire documents into your text.

Suppose you are a lawyer, and you keep the various parts of a standard agreement in separate files, each with appropriate names. To create a customized version of that agreement, you could use the INCLUDE statement to include those sections in the agreement, for example,

«INCLUDE ARBITRAT.DOC»
«INCLUDE CHOICE.DOC»

Those two INCLUDE statements would put the contents of the files AR-BITRAT.DOC (an arbitration clause) and CHOICE.DOC (a choice of law clause) into the contract.

Note that an INCLUDE statement should include a disk drive specification or a path specification if the file being included is not in the current directory.

Included documents may, themselves, be merge documents and may include other documents.

Finally, you may or may not include a document based on an IF statement.

FORMS

Starting with version 4, Microsoft has added new abilities to Word that let you easily work with prepared forms. In fact, you may find Word easier to work with than programs the are dedicated to producing forms.

Designing and Laying Out Your Form

Use Word's line-drawing capabilities to design your forms. By using your imagination, the line draw function (Ctrl-F5), paragraph borders, and vertical tabs, you can easily create forms.

For example, following is the first few lines of an application for employment:

Application for Employment

Last Name»		First Name»	
Address»			
City»		State/Prov»	Postal/Zip Code»

The first line is a separate paragraph, centered, in 14-point Optima bold. The two name blocks are part of a paragraph that has a border around it and a new line command to force the words "Last Name" and "First Name" to the bottom of the box. There is a vertical tab at 2.5" to draw the vertical line and a left-aligned tab at 2.7" to position the words "First Name." The address block is a single paragraph with a border around it. The last line has a border, vertical tabs at 2.5" and 3.8" to draw the vertical lines, and left-aligned tabs at 2.7" and 4.0" to align the text.

As it comes from the printer, this form is ready to be filled out. And, even though you may not have access to a laser printer, Word can produce the best forms your printer can print.

Prepare a similar document and run off a copy on your printer. You will need that document in the next section.

The Double Angle Brackets

The double angle brackets to the right (») in the form have a special function. They are the key to filling out the form on screen.

Position the selection anywhere near the top of your copy. Press and hold Ctrl and simultaneously press the . (period) key. The selection will jump to the first space following the next double angle bracket to the right. Press it again and the selection will jump to the next double angle bracket. By pressing Ctrl-.(Ctrl key and a period), you can advance the selection through your document to each field, filling it in as you go.

The Ctrl-. combination will jump only to double angle brackets that face right.

If you don't want the double angle brackets to print, format them as hidden text, and set the *hidden text* field of the Print Options screen to No.

Standard Forms

You can now use Word's form creation features to automatically fill in standard documents such as the one you first saw at the beginning of this chapter — the solicitation letter:

«SET DATE = ? Enter the date
«ASK TITLE = ? Mr., Ms., Mrs.
«ASK FIRST = ? First name and initial
«ASK LAST = ? Last Name
«ASK ADDRESS1 = ? First line of address
«ASK ADDRESS2 = ? Second line of address
«ASK ADDRESS3 = ? Third line of address

«DATE»

«TITLE» «FIRST» «LAST»
«ADDRESS1»
«ADDRESS2»
«ADDRESS3»

Dear «TITLE» «LAST»,

continued...

...from previous page

As you may know, the Vancouver PC User's Group is trying to raise money to sponsor an exhibit of personal computing technology for the British Columbia Arts, Science and Technology Center. We can't do it without your help. Please send what you can afford today.

Sincerely,

Tim Perrin

Remember that when you merge print that document, Word prompts you for each variable. With some modification, you can make that letter operate like a form. Remember that, in version 4, you can use the Ctrl-. combination to advance to the next ». Remember also that you can set Word so that hidden text appears on the screen but is not printed. So if you modify the letter a bit, you can put "hidden" prompts on the screen. But, because they are hidden, they will not print. Your screen would look something like the following (with the underlined text being hidden text):

DATE»

ADDRESSEE'S NAME HERE»
FIRST LINE OF ADDRESS»
SECOND LINE OF ADDRESS»
THIRD LINE OF ADDRESS (IF ANY)»

Dear title AND LAST NAME»

As you may know, the Vancouver PC User's Group is trying to raise money to sponsor an exhibit of personal computing technology for the British Columbia Arts, Science and Technology Center. We can't do it without your help. Please send what you can afford today.

Sincerely,

Tim Perrin

Each time you press Ctrl-., the selection will jump to the next line that needs some input from you. Your answers, but not the prompts, will print.

For forms that you use regularly but not in big batches, you might find this method easier than using merge with the ASK and SET statements. For example, suppose you had a standard file called INVOICE.DOC that contained a standard invoice. All you would need to do is press CTRL-. and Word would jump to every spot that required your input. If you were a lawyer, you could use this system for preparing standard contracts, filling in the names of the parties, the amounts of money, and other terms as you went along.

SUMMARY

Whether you use Word's merge and form-making abilities frequently or only occasionally, you will find these features to be some of the most valuable features of Word. When you are sipping coffee while Word and your printer do all the work, you will really appreciate word processing.

CHAPTER 18

THE GLOSSARY AND MACROS

GLOSSARY POWER

You have already learned to use Word's Glossary as a tool for shorthand typing; it allows you to store long segments of text in just a few keystrokes. Starting with version 4, the Word Glossary also stores commands as well as text, which allows you to create **macros** — a series of long, complicated commands that normally involve many keystrokes. With the Glossary, you can store macros (which may include dozens of keystrokes) in a single keystroke.

THE STANDARD GLOSSARY

The Standard Glossary allows Word to store large blocks of text in a glossary entry. For example, you might keep a letterhead such as the following in a glossary entry named "letr":

Palmer V. Westhammer   (609) 555-2678
Writer/Producer   6060 S.W. Broadway Ave.
                                                        Seattle, WA 98206

To begin writing a letter, type "letr" and press F3 to expand the glossary entry. Word inserts the letterhead.

The letterhead contains right tabs at the end of each line. The solid line is a paragraph border attached to the first paragraph. (In version 3, a superscripted, bold line can be created with a right tab using the underline character as a leader; see Chapter 16.)

This letterhead is somewhat complicated, but with Word, it can be inserted by pressing just five keys: l, e, t, r, and F3.

HOW TO USE THE GLOSSARY

There are three ways to use the glossary. The most common method is to type the glossary entry name and press F3. Alternatively, you can select the glossary entry from a list or use a shortcut name.

Expand Glossary—F3

The most common method of using the glossary is to type the name of a glossary entry and press F3. Word looks in the glossary and expands the glossary name into the entire glossary entry.

For the F3 key to work, the glossary entry must be preceded by a blank space or be the first word on a line or in a paragraph. Also, the selection should be on the space after the glossary name.

Selecting a Glossary Entry from a List

If you can't remember the name of the glossary entry you want to use, choose the Insert command from Word's main menu. Word will prompt you with the following:

```
INSERT from: {}

Enter glossary name or press F1 to select from list
```

Press F1 (in version 4) or one of the arrow keys (in version 3); Word will list all glossary entries in the current glossary. Use the arrow keys to select one and then press Return.

Version 4 Shortcut

In version 4, you can also use "shortcut" glossary names. For example, you can use ^L (Ctrl-L) as the shortcut name to load the example letterhead; instead of typing "letr" and pressing F3, simply press Ctrl-L.

PLACING TEXT IN THE GLOSSARY

Place text in the glossary by selecting it and then using either the Delete or Copy command. Text stored in the glossary retains all formatting.

The Delete and Copy commands work the same way; Copy will be discussed as an example. When you choose the Copy command, the following appears:

```
COPY to: {}
```

```
Enter glossary name or choose from list
```

Word always proposes the scrap, { }, as the destination for any Copy or Delete command; however, Word also reminds you that you can enter a glossary name. If you press F1 (in version 4) or any of the arrow keys (in version 3), Word lists the names of entries in the current glossary.

GLOSSARY NAMES

To name a glossary entry, type the name under which you want to store the particular block of text. For example, the glossary name for the example letterhead might be entered as follows:

```
COPY to: letr
```

```
Enter glossary name or choose from list
```

Glossary names must be single words, but they may be up to 31 characters long. No spaces or punctuation marks (other than the underline character) are allowed. So, "InsertLetterhead" is a legitimate glossary name, and so is "Insert_letterhead." "Insert Letterhead" is not allowed, however, because it contains a space. It is suggested that glossary names be at least two or three letters long, which makes them easier to identify and allows a greater number of possible names.

Shortcut Names

As mentioned previously, you can also specify a shortcut name — a single key or short sequence of keys — to invoke the glossary entry without pressing the F3 key.

To designate a shortcut name, name the glossary entry as usual. Then, type the caret symbol (ˆ, usually above the 6 on the keyboard) and the shortcut name. For example, to use Ctrl-L as a shortcut to load the letterhead, type "letrˆ" and hold down the Ctrl key while simultaneously pressing L. The screen would resemble the following:

```
COPY to: letrˆ<ctrl l>

Enter glossary name or choose from list
```

A shortcut name must begin with a control character (Ctrl and another key). It may not begin with a letter, number, or Alt character. A shortcut name may be more than one character long. For example, the shortcut name could be Ctrl-L L. Then, if you press Ctrl-L followed by any other key, Word ignores it. If you press Ctrl-L followed by L, however, Word inserts the letterhead. It is suggested that you use shortcut names of at least two characters to allow variety.

To use the caret symbol (ˆ) as part of the glossary name, you must repeat it (ˆˆ).

PLACING MACROS IN THE GLOSSARY

Macros are a new feature of Word version 4.0. A **macro** is a glossary entry that includes commands as well as text. Macros can also pause, prompt you for information, and then perform according to the responses.

There are two ways to place macros in the glossary. First, you can record a macro. Second, you can create a macro using Word's macro programming language.

Recording a Macro

The easiest way to place a macro into the glossary is to record it by pressing Shift-F3. The letters "RM" appear at the bottom of the screen, indicating that Word is recording a macro. Next, press the keystrokes in the exact sequence you want recorded in the macro. When you are done, press Shift-F3 again. Word offers to copy the macro either to the scrap (not very useful) or to the named glossary entry:

```
COPY to:

Enter glossary name or chose from list
```

Name your macro as you would name any glossary entry.

Programming a Macro

Recording is sufficient for most macros, but if you want to include conditional actions in your macro or create a macro that requires input from the user, use the Word macro programming language.

If you have ever written a computer program, you will find it easy to program a Word macro. Even if you haven't tried programming, creating Word macros is a good place to start because the language is so simple.

Creating and Saving a Macro Program

Programmed macros are created by writing the program as a Word document, selecting the program, and then copying (or deleting) it to the glossary. Word recognizes the text as a macro program and converts it into a macro.

Most of a macro program consists of keystrokes. List the keystrokes you want the macro to record. For example, entering

<esc>ts

creates a macro equivalent to pressing Esc, t, and s.

Double Angle Brackets

In a macro program, you again use the double angle brackets covered in the discussion of Word's merge feature. All program statements containing keywords must be enclosed in double angle brackets as follows:

«SET answer = "n"»

In many ways, a macro program resembles a merge file; it can use the SET and ASK keywords to request information. Macros also use the IF. . .ELSE. . .ENDIF structure to control branching. If you enjoy working with Merge, you'll consider macro programming a breeze.

Variables

Word macro programs usually contain variables. A **variable** is a word in your macro program that tells Word to substitute another word, phrase, or numerical value in its place. Variables must be a string of letters (usually a word). Legitimate variables include "PageOne," "TopOfForm," and even "Variable." Uppercase and lowercase letters in variables are treated the same by Word; however, it is suggested that you use a mix of uppercase and lowercase characters to make the variable more readable.

You may not use a keyword or the words "selection" or "field" as a variable.

Macro Programming Keywords

Keywords are assigned special tasks by Word; you cannot use them as variables in a Word macro program.

There are only a few sets of related keywords in Word's macro programming language; however, if used creatively, they are more than enough.

As a rule, type keywords in uppercase letters to make them easier to see when modifying the program.

Following are discussions of the main Word macro keywords.

ASK and SET

Word offers two simple ways of providing values to control macro functions. One is the keyword SET, and the other is the keyword ASK.

If you want the macro to ask the user for the value of a variable, use the following format:

«SET DATE =? What is today's date?»

When Word encounters that line in the macro, it will stop and, at the bottom of the screen, ask for the date:

```
RESPONSE: _

What is today's date?
```

The ASK statement uses a similar format and functions in the same way:

«ASK TITLE =? Mr., Ms., Mrs.»

If you omit the question mark in the SET statement, you will not be asked for the value of a variable; it will be set to the specified value. For example,

«SET RESPONSE = "Hello"»

sets the variable RESPONSE to equal "Hello."

IF . . . ELSE . . . ENDIF

The IF. . .ELSE. . .ENDIF structure works the same in a macro as it does with Merge; it says, "IF a certain condition is met, do this; ELSE, do this."

Word can use the IF. . .ELSE. . .ENDIF structure to check whether a variable is equal to ($=$), greater than ($>$), less than ($<$), or not equal to ($\neq$) a number or a string of characters.

To check whether a variable is equal to a number, use the form IF VARIABLE$=$000. Substitute any variable name for VARIABLE. Substitute any number for 000. For example:

«IF SALARY = 25000»

You may, of course, also use $>$, $<$, and $<>$ as comparators.

You can use IF VARIABLE$=$"match text" to determine whether a variable is the same as a particular string of text.

Note the quotation marks around the text to be matched. You must use the quotation marks; otherwise, Word expects a number.

An Example

Following is an example of a short macro program that uses SET and the IF. . .ELSE. . .ENDIF structure. The following macro will save a file unless you try to name it DUMMY.FIL:

```
«SET filename = ? Enter the name of the file to save»
«IF filename = "DUMMY.FIL"»
   «PAUSE That's not good enough.  Try again.  Press Enter to
continue.»
«ELSE»
   <esc>ts«filename»<enter>
«ENDIF»
```

COMMENT

If you have done any programming, you realize the value of inserting comments in your program so it can be understood months later when it must be modified. The COMMENT keyword allows you to insert such comments. Comments are ignored by Word when the macro is executed; they are there just for you. Following is an example:

«COMMENT This line doesn't do anything»

PAUSE

PAUSE allows you to pause the execution of the macro while you perform another task on the screen, such as marking a block of text. The pause ends when you press the Return key. A pause statement can contain a prompt. Following is an example:

«PAUSE Mark the text you wish to delete then press <return>.»

WHILE . . . ENDWHILE

A WHILE. . .ENDWHILE structure executes the same set of lines again and again, as long as a certain condition exists. The condition is usually the value of a variable. For example:

```
«SET ans="n"»
«WHILE ans="n"»
  «ASK ans=? Is this correct? (Y)es or (N)o»
  «IF ans="N"»
    «SET ans="n"»
  «ENDIF»
«ENDWHILE» !!! CORRECT !!!»
```

REPEAT . . . ENDREPEAT

REPEAT. . .ENDREPEAT has a looping structure; it executes the program lines between the REPEAT and the ENDREPEAT statements a specified number of times. The number is the second element in the REPEAT statement and can be either a variable or a number. Following is an example:

```
«REPEAT 10»
   . . .
  repeat these lines 10 times
   . . .
«ENDREPEAT»
```

Selection

"Selection" is the keyword for the selection, as in the following example:

«SET word = selection»

This line sets the variable word to whatever is in the selection.

Field

"Field" is the keyword for the contents of the current command field. Following is an example:

«SET word = field»

This keyword sets the variable word to the contents of the highlighted field in Word's command area. Following is a macro that reads and reports to you the current page number:

<esc>jp«SET pagenumber = field»<esc>The page number is «pagenumber».

Math Functions

Word macros can also perform simple math functions. For example, the following macro resembles the previous example, but it calculates a number twice the actual page number:

<esc>jp«SET pagenumber = field»<esc>The page number is «pagenumber * 2».

Word macros can add (+), subtract (-), multiply (*), and divide (/). They can also perform percentage calculations. Calculations inside parentheses are performed first, and multiplication and division operations are performed before additions and subtractions. For example, if «pagenumber» is 8, then

«pagenumber * 50%»	is 4 (8*50% = 4)
«(pagenumber * 50% + 1) * 2»	is 10 (8*50% = 4, 4 + 1 = 5, 5*2 = 10)
«(pagenumber * 50%) + (2 * 2)»	is 8 (8*50% = 4, 2*2 = 4, 4 + 4 = 8)

Special Characters

Many characters on the keyboard cannot be directly entered into a Word document. To instruct a macro to insert one of these characters, use the following substitutes:

<enter>	Enter or Return
<esc>	Escape
<ctrl *any*>	Use <ctrl *any*> for any Ctrl key combination, substituting the key to be pressed for *any*. For example, <ctrl T> is the same as pressing Ctrl and then simultaneously pressing T. Use <ctrl esc> if you are not sure whether the selection will be in the text area or the command area.
<tab>	The Tab key. Use <shift tab> for Shift and the Tab key.
<pgdn>	Page Down
<pgup>	Page Up
<home>	Home
<end>	End
<left>	The left arrow on the numeric keypad
<right>	The right arrow on the numeric keypad
<up>	The up arrow on the numeric keypad
<down>	The down arrow on the numeric keypad
<f1>	The function key F1; others are <f2> through <f10> (or <f12> on some computers)
<ins>	Insert

continued...

...from previous page

<del>	Delete
<shift any>	Use this form to signify the Shift key and any other key. For example, <shift tab> is the same as simultaneously pressing the Shift key and the Tab key.
<backspace>	The Backspace key in the upper right corner of the keyboard. This key is not the same as the Left Arrow key.

Repeat Keystrokes

To repeat keystrokes, use a structure such as <tab 5>. This structure repeats the tab key five times and is useful for moving around a menu. Other examples are <pgdn 2> to page down two screens or <del 3> to delete the selection and two more characters.

BUILT-IN GLOSSARY COMMANDS

Word provides six built-in glossary names: page, date, dateprint, time, timeprint, and footnote.

Use the **page** glossary entry to include page numbers on each page. Normally, you will place this entry in a running head. When you type the word "page" and press F3, Word will display "(page)" on the screen, but Word replaces it with the appropriate page numbers when the document prints.

The **date** and **time** built-in glossary entries work in much the same way as the page entry. Press F3 after typing the words "date" or "time," and Word will replace the entries with the current date or time.

The **Dateprint** and **timeprint** entries appear on the screen as "(dateprint)" and "(timeprint)," but Word replaces the entries with the current date or time as it prints the document. The dateprint and timeprint features can be used to keep track of drafts of an article or book. Place both a dateprint and timeprint entry in a document's running head. Then, each version will print with the date and time. You can also use the dateprint feature for form letters. Instead of placing «SET DATE = ?» in the master letter and then filling in the date by hand, use the dateprint built-in glossary function. Word automatically fills in the date on each letter.

Word reads the date and time from the computer's built-in clock. If your system requires that you fill in the date and time each time you turn it on, be sure to do so; otherwise, Word will insert incorrect dates and times. The format for the date and time is set with the Options command.

The final built-in glossary command is **footnote**, which has only one use. If you accidentally delete a footnote reference number from a footnote entry, move the selection to the beginning of the footnote entry, type "footnote," and press F3. The number will be restored.

The footnote feature operates only on the footnote itself, not on the footnote reference in the main text.

MULTIPLE GLOSSARIES

Word can support several glossaries. If you are a lawyer, you can create separate glossaries for standard clauses of separation agreements, contracts for the sale of residential real estate, contracts for the sale of commercial real estate, and so on.

The standard glossary is in a file named NORMAL.GLY. Word searches for the NORMAL glossary when it is first loaded. In Word 3.0 or earlier, the program searches the drive containing Word or the subdirectory of a hard disk containing Word. In later versions, Word searches first in the drive or directory set by the Transfer Options command and then in the drive or directory containing Word. As a result, with version 3.1 or 4.0, you can use several NORMAL.GLY files that load automatically, depending on the disk or directory in use.

TRANSFER GLOSSARY MERGE

If you want to include entries from one glossary in another glossary, use the T(ransfer) G(lossary) M(erge) command to load the glossary into memory and merge it with the glossary already in memory. If a glossary entry in the new file has the same name as an entry in the old file, Word uses the new value.

When you choose the Transfer Glossary Merge command, Word requests the name of the glossary to load into memory. If you press F1 (in version 4) or an arrow key (in version 3), Word lists the .GLY files on the current directory. If you enter a global file name (such as C:\WORD*.GLY) and then press an arrow key, Word lists the .GLY files in that drive or directory. Select a .GLY file from the list or enter the name of the glossary you want to merge with the current entries. Word presumes a file type of .GLY unless you specify otherwise.

TRANSFER GLOSSARY SAVE

Use the T(ransfer) G(lossary) S(ave) command to save the contents of the current glossary on disk. This command gives you an opportunity to create new glossaries under different names. You can, for instance, merge the contents of RESIDENT.GLY (the glossary containing clauses for residential real estate deals) with COMMERCL.GLY (the glossary with the commercial real estate clauses) and then save them as REALESTA.GLY (a single glossary containing all the clauses).

When you choose the Transfer Glossary Save command, Word requests the name of the glossary to save. If you press an arrow key, Word lists the .GLY files on the current directory. If you enter a global file name (such as C:\WORD*.GLY) and then press F1 (in version 4) or an arrow key (in version 3), Word lists the .GLY files in that drive or directory. Select a .GLY file from the list, or enter the name of the glossary you want to save. Word presumes a file type of .GLY unless you specify otherwise.

TRANSFER GLOSSARY CLEAR

Use the T(ransfer) G(lossary) C(lear) command to erase glossary entries or an entire glossary. When you choose Transfer Glossary Clear, Word requests the name of the glossary entry or entries to clear as follows:

```
TRANSFER GLOSSARY CLEAR names:
```

To clear one or more glossary entries, enter the names separated by commas, but don't include spaces after the commas. If you can't remember the names of glossary entries, press an arrow key for a list. Press the arrow keys to select a glossary entry, and press F10 to select it. Word will place the entry on the command line. Type a comma, use the arrow keys to move to another entry, press F10 again, and so on. (If you have selected commas as your decimal character with the Options command, use semicolons in place of the commas in your list.)

To clear an entire glossary, just press Return without entering a glossary name. Word requests confirmation and then clears the entire glossary. You can use this technique to create an empty NORMAL.GLY by first clearing the glossary and then saving the file, or you can use it to load a glossary without merging the new glossary with the old glossary. Clear first and then merge the glossaries.

PRINT GLOSSARY

The final Glossary command is P(rint) G(lossary), which simply sends the contents of the glossary to the printer so you can see the text assigned to each glossary term. Word macros are listed as macro program listings.

VERSION 3.0 BUG

A bug in version 3.0 causes Word to "forget" paragraph formatting when a glossary file is saved. Formatting remains as you make the glossary entry and throughout the editing session, but the next time you load that glossary from disk, paragraph formatting disappears.

This bug does not affect character or division formatting, and it exists only in version 3.0.

GLOSSARY AS A REPLACE ASSISTANT

Word's Replace command cannot recognize character formatting; however, the glossary can recognize character formatting, which allows you to use the glossary for replacing unformatted text with formatted text.

For example, to index a document without constantly switching to hidden text mode each time you want to enter a hidden .i., you can simply enter .i. in normal text, use the Search command to find each occurrence of .i., and press F3 to replace each occurrence with a hidden .i. previously placed in the glossary.

CHAPTER 19

WORD AND NUMBERS

While Word is hardly a spreadsheet program, it is quite adept at handling numbers. Word can perform basic math operations right on screen. It can also automatically number an outline or sections of a document. And, while Word may not be a spreadsheet, it can easily import data from spreadsheets and even go back and update that data as often as you want.

MATH OPERATIONS ON SCREEN

Word's ability as a mathematician, added in version 3.0 and substantially improved in version 4, can come in handy, particularly if you have to prepare financial statements or any kind of tabular information.

Following is an example using the table created in Chapter 16:

Country	Population	Density
Spain	38,234,000	193
Sri Lanka	15,300,000	582
Sudan	20,539,000	19
Suriname	363,000	6
Swaziland	632,000	82
Sweden	8,331,000	48
Switzerland	6,463,000	398
Syria	9,700,00	126

If you want to find out the total population of these eight countries, just move the selection to the first digit in the first number in the column of populations. Press Shift-F6 to turn on Word's Column Selection feature. The letters "CS" will appear at the bottom of the screen. Then extend the selection to include the entire column.

```
1━━[····|····1·········L·········3····R····4·········R········6·········7·]·┓
 |   [····|····1·········L·········3····R····4·········R········6·········7·]·|
 |        Country            Population          Density¶
 |        Spain             38,234,000              193¶
 |        Sri Lanka         15,300,000              582¶
 |        Sudan             20,539,000               19¶
 |        Suriname             363,000                6¶
 |        Swaziland            632,000               82¶
 |        Sweden             8,331,000               48¶
 |        Switzerland       6,463,000              398¶
 |        Syria             9,700,000        ▶       126¶
 |        ¶
 |SP          If you want to find out the total population of these eight
 |        countries, just move the selection to the first digit in the first
 |        number in the column of populations.  Press Shift-F6 to turn on Word's
 |        Column Selection feature.  The letters "CS" will appear at the bottom of
 |        the screen.  Then extend the selection to include the entire column.¶
 |
 |
 |FH                        Figure 19-1 here¶
 |                                                            ━CHAP19.DOC━
 |  Pg1 Li24 Co36    {know·th...n.··¶}   ?               CS     Microsoft Word
```

Figure 19.1

Now press the F2 key. The total population of those eight countries, 99,562,000, will appear in the scrap at the bottom of the screen.

```
1━━[····|····1·········L·········3····R····4·········R········6·········7·]·┓
 |        Country            Population          Density¶
 |        Spain             ▉8,234,000              193¶
 |        Sri Lanka         15,300,000              582¶
 |        Sudan             20,539,000               19¶
 |        Suriname             363,000                6¶
 |        Swaziland            632,000               82¶
 |        Sweden             8,331,000               48¶
 |        Switzerland       6,463,000              398¶
 |        Syria             9,700,000        ▶       126¶
 |        ¶
 |SP          If you want to find out the total population of these eight
 |        countries, just move the selection to the first digit in the first
 |        number in the column of populations.  Press Shift-F6 to turn on Word's
 |        Column Selection feature.  The letters "CS" will appear at the bottom of
 |        the screen.  Then extend the selection to include the entire column.¶
 |
 |FH                        Figure 19-1 here¶
 |                                                            ━CHAP19.DOC━
 |  Pg1 Li17 Co26    {99,562,000}       ?                      Microsoft Word
```

Figure 19.2

You can then move the selection to where you want the total to appear, and then press the Insert key to enter the sum in your text.

What Figures are Manipulated?

Word performs its mathematical magic on whatever numbers are in the selection. It doesn't matter if there are intervening words, so if you select the sentence, "157 is a number, as is 25," then press F2, Word will enter 182 in the scrap because 182 is the sum of 157 and 25.

You can use either the Column Selection mode (Shift-F6) or Word's regular Extend Selection mode (F6).

Functions Allowed

Word can perform addition, subtraction, multiplication, division, and percentages. Word always adds the numbers in the selection unless they have a - (subtraction), * (multiplication), or / (division) character in front of them or a % character after. You may use the + character for addition, but it is not necessary. Numbers in parentheses are negative.

Precedence

In version 3, Word manipulates the numbers as the program comes across them, moving from left to right and top to bottom. It does not perform multiplication or division functions first. So 12 2 3 * 5 2% /7 will give you the result 12.14 (12 + 2 = 14, 14 + 3 = 17, 17*5 = 85, 85 + .02 = 85.02, 85.02/7 = 12.14).

The only exception to the no precedence rule in version 3 is the percent sign. Word divides the number that precedes the percent sign by 100 before doing anything else to it. In other words, 2% is the same as .02.

In version 4, Word performs calculations in parentheses first and performs multiplication and division functions before addition and subtraction. So, 12 2 3 * 5 2% /7 will give you the result 29.00 (12 + 2 = 14, 3*5 = 15 [multiplication has precedence], 2%/7 = 0 [division has precedence and the result, .0028, is rounded off to two decimal places], 14 + 15 + 0 = 29). In more conventional mathematical notation, the result would be 12 + 2 + (3*5) + (.02/7). The calculations are much easier to understand that way also.

Format of Result

If any of the numbers in the selection contain commas, the result will contain commas. The number of decimal places in the result will be the same as the greatest number of decimal places in any of the numbers in the selection, up to a maximum of 14. If there are more than 14 decimal places, Word will give you the error message "Math overflow."

Replacing Raw Figures

You can replace your raw figures with the mathematical result using the Shift-Insert key combination. Select the figures you want to manipulate and press F2 to calculate the result as usual. If you used the Column Selection mode to select the raw figures, you must re-select them now. If you used Word's standard Extend Selection mode, the figures will still be selected. With the raw figures selected, press Shift-Insert. Word will replace the selection containing the raw figures with the result.

LIBRARY NUMBER COMMAND

Word's second mathematical miracle is the ability to quickly and easily number (and renumber) paragraphs and outlines.

For example, if you are a lawyer drafting a contract with multiple, numbered clauses, you don't want to constantly be renumbering parts of your document. Instead, you can use Word's automatic numbering ability. You can also use the numbering ability to "number" paragraphs by letter.

The Library Number command is the key to Word's numbering ability. When you chose the L(ibrary) N(umber) command, you will see a short set of fields:

```
LIBRARY NUMBER: (Update)Remove      restart sequence:(Yes)No
```

Word will update the numbering sequence of the numbered paragraphs in the selection. If the selection is a single character, the command acts on the entire document.

When you tell Word to update the numbers, it will renumber the sequence of numbers, following the numbering style of the first number it encounters. If you tell Word to remove the numbers, it will do so. If you tell Word to restart the numbering sequence, it will start the numbering sequence with 1, A, a, I, or i, depending on the format of the first number it encounters. If you set the *restart* field to No, Word will start the numbering sequence with the first number it encounters.

What is a "Number"?

Word only (re)numbers paragraphs that are already numbered. Word recognizes as "numbers" any of the following characters:

- Arabic numbers (e.g., 1, 2, 3)

- Roman numerals (both uppercase, e.g., I, II, III, and lowercase, e.g., i, ii, iii)

- letters (both uppercase, e.g., A, B, C, and lowercase, e.g., a, b, c)

- legal style numbering (e.g., 1, 1.1, 2, 2.1, 2.1.1)

To be recognized by the Library Number command, a "number" must

- be the first character(s) in a paragraph (except spaces or tabs), and

- be followed by a period or close parenthesis that is, in turn, followed by at least one space or tab character.

Following is an example with five paragraphs:

1. This is the first paragraph. It is numbered.
This second paragraph is not numbered.
7. This third paragraph is numbered but out of sequence.
156745. The number on this paragraph is ridiculously high.
A. Paragraph 5 has a different numbering system.

Now, when those paragraphs are selected and the Library Number command set to *update* and *restart sequence*, the result is the following:

1.   **This is the first paragraph. It is numbered.**
This second paragraph is not numbered.
2.   **This third paragraph is numbered but out of sequence.**
3.   **The number on this paragraph is ridiculously high.**
4.   **Paragraph 5 has a different numbering system.**

Note several of the results. First, the second paragraph is still not numbered, and the last paragraph, which had the letter A as its number, is now numbered with the same system as the others.

The next example is a bit different. This time, the first paragraph is numbered with a letter, and the *restart sequence* field is set to No:

J.   **This is the first paragraph. It is numbered.**
This second paragraph is not numbered.
G.   **This third paragraph is numbered but out of sequence.**
1.1   **The number on this paragraph is in a different system.**
ii.   **Paragraph 5 has a different numbering system.**

Next, Word skipped the second paragraph because it had no number on it to start with. Word also switched in each paragraph to the numbering system of the first "number" it found, but this time Word did not start renumbering at A (or 1) because *restart sequence* was set to No:

J.   **This is the first paragraph. It is numbered.**
This second paragraph is not numbered.
K.   **This third paragraph is numbered but out of sequence.**
L.   **The number on this paragraph is in a different system.**
M.   **Paragraph 5 has a different numbering system.**

Multilevel Numbering

Word separately numbers each level of indent. For example, if one group of paragraphs has its indent set to 0, those paragraphs will be numbered in one sequence while paragraphs with their left indents set to 0.5" will be numbered separately. Following is an example:

1.
2.
       A.
3.
       A.
       B.
4.
5.

In the above example, the first paragraph was numbered with Arabic numbers, but the first paragraph on the second level was numbered with the letter A. You can see the result of the renumbering.

For multilevel numbering to work, the formatting must be set as paragraph formatting, either with the Format Paragraph command, style sheets, or Word's built-in paragraph formats. Indenting with tabs or spaces won't work.

Word always considers outline headings as indented whether Word is in outline view or not.

Numbering Outlines

When Word is in outline view, it presumes that you want to renumber your outline and will apply numbering to outline headings whether or not they have been previously numbered.

Unless you indicate another outline numbering system, Word will use the standard outline numbering system you probably learned in school:

I.
> **A.**
>> **1.**

II.
> **A.**

III.

However, if you place a number 1 and a period in front of the first outline heading, Word will use the legal system of outline numbering:

1.
> **1.1**
>> **1.1.1**

2.
> **2.1**

3.

Experimenting

The best way to find out about the power of Word's Library Number command is to experiment. Try all the various combinations; renumber and then see what happens. You will find that Word's numbering system is smart enough to guess what you want it to do from just a few hints.

LINKING TO SPREADSHEETS

A new feature in version 4 is Word's ability to incorporate numbers from spreadsheets using the Library Link command.

Which Spreadsheets?

Word's Linking ability works with Microsoft's Multiplan or PC Excel programs or with Lotus 1-2-3. If you don't have one of those three spreadsheets, the spreadsheet you do have can probably save files in the format of one of those other spreadsheet programs. For example, if you use SuperCalc 4, that program has the ability to use Lotus files. Just prepare your spreadsheet as usual, but save it in Lotus 1-2-3 format. The Link function should work just fine.

How to Link

Importing figures from your spreadsheet is easy. Just place the selection where you want the spreadsheet information. Then choose the L(ibrary) command. From the Library submenu, choose L(ink).

```
LIBRARY LINK filename:                          area:
```

Enter the name of the spreadsheet file that contains the data you want to import. Be sure to include the complete drive and directory name and the complete file name, for example,

```
LIBRARY LINK filename: C:\SC4\DATA\LINK.WKS     area:
```

In the *area* field, enter the name of the range of spreadsheet cells you want to import into your Word document. (Naming ranges is a function of your spreadsheet; see your spreadsheet documentation.) If you do not specify an area, Word will import the entire spreadsheet.

When you press Return, Word will import the requested information from the spreadsheet.

The Imported Data

The imported data will be set off with two blocks of hidden text. At the beginning of the imported data will be a line that starts with .L. and then lists the name of the file and the name of the range imported. At the end of the imported data, Word places another hidden .L. (see Figure 19.3).

```
▯    [········1·········2·········3·········4·········5·········6·········7·]···
     .L. C:\SC4\DATA\LINK.WKS. test_range↓
     This is a test of Spreadsheet Linking in MS Word↓
     ↓
     4     2.1↓
     5.6   1.2↓
     3.4   4.3↓
     .L.¶
```

Figure 19.3

The first line of hidden text is used by Word to find this particular imported data for later updating. The last line just marks the end of the imported data.

Note that the data, as it is imported, is not formatted. Use the standard formatting commands to insert formatting.

Updating

Every time Word loads a document containing data imported from a spreadsheet, it automatically updates the data to the latest version. So if you have changed the spreadsheet, the information in your document will be updated.

Of course, Word cannot update the data if you have deleted the spreadsheet file or if you have deleted the hidden text at the beginning and end of the imported data.

CHAPTER 20

SORTS, HYPHENATION, AND REDLINING

This chapter will show you how to use Word to sort data in your documents, hyphenate text, and mark text for future revision.

First, using Word's Library Autosort command, you can sort mailing lists by last names, first names, street numbers, cities, states, or zip codes. Word can handle all with equal ease. You can also use this command to put numbered paragraphs in numerical sequence, to put the names of the birds you have spotted in a twenty-year birding career in alphabetical order, or to find out which of your customers has offices on Main Street.

Second, using Word's Library Hyphenate command, you can improve the look of your text by hyphenating words at a end of the line whenever it is practical to do so.

Finally, you can use Word's redlining abilities (new in version 4) to mark text proposed for addition and deletion in a revised version of a document.

LIBRARY AUTOSORT

The basics of Library Autosort command are really quite straightforward. If you choose the Autosort default values, Word sorts the selected paragraphs into alphanumeric order. If the selection is one character, Word sorts all the paragraphs in the document; however, you can use the Library Autosort command to vary the sorts quite a bit. When you choose L(ibrary) A(utosort), you are asked to fill in four fields:

```
LIBRARY AUTOSORT by:(Alphanumeric)Numeric sequence:(Ascending)Descending
              case: Yes(No)              column only: Yes(No)
```

In alphanumeric sort mode, Word will sort the the selection into alphanumeric order, which includes letters, numbers, and punctuation marks in the following order:

<space> ! " # $ % & ' ( ) * + , - . / 0 1 2 3 4 5 6 7 8 9 : ; = ? @ [\ ] ^ _
' a b c d e f g h i j k l m n o p q r s t u v w x y z { | } ˜

Because Word is looking at the sequence of characters and not the value of numbers, Word will not sort numbers into proper numerical order. For example, 125 will come before 13 because 2 is ahead of 3 in alphanumeric order. If you want to sort numbers into numerical order, set the *by* field to Numeric. Numbers may include dollar signs, percent signs, the minus sign, parentheses, decimal points, and commas. Numbers enclosed in parentheses are negative.

The *sequence* field determines whether you sort into a normal ascending order (a,b,c) or into descending order (z,y,x).

If the *case* field is set to Yes, Word places uppercase letters ahead of their lowercase versions, so "Ball" would come before "ball." If you leave this field set to No, Word sorts upper- and lowercase versions of a letter together, leaving them in the order in which they were found.

If the *column only* field is set to Yes, Word will sort a selected column but leave everything around it untouched; however, if this field is set to No, Word will use the column as the key for a sort of the entire line. Read the following section for more details on sorting on a column, one of Autosort's most powerful features.

Sorting on a Column

Because Word sorts what is in the selection, the *column only* field gives Word's sorting ability some interesting powers. First, look at a simple column sort using the default choice of the Library Autosort command. The chart of populations from Chapter 16 will be used again.

Country	Population	Density
Spain	38,234,000	193
Sri Lanka	15,300,000	582
Sudan	20,539,000	19
Suriname	363,000	6
Swaziland	632,000	82
Sweden	8,331,000	48
Switzerland	6,463,000	398
Syria	9,700,000	126

Select the numbers in the population column with the Column Selection command, choose Library Autosort, and without changing any of the fields, press Return. You will see this result:

Country	Population	Density
Sri Lanka	15,300,000	582
Sudan	20,539,000	19
Suriname	363,000	6
Spain	38,234,000	193
Switzerland	6,463,000	398
Swaziland	632,000	82
Sweden	8,331,000	48
Syria	9,700,000	126

The population column has been sorted alphanumerically. Note that the first number starts with 1, the second with 2, and so on. Now, perform the same sort again, but this time set Word to sort numerically.

Country	Population	Density
Suriname	363,000	6
Swaziland	632,000	82
Switzerland	6,463,000	398
Sweden	8,331,000	48
Syria	9,700,000	126
Sri Lanka	15,300,000	582
Sudan	20,539,000	19
Spain	38,234,000	193

Now the countries are in population order, from the smallest to the largest.

For both of those sorts, the *column only* field was set to No. Watch what happens when you do the same sort but set the *column only* field to Yes.

Country	Population	Density
Spain	363,000	193
Sri Lanka	632,000	582
Sudan	6,463,000	19
Suriname	8,331,000	6
Swaziland	9,700,000	82
Sweden	15,300,000	48
Switzerland	20,539,000	398
Syria	38,234,000	126

The numbers in the population column have sorted themselves into order, but everything around them has stayed the same. The country names are still in alphabetical order but no longer have the correct populations next to them.

If you accidentally set the *column only* field to No when you don't want to, use the Undo command immediately after the sort, and Word will put things back in their original order.

A Warning

There is one quirk about column sorting. Word treats each line as a paragraph. So if you have a paragraph that runs more than one line long, when you sort it, Word will split up the lines of the paragraph.

The way around this problem is to temporarily reformat the division in which you are working, setting the page width to the maximum allowed, 22". Then select the material to be sorted, and reformat it as the smallest font possible with your printer. With most printers, you will be able to fit between 250 and 365 characters on a line that way.

Applications

You can use column sorts, for example, to put a mailing list in zip code order, or, by sorting on the street names, you can find out which of your customers has offices on Main Street.

In Chapter 17, "Merge and Forms," you learned that merge data files must have the fields in each record separated by commas or tabs. If you are going to be sorting on fields, be sure to use tabs as your separators so you can align fields for sorting.

Secondary Sorts before Primary

If you are trying to sort a list on two fields, then be sure to perform the lower level (secondary) sort first. For example, to sort the following list of names into both first and last name alphabetical order, first sort on the given names (the secondary characteristic), then on the surnames (the primary characteristic). Following is the original list:

Perrin,	**Timothy**
Cowell,	**Douglas**
Wurts,	**Rosemary**
Butters,	**George**
Cruise,	**David**
Perrin,	**Connie**
Cowell,	**Leslie**

Next is the result of the first sort on the first names:

Perrin,	**Connie**
Cruise,	**David**
Cowell,	**Douglas**
Butters,	**George**
Cowell,	**Leslie**
Wurts,	**Rosemary**
Perrin,	**Timothy**

Following is a second sort, but this time on the column containing the surnames:

Butters,   **George**
Cowell,   **Douglas**
Cowell,   **Leslie**
Cruise,   **David**
Perrin,   **Connie**
Perrin,   **Timothy**
Wurts,   **Rosemary**

Small things can get you into trouble on a sort like the previous one. The first time this sort was performed, "Perrin, Timothy" came out above "Perrin, Connie." The problem occurred because there was a space character entered behind Perrin in Connie's name but not in Timothy Perrin's name. So if you have similar problems, turn the Options *visible* field to Complete so you can see exactly what characters are contained in your sorting field.

Outline Sorts

You can use the Library Autosort command to sort the elements of a Word outline, but the command will only operate on one level of the outline at a time. For instance, you could use Library Autosort to put the level one headings into ascending order and the level two headings into descending order.

Sorting Indices Together for Large Documents

In Chapter 15, "Indexing," you learned that one solution to indexing really large documents was to index the smaller elements of the document, such as the chapters of a book, and then use Word's Library Autosort command to sort the entries together into a single index. Following is an example of this rather difficult sorting problem.

Gathering the Indices

The first step in this sort is to gather all the individual indices, which will be called chapter indices here, into a single master index. Use the Transfer Merge command to bring each chapter index into the master index file. Delete the hidden *.Begin Index.* and *.End Index.* markers; however, DO NOT sort the index entries right away. If you do, Word will separate main index entries and their subentries, placing everything into a single alphabetical sequence, which probably isn't the result you want.

Instead, switch to Word's outline view. In outline view, Autosort sorts only one level of heading at a time, taking each heading's subheadings as it moves.

Next comes the hard work. You must convert each index entry from a text paragraph into an outline heading.

If you are using version 4 with a style sheet that has each of the four index styles defined, use the Format sEarch command to search for each of those styles, and change each one to the correpsonding outline heading. You might want to record a macro to perform these actions in one keystroke.

If you are using a style sheet with version 3 and that style sheet has the paragraph heading levels defined, just apply the appropriate style to each entry by simultaneously pressing the Alt key and the key code for that style.

If you are not using a style sheet, you will need to move the selection to each entry and press Alt-9 to change the entry from text to an outline heading; then press Alt-9 and Alt-0 to move the heading to the right level. Set main entries to level one, subentries to level two, and so on.

The Primary Sort

Now, press Shift-F10 to select the entire master index. Choose the Library Autosort command and execute an alphanumeric sort in ascending order. Because sorts in outline view affect only the highest level in the selection, Word will sort all the major index headings into alphanumeric order.

The Cull

Move through the index and eliminate all duplicate major entries. There will be many of these entries because topics that occurred in Chapter 5 and Chapter 10 will appear once in each index. Now they will be sequential in the index, but the subentries will not be sorted together.

For example, if in a book called *Great Computer Authors of the Twentieth Century* a particular author is mentioned once on page 15 in Chapter 3 and again on page 105 in Chapter 5, the index entries will appear as follows:

```
Perrin, Timothy,  15
  greatest work, 17
Perrin, Timothy,  105
  birth, 105
```

Remove the second main entry and combine the numbers on a single main entry.

```
Perrin, Timothy,  15, 105
  greatest work, 17
  birth, 105
```

Sorting Subentries

The final step is to select the subentries for each main entry and sort them into alphanumeric order. Note that in the previous example, the subentries are in the wrong order. Simply move the selection to the first subentry, press F6 to turn on the Extend Selection mode, and extend the selection to include all subentries at level 2. Perform another alphanumeric sort to list the subentries in order.

```
Perrin, Timothy,  15, 105
  birth, 105
  greatest work, 17
```

You must perform this sort for every level of subentries under every index entry.

Consolidation

Next, edit the index again to consolidate subentries and clean up duplication. When you are finished, you will have a multichapter outline in perfect order.

Final Formatting

The last step is to format the index entries. If you didn't use a style sheet, there should be no final formatting to do. You should have developed your formatting as you went along.

If you are using a style sheet, simply change the formatting of the paragraph heading styles to match the index styles.

If you are using a mouse, choose the Gallery command and then select the first paragraph heading style. Next, use the mouse and scroll bar to scroll the Gallery until the index style you want to copy is in view. Because you used the mouse, the selection will still be on the paragraph heading style you chose earlier. Move the mouse pointer to the selection bar next to the index style you want to copy. Click the left then right mouse buttons. Word will copy the formatting from the index style to the paragraph heading style.

HYPHENATION

The Library Hyphenate command provides an easy way to hyphenate words that appear at the ends of lines. It is most useful when you are using very narrow columns. In narrow columns, the movement of a long word to the next line can make the text look extremely ragged. You can also use this command when you simply need to shorten a particular document by a few lines. Sometimes, you can then tighten up your text a bit.

The L(ibrary) H(yphenate) command contains only two fields:

```
LIBRARY HYPHENATE confirm:(Yes)No     Hyphenate caps: Yes(No)
```

If you set *confirm* to Yes, Word will stop at each word it thinks can be hyphenated and ask for your approval. You can use the arrow keys to move the position of the hyphen. If you set this field to No, Word will insert hyphens where it thinks best.

If you set *Hyphenate caps* to Yes, Word will hyphenate all words. If you set it to No, Word will not hyphenate words beginning with uppercase letters. This setting protects proper names and the first words of sentences from being split at the end of a line.

Limitations on Automatic Hyphenation

Using a computerized hyphenation feature, like using a computerized spelling checker, is a trade-off. What you gain in convenience, you lose in accuracy. Word hyphenates according to the same rules you use when you do it yourself, but you are much more likely to catch the exceptions to the rules.

The standard rules for hyphenation are to divide between doubled letters, divide after prefixes and before suffixes, and divide between consonants with a vowel on either side; however, the actual process is not that simple. For each of those rules, there are innumerable exceptions. Try dividing "bil-ling" between the doubled letters or dividing "str-ing" before the common -ing suffix. The rules don't work too well. There are also words that are spelled the same, but their pronunciation changes with their meaning. For example, consider the sentence "I pre-sent you with the pres-ent."

Just as Word's Spell program can be a great help in catching spelling errors, so can Word's hyphenation program be a great help with automated hyphenation; however, carefully proofread a document after Word hyphenates it, double-checking all the proposed changes. Better yet, hyphenate with the *confirm* field set to Yes.

REDLINING

If you work on documents that need to be revised and reviewed by several people, then you will want to know about **redlining**. In a document that has been redlined, text slated for deletion is struck through while the proposed additions are highlighted in some way. Following is a sample of redlined text from a previsouly unknown early draft of the Declaration of Independence.

> When in the course of human events, it becomes necessary for ~~Americans~~ <u>one people</u> to ~~break away from England~~ <u>dissolve the political bonds which have connected them to another</u>, and to assume among the powers of the earth, the separate and equal station to which the laws of nature and nature's God entitle them, a decent respect for the opinions of mankind require that they declare the causes which impell them to the ~~revolution~~ <u>separation</u>.

The type that is double underlined is the proposed new text. The text that is struck through is the text that is proposed for deletion. The bars at the left margin let you know know exactly where to look in the text for proposed revisions.

The Format revision-Marks Command

The key to redlining is the Format revision-Marks command. Note that you press **Esc**, **F**, then **M** (*not* R). When you choose the Format revision-Marks command, Word will present you with the following short menu:

```
FORMAT REVISION-MARKS: Options Remove-marks Undo-revisions Search
```

Format revision-Mark Options

To start redlining, choose the Format revision-Mark Options command:

```
FORMAT REVISION-MARK OPTIONS
     add revision marks: Yes No
     inserted text: Normal Bold(Underlined)Uppercase Double-underlined
     revision bar position:(None)Left Right Alternate
```

When you set the *add revision marks* field to Yes, Word will highlight everything you type with the style of highlighting selected in the next field, *inserted text*. If you attempt to delete any text, Word will not delete it but will, instead, strike through it. The *revision bar* field determines the position of the left margin bar that indicates there is redlined text nearby.

Tutorial

The following tutorial shows you how to produce the example redlined paragraph presented in the previous section. Type the following paragraph, which is the version of the example paragraph before the redlining was added:

When in the course of human events, it becomes necessary for Americans to break away from England, and to assume among the powers of the earth, the separate and equal station to which the laws of nature and nature's God entitle them, a decent respect for the opinions of mankind require that they declare the causes which impell them to the revolution.

Now, choose the Format revision-Mark Options command from the Word menu. Set the *add revision marks* field to Yes. Then move the selection to the word "Americans." Make sure the entire word is selected, and then press the Delete key. Rather than deleting the word, Word will strike it through.

Next, press the Right Arrow key to move the selection to the space after "Americans" and type

one people

Word will automatically underline these words as you type them. If you set the *inserted text* field to one of the choices other than Underlined, Word will highlight any added text in the format chosen.

Now, use the arrow keys to move the selection to the first letter in "break." Turn on the Extend Select (F6) mode, and select "break away from England." Press Delete. Word will strike through the selected text. Use the Right Arrow key to move the selection to the first space after the text that has been struck through. Type

dissolve the political bonds which have connected them to another

Word will underline this text as you type it.

Finally, select the word "revolution" in the last line. Press Delete. Press the Right Arrow key and then type

separation

You have just created redlined text.

Format revision-Mark Remove-marks

Use the Remove-marks command to accept your proposed changes.

Use F10 to select the entire paragraph you have just created. Then select Format revision-Mark Remove-marks. Word will delete the passages marked for deletion and remove the highlight from the text you have proposed to put in its place. The result will be the revised text:

When in the course of human events, it becomes necessary for one people to dissolve the political bonds which have connected them to another, and to assume among the powers of the earth, the separate and equal station to which the laws of nature and nature's God entitle them, a decent respect for the opinions of mankind require that they declare the causes which impell them to the separation.

Format revision-Mark Undo-revisions

If you decide you liked the original version better, use the Undo-revisions command.

For example, press **Esc** and then **U** to Undo the last editing action you performed, which was to accept the revisions. Word will restore the redlined paragraph.

Make sure the paragraph is selected and choose Format revision-Mark Undo-revisions. Word will delete the proposed revisions and remove the strike through marks from the areas you proposed to change:

When in the course of human events, it becomes necessary for Americans to break away from England, and to assume among the powers of the earth, the separate and equal station to which the laws of nature and nature's God entitle them, a decent respect for the opinions of mankind require that they declare the causes which impell them to the revolution.

Format revision-Mark Search

The final Format revision-Mark subcommand is the Search command, which searches forward through your document for the next occurrence of redlined text. Use it when you are cleaning up a document that has been redlined for correction.

CHAPTER 21

DOCUMENT RETRIEVAL

NEEDLE IN A HAYSTACK

Have you ever spent hours searching for a letter – for example, the one you sent to a client in upstate New York sometime last summer? You know that the letter discusses buying 100 bushels of widgets at a price of $4.95 each, and you know it's on one of many floppies or somewhere on the hard disk. It's just that there are so many files, and they all have names UPSTATLT.DOC and WIDGET.DOC. Which one is the letter?

If you've ever had such an experience – and if you haven't yet, you will soon – you will appreciate the Document Retrieval features in Word. Document Retrieval allows you to select documents based on content. You can search through the document summaries or, if you're willing to spend more time, through the text of your documents themselves.

Document Retrieval is a new feature in Word version 4; if you have version 3, you must buy an upgrade or do without this feature.

LIBRARY DOCUMENT RETRIEVAL COMMAND

The key to Word's document retrieval capabilities is the Library Document-retrieval command. Select this command through the main menu and the Library submenu. After a few seconds, Word displays a listing of the files on the drive and directory specified with the Transfer Options command. Word then presents the following choices:

```
COMMAND: Query Exit Load Print Update View

Select document or press ESC to use menu
```

Query

The key to the Document Retrieval feature is the Query command. Query allows you to select documents according to the contents of their document headers or text.

For example, the titles of a book's chapters might be changed during revision. You can then use Word's Document Retrieval functions to find cross-references that also need changing in other chapters.

As an example, say you want to change the title of Chapter 17 in this book — "Merge and Forms." First, select Library Document-retrieval. Then, when Word has displayed the document retrieval screen, press Esc to use the menu and Q for query. The screen should resemble the following:

```
Path: B:\WORD\
B:\WORD\APPEND-A.DOC               B:\WORD\CHAP14.DOC
B:\WORD\APPEND-B.DOC               B:\WORD\CHAP15.DOC
B:\WORD\APPEND-C.DOC               B:\WORD\CHAP16.DOC
B:\WORD\BUGLET2.DOC                B:\WORD\CHAP17.DOC
B:\WORD\CHANGES.DOC                B:\WORD\CHAP18.DOC
B:\WORD\CHAP00.DOC                 B:\WORD\CHAP19.DOC
B:\WORD\CHAP01.DOC                 B:\WORD\CHAP20.DOC
B:\WORD\CHAP02.DOC                 B:\WORD\CHAP21.DOC
B:\WORD\CHAP03.DOC                 B:\WORD\CHAP22.DOC
B:\WORD\CHAP04.DOC                 B:\WORD\CHAP23.DOC
B:\WORD\CHAP05.DOC                 B:\WORD\COLDEMO.DOC
B:\WORD\CHAP06.DOC                 B:\WORD\COMMAND3.DOC
B:\WORD\CHAP07.DOC                 B:\WORD\COMMAND4.DOC
B:\WORD\CHAP08.DOC                 B:\WORD\COMMANDS.DOC

QUERY path: B:\WORD\
  author:
  operator:
  keywords:
  creation date:             revision date:
  document text:
  case: Yes(No)
Enter list of file specifications
DOCUMENT-RETRIEVAL              ?              Microsoft Word
```

Figure 21.1

At the top of the screen are the current drive and directory. Below these items is a listing of all files in the drive and directory. At the bottom of the screen is a section similar to the document summary discussed in Chapter 3; this is where you enter information that Word will use in searching for a document or documents.

AND/OR Searches

You can search fields for information based on AND/OR logic or for certain dates or date ranges.

To search for one piece of information AND another, separate the words with a space or an ampersand (&). For example, to search for the words "Merge" AND "Forms," enter the search information as follows:

```
Merge Forms
```

or

```
Merge & Forms
```

To search for OR information, separate individual search elements with a comma. To search for "Merge" OR "Forms" enter the search paramenters as follows:

```
Merge,Forms
```

The Query Fields

Following is a description of the types of searches performed by each field:

Path. You can change the path if you want to search another drive and/or directory. If you want a listing of files other than those with the type .DOC, list an ambiguous file specification. For example, *.* lists all the files in the current drive and directory.

Author. To find documents written by a particular person, list that person's name or initials here.

Operator. The *operator* field operates like the *author* field.

Keywords. Enter the keywords for which you want to search. This is not the same as searching the actual text; this field only searches the *keyword* field of the document summary.

Creation date. The creation date is the date to which the computer clock was set when a document was first saved. It may be changed, but only by entering a new date in the document summary. To search this field, enter a date in the format Month/Day/Year or Day/Month/Year, depending on the setting of the *date format* field of the Options command. To search a range of dates, use the < and > symbols.

You can also search the date fields for dates before or after a particular date by using the greater than (>) and less than (<) symbols. For example, to search for all the files originally created in January 1988, enter ">12/31/87 & <2/1/88" in the *creation date* field.

Revision date. The revision date is the date to which the computer clock was set when the file was last saved. Enter dates in the same way as for the creation date.

Document text. If you enter any text in this field, Word searches for the text in the actual document. Because there may be a large amount of text in a group of documents, searching the entire document is slower then simply searching the document summaries.

Case. If this field is set to Yes, Word recognizes the case of words during a document text search. If the field is set to No, Word treats "DoCumEnt" the same as "document" or "DOCUMENT."

Example

In this example, suppose you want to find all chapters of this book that contain the words "Merge and Forms," the title of Chapter 17. To find these words, you would set the fields as follows:

```
QUERY path: B:\WORD\
  author:
  operator:
  keywords:
  creation date:                          revision date:
  document text: Merge & Forms
  case: Yes(No)
Enter query expression
DOCUMENT-RETRIEVAL                    ?                    Microsoft Word
```

Figure 21.2

Note that the only field with an entry is the *document text* field. The other fields are not necessary; filling them will slow down the search because Word will have one more factor to check.

The screen would resemble the following when the search is complete:

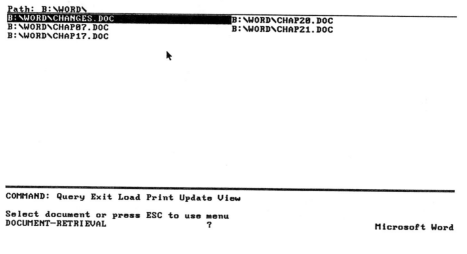

```
Path: B:\WORD\
B:\WORD\CHANGES.DOC                    B:\WORD\CHAP20.DOC
B:\WORD\CHAP07.DOC                     B:\WORD\CHAP21.DOC
B:\WORD\CHAP17.DOC
```

```
COMMAND: Query Exit Load Print Update View

Select document or press ESC to use menu
DOCUMENT-RETRIEVAL                    ?                    Microsoft Word
```

Figure 21.3

The files listed are all the files that contain both the word "merge" and the word "forms." Once they are selected, they can be printed, loaded for editing, or their document summaries updated. But before you learn how to perform those functions, examine the different ways of viewing the list of files.

View

The View command of the Document Retrieval menu is the key to quickly learning more about these files. When you choose View, you will see the following short submenu:

```
VIEW:(Short)Long Full
Sort By:(Directory)Author Operator Revision_date Creation_date Size
```

Types of Views

Word lists files on the Document Retrieval screen in a **short** directory, a **long** directory, or a **full** directory. You have already seen the short directory; it simply lists each file path and name.

The long directory lists not only the file names but also the *title* field and one other field that varies with the *sort* field. In this example, the other field is the *author* field.

```
Path: B:\WORD\                                author        title
B:\WORD\APPEND-A.DOC
B:\WORD\APPEND-B.DOC
B:\WORD\APPEND-C.DOC
B:\WORD\BUGLET2.DOC
B:\WORD\CHANGES.DOC          k           tp              Changes in Word version 4
B:\WORD\CHAP00.DOC                       tap             Power of Word 4.0 - Intro
B:\WORD\CHAP01.DOC                       tp              Chapter 1 - Installing MS
B:\WORD\CHAP02.DOC                       tp              Word Book - Chapter 2
B:\WORD\CHAP03.DOC                       tp              Word book - chapter 3
B:\WORD\CHAP04.DOC                       tp              chap 4 - Printing Basics
B:\WORD\CHAP05.DOC                       tp              chap 5 - Process approach
B:\WORD\CHAP06.DOC
B:\WORD\CHAP07.DOC
B:\WORD\CHAP08.DOC
B:\WORD\CHAP09.DOC
B:\WORD\CHAP10.DOC                       tp              chap 10 - Direct Formatti
B:\WORD\CHAP11.DOC
B:\WORD\CHAP12.DOC
B:\WORD\CHAP13.DOC

COMMAND: Query Exit Load Print Update View

Select document or press ESC to use menu
DOCUMENT-RETRIEVAL                    ?                     Microsoft Word
```

Figure 21.4

A full listing shows the entire document summary for the highlighted document.

```
Path: B:\WORD\
B:\WORD\APPEND-A.DOC                    B:\WORD\CHAP14.DOC
B:\WORD\APPEND-B.DOC                    B:\WORD\CHAP15.DOC
B:\WORD\APPEND-C.DOC                    B:\WORD\CHAP16.DOC
B:\WORD\BUGLET2.DOC                     B:\WORD\CHAP17.DOC
B:\WORD\CHANGES.DOC        ▸           ▐B:\WORD\CHAP18.DOC▌
B:\WORD\CHAP00.DOC                      B:\WORD\CHAP19.DOC
B:\WORD\CHAP01.DOC                      B:\WORD\CHAP20.DOC
B:\WORD\CHAP02.DOC                      B:\WORD\CHAP21.DOC
B:\WORD\CHAP03.DOC                      B:\WORD\CHAP22.DOC
B:\WORD\CHAP04.DOC                      B:\WORD\CHAP23.DOC
B:\WORD\CHAP05.DOC                      B:\WORD\COLDEMO.DOC
B:\WORD\CHAP06.DOC                      B:\WORD\COMMAND3.DOC

filename: B:\WORD\CHAP18.DOC                  char count: 22609
title: chap 18 - glossary and macros         version number: 1
author: tp                                    creation date: 8/25/87
operator: tp                                  revision date: 10/13/87
keywords: glossary macros word
comments:

COMMAND: Query Exit Load Print Update View

Select document or press ESC to use menu
DOCUMENT-RETRIEVAL                  ?                  Microsoft Word
```

Figure 21.5

Sorts

The View command also offers you six ways to sort the directory listing:

```
VIEW:(Short)Long Full
Sort By:(Directory)Author Operator Revision_date Creation_date Size
```

The default directory listing is in alphanumeric order.

The author and operator sorts list the documents in alphanumeric order but with all documents by the same author or operator grouped together. The Revision__date and Creation__date sorts also group documents together by dates.

When you instruct Word to sort by size, it lists the documents from shortest to longest.

Whenever you set the *Sort By* field to anything other than Directory or Author, the third field of a long directory listing is changed to the appropriate field. So if you set the *Sort By* field to Size, the long directory listing would resemble the following:

```
Path: B:\WORD\                          char count      title
B:\WORD\APPEND-C.DOC                        128
B:\WORD\MERGE.DOC                           338
B:\WORD\OUTLINE.DOC                         534
B:\WORD\COMMAND4.DOC                        2533         MS Word Version 4 Commands
B:\WORD\COMMAND3.DOC                        2542         MS Word Version 3 Commands
B:\WORD\LITTLE1.DOC                         2944
B:\WORD\APPEND-A.DOC                        4224
B:\WORD\BUGLET2.DOC                         4585
B:\WORD\COMMANDS.DOC                  ▶     5120
B:\WORD\CHANGES.DOC                         5151         Changes in Word version 4
B:\WORD\CHAP13.DOC                          6122
B:\WORD\MSLETTER.DOC                        6144
B:\WORD\CHAP11.DOC                          7306
B:\WORD\CHAP00.DOC                          10438        Power of Word 4.0 - Introduct
B:\WORD\APPEND-B.DOC                        10888
B:\WORD\CHAP19.DOC                          12261
B:\WORD\CHAP02.DOC                          12334        Word Book - Chapter 2
B:\WORD\CHAP14.DOC                          12835
B:\WORD\CHAP05.DOC                          15186        chap 5 - Process approach to

COMMAND: Query Exit Load Print Update View

Select document or press ESC to use menu
DOCUMENT-RETRIEVAL                            ?              Microsoft Word
```

Figure 21.6

Load

Once you have used Word's Document Retrieval capabilities to find the documents you want, you can use the Load command on the Document Retrieval menu to load the highlighted document for editing. Word prompts you by asking for the file name as follows:

LOAD filename:

If there is currently an unsaved document in the active editing window, Word will offer you a chance to save that document before loading the new one.

Print

Use the Print command to print one or more documents or document summaries. When you choose Print from the document retrieval window, Word displays the following choices:

PRINT: Summary Document Both   range:(Selection)All

Decide whether you want to print the document summary, the document only, or both. The default choice is to print just the document summary. The *range* field lets you choose to print only the selected document or all documents listed on the screen.

Word will print the documents using the option values (number of copies, pages, etc.) previously specified with the Print Options command.

Update

If you choose Update from the Document Retrieval menu, Word allows you to update the document summary for the highlighted document.

Exit

The final command on the Document Retrieval menu is Exit. Select Exit from the Document Retrieval menu to return to editing.

PART VI

WORD AND PRINTERS

Chapters 22 and 23 are completely optional. Microsoft's legendary printer support will probably cover your printing needs, but if Word will not run your printer correctly, or if you can't seem to get the computer and printer to even communicate, read these chapters for details on how Word works with printers.

CHAPTER 22

WORD AND PRINTERS

COMPUTERS AND PRINTERS

The first thing you must understand about printers is that they are, in fact, computers — computers dedicated to the particular task of printing ink on a page, but computers nonetheless.

To instruct the printer what to print, the computer sends it a sequence of printable characters and other commands. The computer sends the characters or commands requested by the software (such as Word) running the computer.

When a printer receives a character to print, it searches its own memory to determine what to do. If it is a daisywheel printer, the memory instructs it to spin the daisywheel to a certain position and strike the hammer. If it is a dot matrix or laser printer, it searches its memory to find the pattern of dots representing the requested character.

The commands sent by the computer instruct the printer to perform tasks such as printing on the next line, changing fonts, printing in boldface, or advancing the print position to a specific spot on the page.

What is a Printer Driver?

When you install Word on your computer (see Chapter 1, "Installing Microsoft Word"), you inform Word of the type of printer you are using, and the program copies a **printer driver** file to the Word disk or directory. A printer driver file informs Word of the commands to use with the printer as well as other information Word requires to print correctly.

Word requires a different printer driver for each printer because different printers respond to different sets of commands. For example, the command that instructs an Epson FX-100 printer to start printing in enhanced print tells a Hewlett-Packard LaserJet + to reset itself.

Printer drivers are in files with .PRD extensions. The driver you use determines how much of the printer's potential will be available to you.

The MAKEPRD.EXE program converts a printer driver file into a text file of a particular format so you can make changes to it. MAKEPRD then converts the text file back to a printer driver file. Chapter 22, "MAKEPRD and How To Use It," details the structure of printer drivers.

Emulations

Many printers today **emulate** other printers, which means they respond to the same set of commands.

If there is no driver for your printer, you must determine the printer it emulates and install the driver for that printer. Unfortunately, some printer manufacturers never document the printer being emulated. Often, the only way to find out such information is to call or write the manufacturer.

Bits and Bytes

When two computers (such as a PC and a printer) communicate, they do so in characters called **bytes**. Each byte is actually a number between 0 and 255. These are not numbers as you normally see them; they are **binary** numbers, which consist of eight ones and zeros. Each 1 or 0 is called a **bit**.

Inside each computer (and in the cables that connect them), a 1 is represented by a high voltage (about 5 volts), and a 0 is represented by a low voltage (0 volts).

It is not necessary for you to understand all the details of bits and bytes, but understand that the eight bit positions in each byte carry a different value. The leftmost column is worth 128, the next worth 64, and so on down to 1 as follows:

       128   64   32   16   8   4   2   1

If a column contains a 1, the number takes the value of that column. So a byte with the following bit pattern

       1   0   0   1   1   1   0   0

represents 156 because there is a 1 in the 128, 16, 8, and 4 columns, and 128 + 16 + 8 + 4 = 156.

ASCII

If computers communicate in numbers, how does the printer know what characters to print?

A code named the **American Standard Code for Information Interchange** (ASCII) assigns each of the first 128 numbers to a particular printed character. So the number 65 represents the letter A, and the number 97 represents the letter a. ASCII codes are listed in Appendix A.

Control Codes

The first 32 ASCII characters are called the **control codes** because they are generated at your keyboard when you press and hold the Control (Ctrl) key and then simultaneously press another key.

Control codes are one class of commands that a computer can send to your printer. Examine the ASCII table in Appendix A. Note that each entry has an abbreviation that stands for a name given to that control code back when all computers were telex terminals working on paper rather than electronic screens. For example, number 13, ^M (Ctrl-m), is also named "carriage return" because its function is to move the print position back to the left-hand margin. Number 10, ^L, is the line feed character because it advances the print position one line by feeding the paper through the printer. Many functions performed by the control codes are obsolete or used only in very specialized circumstances. Control codes such as Data Link Escape (^P) have been given new functions in most printers.

Escape Sequences

One control code has a special job: number 27, the Escape code. A computer and printer use Escape to change the meaning of the other characters. For example, if an Epson FX-100 printer receives the E character from the computer, it will normally print the letter E on the page; however, if it first receives Escape and then E, it will switch into enhanced print mode. Escape tells the printer that the next character is a command and not a character to be printed.

THE INTERFACE

Computers and printers communicate with each other through the **interface**. The interface consists of a special plug on the computer, a cable, and another special plug on the printer.

There are two types of printers: **parallel** and **serial**. The difference will be discussed shortly. Use the *setup* field of the Printer Options command to inform Word of the type of printer in use and where (electronically) it is connected to the computer.

If you are using a parallel printer, your choices for the Printer Options *setup* field are LPT1:, LPT2:, and LTP3:. You must include the colons in these choices. The three ports correspond to the three *Line PrinTer* ports recognized by MS-DOS.

If you are using a serial printer, you can connect it to COM1: or COM2:. Enter your choice in the *setup* field of the Printer Options command.

Parallel Interface

There are ten essential wires in a parallel printer interface. Eight of these wires are the **data lines**. The computer places the bits that make up the byte on these wires — a high voltage (5 volts) for a 1 and a low voltage (0 volts) for a 0. When the voltages are ready, the computer pulses the voltage on the ninth line, the strobe line, to instruct the printer to read the byte.

As an analogy, think of a small man sitting inside the printer watching nine lights on the wall. Eight of the lights are green, and the ninth light is red. Whenever the red light flashes, the man writes down the pattern of the green lights, counting a 1 for each light that is shining and a 0 for each light that is not shining. This pattern of ones and zeros informs him of the character to be printed.

There is also a tenth wire in the parallel interface that the printer uses to inform the computer that it is ready to receive another character. While it is processing the last character, the printer keeps the voltage on this wire high. As soon as it is ready, the printer changes the voltage on this wire to low, instructing the computer to continue.

Using a parallel interface, a computer can send about 3,000 characters to the printer each second.

Serial Interface

A serial printer interface is a bit more complex. Instead of nine lights on the wall as in the previous analogy, the small man now watches only one light and a clock. He watches the clock and, at certain intervals, looks up at the light. If the light is lit, he writes down a 1; if it is not, he writes down a 0. When he collects eight bits, they form a byte, and he starts keeping track of the next byte.

In this analogy, it is critical that the man in the printer keep close track of the lights. If he is off by even one bit, the results will be gibberish. One method of maintaining accuracy is to make sure that the clocks in the computer and printer are very accurate so they can stay closely synchronized. This is called **synchronous communication**. The other way is to use a series of **start** and **stop bits** (discussed later in this chapter) to let the printer know when each byte starts and stops. This is called **asynchronous communication**. Microcomputers use asynchronous communication when dealing with printers.

Serial Parameters

A serial connection has four parameters: speed, data bits, stop bits, and parity. For example, a serial interface might be set to 1200 baud (speed), 8 data bits, 1 stop bit, and no parity.

The secret of serial interfacing is that it doesn't matter what these settings are, but the computer and printer must be using the same parameters.

Speed

When a computer and printer are sharing information over a serial interface, the first thing they each must know is how fast the information will be transferred. In the previous analogy, this value instructs the man in the printer how often to look at the wall.

The speed of a serial interface is measured in **bits per second** (bps), also called the **baud rate**. Though bps and baud rates are not technically identical, they are for practical purposes, so don't worry about purists who claim you are using the wrong term.

Common baud rates are 110, 300, 600, 1200, 2400, 4800, and 9600 bps.

Data Bits

There are 256 possible combinations of eight ones or zeros, so there are 256 possible bytes the computer can send to the printer. If you examine the ASCII chart in Appendix A, however, you will notice that only the first 128 bytes have been assigned characters. Because these 128 characters contain the entire alphabet, numerals, and punctuation, many printers require only these characters.

Consider the discussion of bits and bytes earlier in this chapter. Remember, the position of a bit in a byte determined its value. A bit must be in the first column to have a value of 128. If you add up the other columns, you will see that the other seven columns can produce any number between 0 (00000000) and 127 (01111111). So you only need seven bits to transmit all the characters in the ASCII code from the computer to the printer.

A serial interface can use seven or eight data bits. Seven is adequate for transmitting text only. If you are sending programs (as you might do between two computers) or if the printer requires characters between 128 and 255, you must use eight.

Stop and Start Bits

In the previous analogy, things can become messy if the man in the printer loses track of which byte he is working on. After all, the only thing telling him which bit goes in which byte is his careful record-keeping. If he loses track, the result is chaos.

For this reason, most serial interfaces use a system of start bits and stop bits. When the computer finishes sending one byte, it places a 0 on the line and leaves it there until it is ready to start sending the next byte. The computer then switches the 0 to a 1, and the man in the printer knows to start counting off another eight bits at regular intervals. The 0 at the end of every byte is the stop bit, while the 1 at the beginning of the next byte is the start bit.

Because personal computers and serial printers use start and stop bits, it is not necessary that they stay exactly in sync; they reestablish their timing with every new byte.

Parity Bits

If you are using only seven data bits, the eighth bit in each byte is available for another job. Occasionally, you will see this bit acting as a second stop bit, but more frequently it will be serving as a parity bit.

A **parity bit** is either a 1 or a 0 — whatever will make the byte an odd or even number. You might have heard of **odd parity** and **even parity**. The third common choice on parity is **ignore parity**.

Of course, if an interface is using eight data bits, it will almost always have no parity.

Handshaking

Handshaking is how the printer instructs the computer to stop sending data for a moment while it deals with information already received, which is necessary because computers can send data much faster than even a speedy laser printer can process it.

Like serial parameters, it doesn't matter which handshaking system you use as long as both the computer and printer use the same system.

Hardware Handshaking

In hardware handshaking, there is an extra wire in the cable between the computer and printer. When the printer sets the voltage on this wire to either high or low (depending on what the computer is expecting), the computer will stop sending data until the voltage changes again.

Software Handshaking

In software handshaking, the printer sends the computer a character that is the signal to stop sending data. Then, when the printer is ready for more information, it sends another character to say "Start again."

Two characters often used for software handshaking are named XON and XOFF. When a computer set for XON/XOFF handshaking receives the XOFF character (^S), it stops sending data until it receives the character XON (^Q).

Another set of characters occasionally used for software handshaking is ETX/ACK (^C/^F). Check your printer manual to see which protocol(s) your printer supports. In the unlikely event that you ever adjust the software handshaking used by your printer, you must change the printer driver file (see Chapter 23, "MAKEPRD and How To Use It").

Setting the Serial Interface

If you are using a serial interface, you must use the DOS MODE.COM program to set the serial port parameters. The syntax for using the MODE command to set a serial printer port is as follows:

MODE COM*n***, *baud, parity, databits, stopbits*, P**

n is the number of the serial port (COM1 or COM2).

Baud is the speed, in bits per second, of the connection. Valid values are 110, 150, 300, 600, 1200, 2400, 4800, or 9600 bits per second. Only the first two characters are recognized, so a baud rate of 96 instructs the computer to use 9600 bits per second.

Parity informs the computer of the parity this connection is using — None, Odd, or Even. The default is Even.

Databits is the number of databits used in this connection — 7 or 8. The default is 7.

Stopbits instructs the computer whether to use 1 or 2 stop bits. At 110 baud, the default is 2. At other speeds, the default is 1.

P tells the computer that this serial port is being used as a printer port.

Thus, a typical MODE command would read as follows:

```
MODE COM1,96,n,8,1,P
```

The details of the MODE command may vary slightly in your version of MS-DOS. Check the DOS manual.

You must reset the serial port each time you use your computer. You will probably want to put the MODE command in your AUTOEXEC.BAT file so it executes automatically each time you turn on the computer.

TAKING DIRECT CONTROL OF THE PRINTER

There are things that printer drivers simply will not do. For example, a printer may be able to print inverse or reversed print; however, Word's printer drivers make no provision for this feature. Some printers can also print patterns of lines or gray scales, but Word's printer drivers do not take advantage of these features either.

Alt-27 For Escape

Most printer commands consist of the Escape character followed by one or more printable characters. To directly give a command to the printer, you must place the Escape character in the text. Press and hold the Alt key and simultaneously press the 2 and 7 keys on the numeric keypad. Next, release the Alt key. A small arrow (facing left) will appear on your screen, which means the Escape character is now part of your text. (If you are using a keyboard macro program like Superkey or ProKey, simultaneously hold and press the Shift and Alt keys.)

Next, type the remainder of the command. When you print the page, the Escape character will inform your printer that the following character(s) is not to be printed but is part of a command sequence.

Printer Commands

Commands are specific to each printer. You must examine a printer's manual(s) for a listing of printer commands and their functions.

FOREIGN AND OTHER UNUSUAL CHARACTERS

Although Word normally restricts itself to standard ASCII characters, if your printer is capable of it, Word can also print a wide variety of foreign characters. Placing these characters on the screen is not difficult, but whether or not they will print as the same characters (or print at all) depends on your printer and the translation tables in your printer driver. Translation tables are explained in the next chapter. The characters your printer can produce are listed in most printer manuals. Following is a list of all the special characters Word can display on the screen and, if all goes well, that the printer will be able to print.

To display these characters on your screen, use the same technique used to enter the Escape character: press and hold the Alt key and then simultaneously press the appropriate numbers on the numeric keypad (see Figure 22.1 on following page).

1	☺	140	î	179	│	218	┌
2	☻	141	ì	180	┤	219	█
3	♥	142	Ä	181	╡	220	▄
4	♦	143	Å	182	╢	221	▌
5	♣	144	É	183	╖	222	▐
6	♠	145	æ	184	╕	223	▀
7	•	146	Æ	185	╣	224	α
8	◘	147	ô	186	║	225	β
14	♫	148	ö	187	╗	226	Γ
15	☼	149	ò	188	╝	227	π
16	►	150	û	189	╜	228	Σ
17	◄	151	ù	190	╛	229	σ
18	↕	152	ÿ	191	┐	230	µ
19	‼	153	Ö	192	└	231	τ
20	¶	154	Ü	193	┴	232	Τ
21	§	155	¢	194	┬	233	θ
22	▬	156	£	195	├	234	Ω
23	↨	157	¥	196	─	235	δ
24	↑	158	₧	197	┼	236	∞
25	↓	159	ƒ	198	╞	237	ø
26	→	160	á	199	╟	238	∈
27	←	161	í	200	╚	239	∩
28	∟	162	ó	201	╔	240	≡
29	↔	163	ú	202	╩	241	±
30	▲	164	ñ	203	╦	242	≥
31		165	Ñ	204	╠	243	≤
127	⌂	166	ª	205	═	244	⌠
128	Ç	167	º	206	╬	245	⌡
129	ü	168	¿	207	╧	246	÷
130	é	169	⌐	208	╨	247	≈
131	â	170	¬	209	╤	248	°
132	ä	171	½	210	╥	249	·
133	à	172	¼	211	╙	250	·
134	å	173	¡	212	╘	251	√
135	ç	174	«	213	╒	252	ⁿ
136	ê	175	»	214	╓	253	²
137	ë	176	░	215	╫	254	■
138	è	177	▒	216	╪		
139	ï	178	▓	217	┘		

Figure 22.1

CHAPTER 23

MAKEPRD AND HOW TO USE IT

THE MAKEPRD PROGRAM

The MAKEPRD program supplied with Microsoft Word allows you to create your own printer drivers or to modify existing ones. The program works by converting a .PRD driver file into a text file that you can edit with Word. After editing, the text file is converted back to a PRD file.

It is not necessary to use MAKEPRD if Microsoft has supplied a printer driver file for your printer, unless you want to modify the driver to take advantage of a printer feature that Microsoft doesn't support. That is not very likely; one of Word's greatest strengths is extensive printer support.

The *Printer Information for Microsoft Word* manual included with the program outlines features supported for each printer.

Word Versions Prior to 3.0

Versions of Word prior to 3.0 do not include a MAKEPRD program; the equivalent program in version 2 was named CONVPRD.

You cannot use version 2 printer drivers with later versions of Word; they use a different format. You can, however, use MAKEPRD to convert them.

Do You Need MAKEPRD?

If you cannot find a printer driver for your printer, check to see what printer your printer emulates. There is probably a driver for the printer being emulated.

If there is no driver, you must create one from scratch (which is very difficult) or modify an existing one. While performing this task, you will probably learn more about printers than you thought you ever wanted to know. It is also likely that you will spend a fair amount of time experimenting until you get a properly working printer driver.

Microsoft supports every printer of which the company is aware. If yours is not supported, it may be because some mad engineer at the printer company decided he or she could do a better job of re-inventing the wheel.

You are most likely to use MAKEPRD to add features to a printer driver that supports only part of the your printer's power. For example, a Mannesmann-Tally MT910 laser printer emulates the Hewlett-Packard LaserJet+, but it also has many features that the LaserJet+ does not. For example, the LaserJet+ only has one font cartridge slot, and the MT910 has two. Since LaserJet printer drivers require various font cartridges, no matter what driver is selected, the LaserJet driver does not support all fonts installed on the MT910. Also, the MT910 can support more fonts in more character sets than the LaserJet+.

In such a case, you can use MAKEPRD to create a custom printer driver that supports all the MT910's features.

A Warning

Changing printer drivers can be very difficult. The required level of knowledge is more than one chapter can provide.

In other words, this is not a job for beginners. Make sure you know what you are doing before you plunge in to modify printer drivers, and *always* keep a backup of the original one — the one that still works.

RUNNING MAKEPRD

To run MAKEPRD, exit Word or any other application program currently running. Your computer should display the DOS prompt (e.g., A> or C>).

The MAKEPRD program is in a file called MAKEPRD.EXE on the original Word Utilities diskette. Use that diskette to make a copy of the program if it is not already on a working diskette. For example, to copy the file MAKEPRD.EXE from the Word Utilities diskette in drive A: to the Word subdirectory of your hard disk, drive C:, type

COPY A:MAKEPRD.EXE C:\WORD

and press the Return key. When you are done, remove the original Word Utilities master diskette and return it to a safe place.

Start MAKEPRD by typing

MAKEPRD

and pressing the Return key. If the MAKEPRD.EXE file is not in the current directory of the current drive, be sure to include the path name. For example, type

C:\WORD\MAKEPRD

if the program is in the Word subdirectory of your hard disk, or

A:MAKEPRD

if the program is on the diskette in drive A.

When MAKEPRD loads, it requests all necessary information. Following is an example of a user entry (underlined) and the MAKEPRD program's response (normal) when MAKEPRD is used to turn an existing PRD file into a text file:

```
C:\WORD>makeprd

PRD Editor 1.50 of July 14, 1987
Name of PRD file : mt910.prd
Name of Text file: mt910.txt
Select PRD to Text conversion (Press T)
    or Text to PRD conversion (Press P): t
Enter Y to confirm overwriting of existing file mt910.txt :y
Conversion Complete
```

Word asks you to confirm overwriting only when a file of the requested name already exists.

When you convert a PRD file to a text file, you can load it into Word (or another text editor) and modify it. Use MAKEPRD to convert the text file back into the PRD file.

MODIFYING A PRD FILE

Before you begin modifying a PRD file, make sure you have all the necessary information. In particular, you must have a copy of the manual containing the commands for your printer.

Following is some general information about working with PRD files.

Standard Measurements

The standard measuring units for most printer drivers are **twips.** A twip is 1/1440".

In a laser printer driver, the standard unit is the resolution of the laser printer, usually 1/300".

Special Characters in PRD File

Since many printer commands contain control characters, you must include these characters in your PRD files. Just use the caret symbol (ˆ) to indicate that a particular command is a control character. For example, ˆA indicates Ctrl-A, which is number 01 on the ASCII table in Appendix A. The code for escape is ˆ[. To enter the caret character itself, use ˆ0136 followed by a space. To enter a quotation mark, use ˆ0042 followed by a space.

Some printers also recognize a set of control characters between 128 and 159, which is just above the ASCII code. To enter these characters, you must use a base 8 number system called **octal**. Each octal entry consists of a caret, a four digit number beginning with zero, and a final space. Use the following chart to convert (don't forget the space):

Decimal	Octal	Decimal	Octal	Decimal	Octal
128	^0200	139	^0213	150	^0226
129	^0201	140	^0214	151	^0227
130	^0202	141	^0215	152	^0230
131	^0203	142	^0216	153	^0231
132	^0204	143	^0217	154	^0232
133	^0205	144	^0220	155	^0233
134	^0206	145	^0221	156	^0234
135	^0207	146	^0222	157	^0235
136	^0210	147	^0223	158	^0236
137	^0211	148	^0224	159	^0237
138	^0212	149	^0225		

PARTS OF A PRD FILE

A PRD file has five parts: the header, font descriptions, width tables, translation tables, and print control sequence descriptions (PCSDs).

A typical PRD file is listed in Appendix B.

A **header** is a general description of the printer and informs Word of the type of printer interface.

The **font description** informs Word of the size of each font and the commands used to select each font.

Width tables provide Word with the width of each character in a proportionally spaced font, which allows Word to justify lines and mix fonts of differing sizes on the same line.

Translation tables instruct Word to send the printer a sequence of characters for each character in your document. For example, your printer may not normally be able to print the Japanese Yen symbol (¥), but it might be able to do so if you sent a Y, a backspace, and an =. The translation table informs Word that it must send those three characters to print a ¥.

The **Printer Control Sequence Descriptions** instruct Word how to select variations of fonts (bold, italics), how to set the line spacing, and other general tasks that apply to all fonts.

Header

A typical PRD file header resembles the following (after it's been converted to a text file by MAKEPRD):

```
MAKEPRD 1.50
dxaMin:300 dyaMin:30
PrinterType:5 Microspace:0 SpecialFlags:0 Serial Interface:40960
WidthTSwap:0 DownloadFlag:0 Linedraw:0
```

The words MAKEPRD 1.50 indicate that this printer driver was created with version 1.50 of the MAKEPRD program — the version that comes with Word 4.0. Version 3 of Word uses version 1.40 of MAKEPRD. There are slight differences in the two versions, and you cannot use version 1.40 of MAKEPRD to convert a .PRD file created with version 1.50.

dxaMin

dxaMin is the smallest horizontal movement the printer can make. For most printers, this value is measured in twips (1/1440"). A typical value for a dot matrix or daisywheel printer is 12, since most of those printers must move the print position a minimum of 1/120" (12/144") at a time.

For laser printers, the dxaMin is the resolution (dots per inch), which is typically 300. Newer laser printers have resolutions of 400, 600, and even 1200 dots per inch. For such printers, dxaMin would be 400, 600, and 1200 respectively.

The example printer is an MT910 laser printer; the dxaMin is 300.

dyaMin

dyaMin is the smallest vertical motion the printer can make. Again, for most printers, this value is measured in twips. A typical value is 20 twips (1/72"). For laser printers, the value is measured in the standard measure for that printer, usually 1/300".

PrinterType

The *printer type* field is a single digit between 0 and 5 that describes the basic printer type:

PrinterType	Type of Printer
0	MSPRINT type PRD file. MSPRINT is a PRD file that produces a generic output for tasks that are too complicated for a standard PRD file. The chances of you ever needing to use MSPRINT are slim, but if you do, contact Microsoft for information on how to use MSPRINT or see *Printer Information for Microsoft Word*, which came with your copy of Word.
1	Dot matrix printers.
2	Daisywheel printers.
3	Any printer not otherwise provided for on this list.
4	This value is used only if this PRD file is PLAIN.PRD.
5	Laser printers.

Microspace

Use the Microspace flag to inform Word whether or not your printer can use **microspacing** to justify lines. In microspacing, a printer divides the total amount of added space necessary to justify a line into equal amounts between every pair of words. Not all printers can make such small printhead movements.

Value	Effect
0	The printer can perform microspace justification.
1	The printer cannot perform microspace justification.
2	The printer cannot perform microspace justification when it is running in draft mode.
4	The printer uses half-width correction for proportionally spaced fonts.
6	The printer uses half-width correction for proportionally spaced fonts and allows no microjustification in draft mode.
8	dxaMin and dyaMin have been set to minimum head movement units (in fractions per inch), which is similar to the way dxaMin on a laser printer is specified as 300 for 1/300". This flag, however, indicates that both dxaMin and dyaMin have been specified that way.
16	Use Width Table Scaling. See the section on Character Width Tables later in this chapter for an explanation of width table scaling.

SpecialFlags

Through version 4.0, Word contains only two SpecialFlags. 0 indicates that the printer does not use Postscript (Adobe Systems' page description language – the industry standard). 2 indicates that the printer uses Postscript, but if this PRD file is for a type 0 printer (MSPRINT), the driver should use a backslash instead of an apostrophe as a Postscript control character.

SerialInterface

If you are using a parallel printer, set this field to 0. If your serial printer uses XON/XOFF handshaking, set this field to 40960. If your printer uses ETX/ACK, set this field to 49152.

WidthTSwap

Large printer drivers may have several width tables. Each width table requires a fair amount of memory. If you set this flag to 1, Word will load only the necessary width table into the computer's memory. Set this field to 0, and Word will load all width tables each time.

DownloadFlag

This flag has two uses. Some printers require receiving a file containing a series of commands to set up the printer in a certain mode. This flag can instruct Word to request the setup file when it starts a print job.

Also, many printers can use **downloadable fonts**, which are character fonts stored in your computer and then loaded into printer memory as needed. If this flag is set properly, Word will automatically download those fonts as needed, which saves printer memory. The DLF field of the font description informs Word of the fonts that must be downloaded:

Value	Effect
0	No setup file and no downloadable fonts
1	Downloadable fonts
2	Setup File
3	Both

LineDraw

This field informs Word of the font to use for line drawing. Since line drawing is a new feature in Word 4.0, this field is a new feature of MAKEPRD version 1.50.

Following are the various values you can place in this field:

<u>Value</u>	<u>Effect</u>
0-63	A value in this range instructs Word to use line-drawing characters from the font with the corresponding font number. The font number is the first element in the font description (discussed below).
64-127	A value in this range instructs Word to use the vertical bar (|) and hyphen (-) characters from the font with the font number 64 less than the number in this field. For example, if you enter a 64 in this field, Word will use font 0 (64 - 64 = 0). With values in this range, Word adjusts vertical line spacing when drawing boxes and line-drawing characters.
128-191	A value in this range instructs Word to use the vertical bar and hyphen characters from the font with the font number 128 less than the number in this field. For example, if you enter a 128 in this field, Word will use font 0 (128 - 128 = 0). With values in this range, Word does not adjust vertical line spacing of boxes and line-drawing characters.

Font Description

The font description portion of a PRD file, in addition to a general description of each font, includes pointers to width and translation tables.

Technically, a **font** is a collection of type of one size and one typeface. In PRD files, however, a "font" is all fonts of the same typeface. So, a Helvetica font might contain 8-, 10-, 12-, and 14-point variations.

{F#

The first element in any font description is the opening {F #, where # is a number between 0 and 63 unique to this font (or typeface). The font number should be on a line by itself.

The number assigned to a font determines its **generic name**, which is the name that remains identical from printer driver to printer driver.

The font numbers are divided into six subgroups: Modern, Roman, Script, Foreign, Decor, and Symbol.

Generic Names	Fonts
0 - 15 Modern a - p	Modern fonts include most typewriter fonts such as Courier, Prestige, and Pica. Other designs include popular typefaces such as Helvetica and Avant Garde. The key element in their design is that all lines are of the same thickness.
16 - 31 Roman a - p	Roman fonts are classic designs based on type styles that were popular in the Roman Empire (hence the name). They generally contain lines of varying width and usually include serifs. Roman fonts include Times Roman, Palatino, Bookman, Century Schoolbook, Garamond, Bodoni, Baskerville, and Trump Medieval.
32 - 39 Script a - h	Script fonts imitate handwriting. Examples are Regency Script, Park Avenue, and Missive.
40 - 47 Foreign a - h	Foreign fonts use charcters other than the Latin alphabet used in English. Examples are Greek, Cyrillic, and Kana. If a font merely includes extra characters using accents or other diacritical marks, it is *not* considered a foreign font.

continued...

48 - 55	These are decorative fonts primarily used for titles.
Decor a - h	Examples include Frontier, Lynz, Broadway, and Old English.
56 - 63	Symbol fonts are nonalphabetical. They include
Symbol a - h	special characters used in mathematics, science, law, and other fields.

Consider an example. In the MT910 printer driver, modern a (font 0) is Courier. In the Epson FX printer driver in Appendix B, modern a (still font 0) is Pica.

CTP:

The next element in a font description is the Character Translation Pointer, which should be on a line by itself just below the font number. The translation table number always begins with an uppercase T. For example, if a font uses translation table number 1, the line would read as follows:

CTP:T1

If a font does not require character translation, enter a translation table name of NIL, as in the following:

CTP:NIL

The function of a character translation table is explained later in this chapter.

cPSDs:

This is the total count of Printer Sequence Descriptions; there is one Printer Sequence Description for each size of each typeface. For example, if your printer has 8-point, 10-point, and 12-point Times Roman type, the cPSD entry for the Times Roman font would be as follows:

cPSD:3

Printer Sequence Descriptions

In the PSDs, you instruct Word how to make the printer print in a particular font or size. PSDs should be arranged in order from the smallest to the largest font using that particular typeface.

FontSize:#

is the size of the font in half-points; the value of FontSize for a 12-point font is 24. For an 8-point font, the value is 16.

For fixed-pitch fonts, divide the pitch into 120 and multiply it by 2. For example, the FontSize for a 12-pitch font is 20 (120/12 * 2 = 20).

A typical FontSize line for a 10-point font would read as follows:

FontSize:20

Wtps:# # #

This field informs Word how wide the characters are. The four # symbols each describe one variation of the font. The first is the width of the regular version, the second is the width of the italic version, the third is the width of the bold version, and the fourth is the width of the bold/italic version.

For fixed-pitch fonts, the width is expressed in dxaMin units. For example, if dxaMin is 12 twips (1/120"), a font that prints charcters 1/10" wide would have a Wtps value of 12 (12/120 = 1/10). If all four variations of the font were of the same width, the Wtps line would read as follows:

Wtps: 12 12 12 12

For proportionally spaced fonts, the Wtps field points to a Character Width Table (CWT) in the PRD file. CWT numbers start with the letter W, so a font that used CWT W1 for the regular and italic versions of the font but CWT W2 for the bold and bold italic versions would have a Wtps line such as the following:

Wtps: W1 W1 W2 W2

Font Selectors

The next part of every PSD is a group of eight **font selectors**. The eight selectors are divided into four sets of two, with each pair instructing Word how to select a particular variation of the font and how to deselect that variation.

Each font selector takes the following form:

beginmod: *mod value* **"code"**

beginmod informs Word that this commmand line is an instruction to select one version of a font of a specific size.

The *mod value* is a number from 0 to 5 that provides particular information about a specific font.

"code" is the printer command instructing the printer to switch into the font or variation. If the printer uses a standard command to switch to a variation, it needn't be listed here; standard methods of switching are listed in the final section of the PRD file — the Printer Control Sequence Description.

Examine each section individually. An example will be given to pull it all together.

Beginmod

Beginmod can take one of eight forms:

Form	Effect
beginmod:	How to start this font.
endmod:	How to end this font. Usually, this will be the code to start the regular, 10-pitch font on this printer.
beginItalicmod:	Start the italic version of this font.
endItalicmod:	End the italic version of this font.
beginBoldmod:	Start the bold version of this font.
endBoldmod:	End the bold version of this font.
beginItalBoldmod:	Start the bold italic version of this font.
endItalBoldmod:	End the bold italic version of this font.

The *beginmod* label informs Word that this command is for a particular variation of this font.

Mod Value

The *mod value* is a number from 0 to 5 that provides special information about the font and its capabilities.

Mod	Effect
0	This is the default and means that no special modifications are required.
1	Use this value if this font cannot be set to bold. For example, on an Epson printer, you cannot set to bold a typeface named *enhanced*.
2	The printer needs a *set character spacing* command when switching to this font. Use this value when the command to switch to the font does not necessarily switch to the correct spacing also.
3	no effect
4	The printer needs a *set character spacing* command but will double it.
5	Word should not send the command to start this font when you have specified *draft* mode on the Printer options menu.

"Code"

"code" is the command that instructs the printer to switch to this font and size. Usually, this command is a sequence of one or more control characters or a group of characters beginning with Escape.

The *"code"* entry must be enclosed in double quotation marks. Remember that use the caret symbol to enter control characters (including Escape) into a command in a PRD file. For example, use ^[for Escape. (See the ASCII table in Appendix A.)

For most printers, the only *"code"* you must enter will be at *beginmod* and *endmod* because most printers use standard commands to switch into italic, bold, and italic bold variations. These standard codes are listed in the Printer Control Sequence Description section of the PRD file.

Some printers, however, such as Hewlett-Packard LaserJets, actually use different fonts for bold and italic. For such a printer, you must list the command to switch to each font.

DLF:#

Many printers can use fonts sent to the printer from the computer and stored in the printers's RAM. This process is called **downloading**. Word can automatically download fonts if three conditions are met. First, the Download Flag in the PRD header must be set to indicate downloadable fonts. Second, there must be a special program that accompanies a particular printer driver (and has a similar name) and knows how to download fonts for that printer. Third, you must tell Word, through the DLF field in a printer sequence description, which versions of a particular font are to be downloaded.

For example, Microsoft provides a printer driver named HPDWNSFP.PRD for use with Hewlett-Packard LaserJets using downloaded fonts. Microsoft also provides an accompanying HPDWNSFP.EXE program that will automatically download the fonts to the printer as needed.

The DLF (DownLoad Fonts) flag is a number between 0 and 15 informing Word which variations of a particular font are available for downloading. The value of the DLF flag is the sum of the numbers assigned to each variation as follows:

1	Normal
2	Italic
4	Bold
8	Italic Bold

For example, if a particular font was available for downloading in an italic version only, the value of the DLF flag would be 2. If italic and bold italic versions were available, the value of the DLF flag would be 10 (2 + 8).

More PSDs

Many printers allow several size variations of a font. For each size variation, the PRD file must contain a separate PSD including everything from the FontSize field through the DLF field.

FontName

The next element in the font description is the font's name. This description is not the generic name determined by the font number; instead, it is the common name of the font, such as Times Roman, Helvetica, Garamond, or Avant Garde.

The font name must not contain spaces. If the name is normally two words, delete the space (TimesRoman) or use the underline character (Times__Roman).

}F

Finally, end each font description with the characters }F on a separate line.

Sample Font Description

Following is an example of a font description. It describes a font on the MT910 laser printer that is available in two sizes — 16.66 pitch and 12 pitch. Remember, since this description is for a laser printer, the font widths (Wtps) are in units of 1/300":

```
{F7
CTP:TO
cPSDs:2
```

continued...

...from previous page

```
FontSize:17
Wtps:18 18 18 18
beginmod:0 "^[{apcX^[{s0t8.5vp16.66H"
endmod:0 "^[(st12vp10H"
beginItalicmod:0
endItalicmod:0
beginBoldmod:0
endBoldmod:0
beginItalBoldmod:0
endItalBoldmod:0
DLF:0

FontSize:24
Wtps:25 25 25 25
beginmod:0 "^[(8U^[(s0p12h12v0s0b6T"
endmod:0 "^[(st12vp10H"
beginItalicmod:0
endItalicmod:0
beginBoldmod:0
endBoldmod:0
beginItalBoldmod:0
endItalBoldmod:0
DLF:0
FontName:Gothic
}F
```

Character Width Tables

If your printer uses proportional type (with varying character widths), you must use Character Width Tables to inform Word of the space to allocate for each character. If a particular font uses a width table, the *Wtps* field in the font description must include the width table number.

{W#

The first element in a width table is the width table number, which is on a line by itself. A typical example would be as follows:

```
{W1
```

FontSize:# chFirst:# chLast:#

FontSize is the size (in half points) of the font that uses this table; for a 10-point font, *FontSize* is 20.

A single width table can accomodate several fonts of differing sizes if width table scaling has been turned on by setting the *Microspace* flag in the PRD file header to 16. Then, Word will compare the *FontSize* of each PSD to the *FontSize* for the width table and scale the widths in the table accordingly. For example, if the *FontSize* of the width table is 20 (for a 10-point font), Word will multiply the values in the font table by 1.2 for a 12-point font.

chFirst is the ASCII number of the first character whose width is indicated by this width table.

chLast is the ASCII number of the last character whose width is indicated by this width table.

FontSize, *chFirst*, and *chLast* appear on a single line at the head of the width table as follows:

```
FontSize:24 chFirst:32 chLast:127
```

The Table Itself

The table consists of entries including ASCII character numbers, a colon, and the width of that character. The width is in dxaMin units. Following is an example:

```
32:13 33:16 34:16 35:38 ...
```

}W

Each width table must end with }W on a separate line.

Translation Tables

A **translation table** informs Word of the sequence of characters to send to the printer for each character in the document. Translation tables are used to print characters not normally found on the keyboard. For example, to create the Japanese Yen symbol (¥), you could send a Y, a backspace, and an = to the printer.

{T#

is the number of this translation table.

cCSD:# chFirst:# chLast:#

cCSD is the count of Character Sequence Descriptions. A character sequence description is a sequential group of translations. Normally, there will be only one CSD in a translation table, but there may be more. For example, if you define translations for characters from 20 to 32 and then for 128 to 255, you would have two CSDs.

chFirst is the ASCII number of the first character whose translation is indicated by this translation table.

chLast is the ASCII number of the last character whose translation is indicated by this translation table.

cCSD, *chFirst*, and *chLast* appear on a single line at the head of the translation table as follows:

cCSD:1 chFirst:32 chLast:127

The Table Itself

The table consists of entries of ASCII character numbers, a colon, and the string of characters Word sends to the printer for that character. The string should be enclosed in double quotation marks. For example, to replace the tilde character (˜) with ¥, create the following table entry:

126:"Y^H="

The entry informs Word that when it encounters the ˜ character in the file, it should send a Y, then a backspace, and finally an =.

}T

Each translation table must end with the characters }T on a separate line.

Printer Control Sequence Description (PCSD)

The final element in any PRD file is the Printer Control Sequence Description, which is a collection of commands instructing the printer how to perform such tasks as switching to bold print, resetting itself, setting line spacing, and so on.

Each PCSD begins at a particular byte location. For example, the PCSD beginning at byte 128 instructs the printer how to turn on boldfacing.

The Short and Long of It

There are two types of PDSDs. **Short PCSDs** have three elements: *byte:#*, *mod:#*, and *"code"*. **Long PCSDs** contain two extra fields: *byte:#*, *mod:#*, *magic:#*, *value:#*, and *"code"*.

byte:# specifies the starting byte for this PCSD and defines its function. For example, if the byte number is 128, this PCSD is the command to start bold print.

mod:# varies in function with the PCSD.

magic: # is an offset value if your printer requires it. For example, to instruct your printer to advance the print position five lines, most printers require a command containing the number 5; however, if your printer needs an offset of 32, you must send 37 to indicate 5. The *magic* number for that printer function would be 32. Most printers do not require a *magic* number, so this field will usually be 0.

value: # is the maximum value a certain parameter can accomodate. For example, on some printers, the page length cannot exceed 120 lines. In such a case, the *value* would be 120. Normally, this value is 0, which means no limit.

"code" is the actual command this printer uses for a particular function. As with other commands in PRD files, use the caret (ˆ) and a letter to signify a control character, for example, ˆ[for Escape.

Example

Following is an example of two short PCSDs from the printer driver for the MT910 printer:

```
byte:128 mod:0 "ˆ[(s3B"
byte:132 mod:0 "ˆ[(s0B"
```

These two PDSDs switch from a regular font to a bold font and back.

{P

The characters {P on a separate line signal the beginning of the PCSD section of a PRD file.

The Order of the PCSDs

0-3   This is the command to reset the printer.

4-7   This command string resets the printer when it is done printing a document. If mod = 1, Word will not issue a form feed command to eject the page when you cancel a print order.

8-13   This PCSD works together with the next (14-17) to inform the printer of the length of paper (in lines). Normally, this kind of command will consist of an escape sequence, a parameter (a number giving the length of the paper), and sometimes a closing character or two. This PCSD is the escape sequence that is sent before the parameter. The PCSD at byte 14 contains the closing character(s).

                 If mod = 0 and no "*code*" is specified, Word will use line feeds when it finishes printing in order to get to the bottom of a page.

                 If mod = 1, Word sends a form feed character to the printer at the end of each page regardless of "*code*".

                 If mod = 2, Word recognizes that the printer expects the parameter as two ASCII charcters in hexadecimal format. This command is used with many Qume printers.

                 Use mod = 3 with the NEC7710 and compatible printers.

                 If mod = 4, Word recognizes that this printer expects the form length parameter as ASCII characters in decimal.

14-17   This is the terminator section of the *set form length* command.

18-23   This PCSD works together with the next (24-27) to inform
             the printer of the line height (in dyaMin units). Normally,
             this type of command will consist of an escape sequence, a
             parameter (a number giving the line height), and sometimes
             a closing character or two. This PCSD is the escape
             sequence that is sent before the parameter. The PCSD at
             byte 24 contains the closing character(s).

             Use mod=1 for an Epson MXG printer.

             If mod=2, Word does not send a newline (line feed)
             character after it sends a carriage return.

             If mod=3, Word sends a newline (line feed) character but
             no carriage return.

             If mod=4, this printer expects the parameter in ASCII.

             Use mod=5 if your printer is a Xerox 2700.

             If mod=7, this printer advances the line position by sending
             a series of commands, each one advancing the line position
             by one unit of dyaMin.

24-27   This is the terminator section of the set line height command.
             Use mod=7 if your printer is a Tandy model that uses a
             control sequence to send the carriage back for overprinting.

28-33   This PCSD works together with the next (34-37) to tell the
             printer the character spacing expressed in dxaMin units
             (plus the *magic*). Normally, this type of command will
             consist of an escape sequence, a parameter (a number
             giving the character spacing), and sometimes a closing
             character or two. This PCSD is the escape sequence that is
             sent before the parameter. The PCSD at byte 34 contains
             the closing character(s).

             If you request spacing larger than the printer can provide,
             Word inserts extra space characters to pad out the line.

             If mod=1, this printer uses relative movement commands
             to change print spacing.

Use mod = 3 if your printer is an Epson dot matrix model (other than an LQ model) or a compatible printer.

Use mod = 4 if your printer expects the character spacing parameter in ASCII format.

Use mod = 6 if your printer is an Okidata dot matrix model or a compatible printer.

Use mod = 8 if your printer is a Hewlett-Packard LaserJet or a compatible printer.

Use mod = 9 if your printer is a DEC LN03 or an Xerox 2700.

Use mod = 10 if your printer is an Epson LQ model.

Use mod = 11 for a Brother printer.

34-37	This is the terminator portion of the character width command.
	Use mod = 1 if you have a Brother printer.
38-41	This is the command to select paper feeder Bin 1.
42-45	This command is issued when Word is done printing a page from Bin 1.
45-49	This is the command to select paper feeder Bin 2.
50-53	This command is issued when Word is done printing a page from Bin 2.
54-57	If your printer needs a command sent at the beginning of each line, place it here.
58-61	If your printer needs a command sent at the end of each line, place it here.
62-65	Use this command only if you are using the MSPRINT driver. It is sent to indicate that this is the beginning of the text.

66-69	For an MSPRINT driver, this command signifies the end of text.
70-73	This is the command to select paper feeder Bin 3.
74-77	This command is issued when Word is done printing a page from Bin 3.
78-127	Reserved for future development.
128-131	Begin bold printing.

Use mod = 1 if you printer prints bold by issuing a backspace and pressing a character a second time (most daisywheel printers).

Use mod = 2 if your printer bold prints by issuing a carriage return and reprinting portions of the line (many dot matrix printers).

Use mod = 3 if your printer needs a special print wheel to print bold characters.

Use mod = 6 if your printer is a C. Itoh F10 or another printer that prints bold by issuing a carriage return, moving one dxaMin unit to the right, and then reprinting portions of the line.

Use mod = 7 for the IBM Quietwriter.

132-135	This is the command to terminate bold printing and resume normal printing.
136-139	This is the command to start printing in italic.

Use mod = 3 if this printer requires a special print wheel to print in italic.

Use mod = 4 if this printer cannot print in italic and you want to substitute underlining in its place.

140-143   This is the command to terminate italic print and resume normal print.

144-149   This is the command to start printing in underlined characters.

Use mod = 1 if your printer underlines by issuing a backspace character and then typing an underline character.

Use mod = 2 if your printer underlines by issuing a carriage return and then adding in underline characters on a second pass.

Use mod = 3 to instruct Epson printers to use their graphics mode to perform underlining.

Use mod = 4 to inform Word that your printer does not underline spaces, so Word must use the underline character for leading underlines or the line above footnotes.

Use mod = 6 to inform Word that your printer underlines by issuing a carriage return with a backspace correction.

150-153   This is the command to end underlining.

154-159   This is the command to begin strike-through characters.

Use mod = 1 if your printer prints strike-through characters by issuing a backspace character and then typing a hyphen.

Use mod = 2 if your printer prints strike-through characters by issuing a carriage return and then printing hyphens on a second pass.

Use mod = 3 to make Epson printers use their graphics mode to print strike-through characters.

160-163   This is the command to end strike-through printing.

164-169   This is the command to begin double underlining.

Use mod=1 if your printer double underlines by issuing a backspace character and then typing two underline characters (unless you also specify a "code").

Use mod=2 if your printer double underlines by issuing a carriage return and then adding in underline characters on a second pass.

Use mod=3 to make Epson printers use their graphics mode to perform underlining.

Use mod=4 to inform Word that your printer double underlines using the underline.

Use mod=6 to inform Word that your printer double underlines by issuing a carriage return with a backspace correction.

170-173	This is the command to end double underline.
174-179	This is the command to begin superscript.

Use mod=2 if your printer superscripts by issuing a carriage return, adjusting the line position, and then making a second pass to print the superscript characters.

180-183	This is the command to end superscript.
184-189	This is the command to begin subscript.

Use mod=2 if your printer subscripts by issuing a carriage return, adjusting the line position, and making a second pass to print the subscript characters.

190-193	This is the command to end subscript.
194-255	Reserved for future development.

}P

The PDSC section of the PRD file must end with the characters }P on a separate line.

END OF THE PRD FILE

The entire PRD file must end with *E* on a separate line.

APPENDICES

APPENDIX A: ASCII TABLE

01	01	^A	SOH	31	1F	^–	US	61	3D	=		
02	02	^B	STX	32	20	SPACE		62	3E	>>		
03	03	^C	ETX	33	21	!		63	3F	?		
04	04	^D	EOT	34	22	"		64	40	@		
05	05	^E	ENQ	35	23	#		65	41	A		
06	06	^F	ACK	36	24	$		66	42	B		
07	07	^G	BEL	37	25	%		67	43	C		
08	08	^H	BS	38	26	&		68	44	D		
09	09	^I	HT	39	27	'		69	45	E		
10	0A	^J	LF	40	28	(		70	46	F		
11	0B	^K	VT	41	29	)		71	47	G		
12	0C	^L	FF	42	2A	*		72	48	H		
13	0D	^M	CR	43	2B	+		73	49	I		
14	0E	^N	SO	44	2C	,		74	4A	J		
15	0F	^O	SI	45	2D	–		75	4B	K		
16	10	^P	DLE	46	2E	.		76	4C	L		
17	11	^Q	DC1	47	2F	/		77	4D	M		
18	12	^R	DC2	48	30	0		78	4E	N		
19	13	^S	DC3	49	31	1		79	4F	O		
20	14	^T	DC4	50	32	2		80	50	P		
21	15	^U	NAK	51	33	3		81	51	Q		
22	16	^V	SYN	52	34	4		82	52	R		
23	17	^W	ETB	53	35	5		83	53	S		
24	18	^X	CAN	54	36	6		84	54	T		
25	19	^Y	EM	55	37	7		85	55	U		
26	1A	^Z	SUB	56	38	8		86	56	V		
27	1B	^[	ESC	57	39	9		87	57	W		
28	1C	^\	FS	58	3A	:		88	58	X		
29	1D	^]	GS	59	3B	;		89	59	Y		
30	1E	^^	RS	60	3C	<<		90	5A	Z		

91	5B	[		121	79	y
92	5C	\		122	7A	z
93	5D	]		123	7B	{
94	5E	^		124	7C	|
95	5F	_		125	7D	}
96	60	`		126	7E	~
97	61	a		127	7F	DEL
98	62	b				
99	63	c				
100	64	d				
101	65	e				
102	66	f				
103	67	g				
104	68	h				
105	69	i				
106	6A	j				
107	6B	k				
108	6C	l				
109	6D	m				
110	6E	n				
111	6F	o				
112	70	p				
113	71	q				
114	72	r				
115	73	s				
116	74	t				
117	75	u				
118	76	v				
119	77	w				
120	78	x				

NUL	Null	ESC	Escape
SOH	Start of Head	FS	File Separator
SOT	Start of Text	GS	Group Separator
ETX	End of Text	RS	Record Separator
EOT	End of Trans.	US	Unit Separator
ENQ	Enquiry	DEL	Delete
ACK	Acknowledge		
BEL	Bell (Beeper)		
BS	Backspace		
HT	Horizontal Tab		
LF	Line Feed		
VT	Vertical Tab		
FF	Form Feed		
CR	Carriage Return		
SO	Shift Out		
SI	Shift In		
DLE	Data Link Escape		
DC1	Dev Ctrl 1 (XON)		
DC2	Device Control 2		
DC3	Dev Ctrl 3 (XOFF)		
DC4	Device Control 4		
NAK	Negative Ack.		
SYN	Synchronous Idle		
ETB	End Trans. Block		
CAN	Cancel		
EM	End of Medium		
SUB	Substitute		

APPENDIX B: SAMPLE PRD FILE

Following is the text version of the printer driver used for a Mannesmann-Tally MT910 laser printer:

```
MAKEPRD 1.50
dxaMin:300 dyaMin:30 PrinterType:5
Microspace:0 SpecialFlags:0 SerialInterface:40960
WidthTSwap:1 DownloadFlag:0 LineDraw:0


{F0
CTP:T0
cPSDs:1

FontSize:24
Wtps:30 30 30 30
beginmod:0 "^[{apcX^[{s3t12vp10H"
endmod:0 "^[(st12vp10H"
beginItalicmod:0
endItalicmod:0
beginBoldmod:0
endBoldmod:0
beginItalBoldmod:0
endItalBoldmod:0
DLF:0
FontName:Courier
}F

{F1
CTP:NIL
cPSDs:1
```

continued...

...from previous page

```
FontSize:20
Wtps:25 25 25 25
beginmod:0 "ˆ[{apcXˆ[{s8t10vp12H"
endmod:0 "ˆ[(8Uˆ[(st12vp10H"
beginItalicmod:0
endItalicmod:0
beginBoldmod:0
endBoldmod:0
beginItalBoldmod:0
endItalBoldmod:0
DLF:0
FontName:Prestige
}F

{F7
CTP:TO
cPSDs:2

FontSize:17
Wtps:18 18 18 18
beginmod:0 "ˆ[{apcXˆ[{s0t8.5vp16.66H"
endmod:0 "ˆ[(st12vp10H"
beginItalicmod:0
endItalicmod:0
beginBoldmod:0
endBoldmod:0
beginItalBoldmod:0
endItalBoldmod:0
DLF:0
```

continued...

...from previous page

```
FontSize:24
Wtps:25 25 25 25
beginmod:0 "ˆ[(8Uˆ[(s0p12h12v0s0b6T"
endmod:0 "ˆ[(st12vp10H"
beginItalicmod:0
endItalicmod:0
beginBoldmod:0
endBoldmod:0
beginItalBoldmod:0
endItalBoldmod:0
DLF:0
FontName:Gothic
}F

{F9
CTP:NIL
cPSDs:5

FontSize:16
Wtps:W0 W0 W1 W1
beginmod:0 "ˆ[&l00ˆ[(0Uˆ[(s1p33h8v0s0b17T"
endmod:0 "ˆ[(8Uˆ[(st12vp10H"
beginItalicmod:0
endItalicmod:0
beginBoldmod:0
endBoldmod:0
beginItalBoldmod:0
endItalBoldmod:0
DLF:5
```

continued...

...from previous page

```
FontSize:20
Wtps:W2 W3 W2 W2
beginmod:0 "^[&l00^[(OU^[(s1p27h10v0s0b17T"
endmod:0 "^[(8U^[(st12vp10H"
beginItalicmod:0
endItalicmod:0
beginBoldmod:0
endBoldmod:0
beginItalBoldmod:0
endItalBoldmod:0
DLF:3

FontSize:24
Wtps:W4 W5 W4 W4
beginmod:0 "^[&l00^[(OU^[(s1p21h12v0s0b17T"
endmod:0 "^[(8U^[(st12vp10H"
beginItalicmod:0
endItalicmod:0
beginBoldmod:0
endBoldmod:0
beginItalBoldmod:0
endItalBoldmod:0
DLF:3
```

continued...

...from previous page

```
FontSize:28
Wtps:W6 W7 W6 W6
beginmod:0 "^[&l00^[(0U^[(s1p19h14v0s0b17T"
endmod:0 "^[(8U^[(st12vp10H"
beginItalicmod:0
endItalicmod:0
beginBoldmod:0
endBoldmod:0
beginItalBoldmod:0
endItalBoldmod:0
DLF:3

FontSize:48
Wtps:W8 W8 W8 W8
beginmod:0 "^[&l00^[(0U^[(s1p11h24v0s0b17T"
endmod:0 "^[(8U^[(st12vp10H"
beginItalicmod:0
endItalicmod:0
beginBoldmod:0
endBoldmod:0
beginItalBoldmod:0
endItalBoldmod:0
DLF:4
FontName:Optima
}F

{F16
CTP:T0
cPSDs:3
```

continued...

...from previous page

```
FontSize:16
Wtps:W9 W10 W11 W11
beginmod:0 "^[(0U^[(s1p8v0s0b5T"
endmod:0 "^[(st12vp10H"
beginItalicmod:0
endItalicmod:0
beginBoldmod:0
endBoldmod:0
beginItalBoldmod:0
endItalBoldmod:0
DLF:7

FontSize:20
Wtps:W12 W13 W14 W13
beginmod:0 "^[(8U^[(s1p10v0s0b5T"
endmod:0 "^[(st12vp10H"
beginItalicmod:0
endItalicmod:0
beginBoldmod:0
endBoldmod:0
beginItalBoldmod:0
endItalBoldmod:0
DLF:0
```

continued...

...from previous page

```
FontSize:24
Wtps:W15 W16 W17 W17
beginmod:0 "^[&l00^[(0U^[(s1p23h12v0s0b5T"
endmod:0 "^[(8U^[(st12vp10H"
beginItalicmod:0
endItalicmod:0
beginBoldmod:0
endBoldmod:0
beginItalBoldmod:0
endItalBoldmod:0
DLF:7
FontName:Roman
}F

{W0
FontSize:16 chFirst:32 chLast:127
 32:9   33:9   34:9   35:9   36:18  37:25  38:24  39:9
 40:11  41:11  42:16  43:28  44:9   45:11  46:9   47:16
 48:18  49:18  50:18  51:18  52:18  53:18  54:18  55:18
 56:18  57:18  58:9   59:9   60:28  61:28  62:28  63:15
 64:33  65:21  66:19  67:22  68:25  69:16  70:15  71:24

 72:25  73:9   74:9   75:20  76:14  77:30  78:23  79:27
 80:17  81:27  82:19  83:17  84:17  85:25  86:21  87:32
 88:18  89:16  90:20  91:11  92:16  93:11  94:18  95:16
 96:9   97:16  98:19  99:16  100:18  101:17  102:10  103:17
 104:18  105:8  106:8  107:17  108:8  109:28  110:18  111:18
 112:19  113:19  114:12  115:15  116:10  117:17  118:16  119:25
 120:15  121:16  122:16  123:17  124:16  125:17  126:28  127:33

}W
```

continued...

...from previous page

```
{W1
FontSize:16 chFirst:32 chLast:127
 32:9   33:9   34:9   35:9   36:9   37:27  38:24  39:9
 40:11  41:11  42:16  43:28  44:9   45:11  46:9   47:17
 48:18  49:18  50:18  51:18  52:18  53:18  54:18  55:18
 56:18  57:18  58:9   59:9   60:28  61:28  62:28  63:14
 64:33  65:20  66:20  67:23  68:25  69:16  70:16  71:25
 72:26  73:11  74:11  75:21  76:16  77:28  78:24  79:28
 80:20  81:28  82:21  83:18  84:17  85:24  86:21  87:32
 88:19  89:18  90:20  91:11  92:17  93:11  94:18  95:16
 96:9   97:17  98:20  99:16  100:20  101:18  102:10  103:17
 104:20  105:9   106:9   107:18  108:9   109:29  110:20  111:19
 112:20  113:20  114:13  115:14  116:11  117:20  118:16  119:25
 120:16  121:16  122:17  123:17  124:16  125:17  126:28  127:33

}W

{W2
FontSize:20 chFirst:32 chLast:127
 32:11  33:11  34:11  35:11  36:22  37:32  38:28  39:11
 40:13  41:13  42:20  43:34  44:11  45:13  46:11  47:21
 48:22  49:22  50:22  51:22  52:22  53:22  54:22  55:22
 56:22  57:22  58:11  59:11  60:34  61:34  62:34  63:18
 64:41  65:25  66:25  67:28  68:31  69:20  70:18  71:30
 72:31  73:12  74:12  75:25  76:19  77:37  78:31  79:34
 80:23  81:34  82:23  83:22  84:22  85:31  86:26  87:39
 88:23  89:22  90:25  91:13  92:21  93:13  94:22  95:20
 96:11  97:21  98:23  99:20  100:23  101:21  102:12  103:21
 104:23  105:9   106:10  107:21  108:10  109:35  110:23  111:23
```

continued...

...from previous page

```
112:23  113:23  114:14  115:17  116:13  117:23  118:20  119:31
120:19  121:20  122:20  123:22  124:20  125:19  126:34  127:41


}W


{W3
FontSize:20 chFirst:32 chLast:127
 32:11   33:11   34:14   35:32   36:22   37:33   38:27   39:11
 40:11   41:11   42:21   43:34   44:11   45:13   46:11   47:20
 48:22   49:22   50:22   51:22   52:22   53:22   54:22   55:22
 56:22   57:22   58:11   59:11   60:34   61:34   62:34   63:18
 64:41   65:25   66:23   67:28   68:30   69:20   70:19   71:30
 72:30   73:10   74:10   75:22   76:18   77:34   78:30   79:33
 80:22   81:33   82:22   83:20   84:19   85:29   86:22   87:36
 88:21   89:19   90:23   91:11   92:20   93:11   94:22   95:20
 96:11   97:20   98:23   99:20  100:23  101:20  102:11  103:19
104:23  105:10  106:10  107:20  108:10  109:35  110:23  111:23
112:23  113:23  114:14  115:16  116:13  117:23  118:18  119:30
120:18  121:19  122:19  123:21  124:20  125:21  126:34  127:41


}W
```

continued...

...from previous page

```
{W4
FontSize:24 chFirst:32 chLast:127
 32:14   33:14   34:14   35:14   36:14   37:14   38:14   39:14
 40:14   41:14   42:24   43:42   44:13   45:16   46:13   47:25
 48:27   49:27   50:27   51:27   52:27   53:27   54:27   55:27
 56:27   57:27   58:13   59:13   60:42   61:42   62:42   63:22
 64:50   65:30   66:29   67:33   68:38   69:25   70:24   71:37
 72:38   73:13   74:13   75:30   76:22   77:45   78:36   79:41
 80:27   81:41   82:28   83:26   84:27   85:37   86:31   87:48
 88:28   89:29   90:30   91:16   92:25   93:16   94:27   95:25
 96:13   97:24   98:28   99:24  100:28  101:26  102:13  103:25
104:29  105:11  106:11  107:24  108:12  109:44  110:28  111:27
112:28  113:28  114:17  115:22  116:16  117:29  118:24  119:39
120:24  121:24  122:24  123:25  124:25  125:25  126:42  127:50

}W

{W5
FontSize:24 chFirst:32 chLast:127
 32:14   33:14   34:14   35:14   36:14   37:38   38:34   39:13
 40:14   41:14   42:25   43:42   44:13   45:16   46:13   47:25
 48:27   49:27   50:27   51:27   52:27   53:27   54:27   55:27
 56:27   57:27   58:13   59:13   60:42   61:42   62:42   63:22
 64:50   65:30   66:28   67:32   68:37   69:24   70:23   71:36
 72:37   73:13   74:13   75:28   76:22   77:43   78:37   79:41
 80:26   81:41   82:28   83:25   84:24   85:36   86:27   87:43
 88:26   89:24   90:29   91:14   92:25   93:14   94:27   95:25
 96:13   97:24   98:29   99:23  100:28  101:24  102:13  103:24
104:28  105:12  106:12  107:25  108:12  109:43  110:28  111:28
112:29  113:28  114:17  115:20  116:16  117:28  118:22  119:37
120:23  121:22  122:24  123:25  124:25  125:25  126:42  127:50
```

continued...

...from previous page

```
}W

{W6
FontSize:28 chFirst:32 chLast:127
 32:16   33:16   34:16   35:45   36:32   37:44   38:40   39:16
 40:19   41:19   42:29   43:48   44:16   45:19   46:16   47:29
 48:32   49:32   50:32   51:32   52:32   53:32   54:32   55:32
 56:32   57:32   58:16   59:16   60:48   61:48   62:48   63:26
 64:58   65:35   66:34   67:39   68:45   69:28   70:27   71:44
 72:45   73:16   74:16   75:35   76:27   77:52   78:43   79:48
 80:31   81:48   82:33   83:30   84:32   85:43   86:36   87:56
 88:32   89:30   90:35   91:19   92:29   93:19   94:32   95:29
 96:16   97:27   98:32   99:27  100:32  101:30  102:16  103:29
104:32  105:13  106:13  107:29  108:13  109:49  110:32  111:32
112:32  113:32  114:21  115:23  116:18  117:32  118:28  119:45
120:27  121:29  122:27  123:28  124:29  125:28  126:48  127:58

}W

{W7
FontSize:28 chFirst:32 chLast:127
 32:16   33:16   34:20   35:45   36:32   37:47   38:40   39:16
 40:16   41:16   42:29   43:48   44:16   45:19   46:16   47:29
 48:32   49:32   50:32   51:32   52:32   53:32   54:32   55:32
```

continued...

...from previous page

```
56:32   57:32   58:16   59:16   60:48   61:48   62:48   63:25
64:58   65:34   66:32   67:37   68:43   69:28   70:26   71:42
72:43   73:16   74:16   75:32   76:25   77:50   78:44   79:47
80:31   81:47   82:32   83:28   84:29   85:42   86:31   87:50
88:29   89:28   90:33   91:16   92:29   93:16   94:32   95:29
96:16   97:28   98:32   99:27   100:33  101:29  102:16  103:27
104:33  105:14  106:13  107:28  108:14  109:51  110:32  111:33
112:32  113:32  114:18  115:23  116:18  117:32  118:26  119:43
120:26  121:26  122:27  123:29  124:29  125:29  126:48  127:58
```

}W

{W8
FontSize:48 chFirst:32 chLast:127
```
32:27   33:27   34:27   35:77   36:55   37:82   38:71   39:27
40:33   41:33   42:50   43:83   44:27   45:33   46:27   47:50
48:55   49:55   50:55   51:55   52:55   53:55   54:55   55:55
56:55   57:55   58:27   59:27   60:83   61:83   62:83   63:44
64:100  65:61   66:59   67:66   68:75   69:51   70:50   71:73
72:76   73:31   74:32   75:62   76:47   77:89   78:73   79:82
80:58   81:82   82:61   83:55   84:55   85:73   86:61   87:97
88:58   89:55   90:61   91:33   92:50   93:33   94:55   95:50
96:27   97:52   98:59   99:48   100:59  101:53  102:31  103:51
104:59  105:29  106:29  107:55  108:29  109:89  110:59  111:57
112:60  113:59  114:38  115:42  116:33  117:59  118:49  119:77
120:47  121:48  122:49  123:50  124:50  125:50  126:83  127:100
```

}W

continued...

...from previous page

```
{W9
FontSize:16 chFirst:32 chLast:127
  32:9   33:11   34:12   35:25   36:16   37:31   38:27   39:8
  40:13  41:13   42:16   43:28   44:8    45:11   46:8    47:16
  48:16  49:16   50:16   51:16   52:16   53:16   54:16   55:16
  56:16  57:16   58:9    59:9    60:28   61:28   62:28   63:16
  64:33  65:25   66:23   67:23   68:27   69:23   70:20   71:27
  72:27  73:12   74:14   75:24   76:21   77:31   78:25   79:27
  80:20  81:27   82:25   83:18   84:22   85:27   86:25   87:32
  88:25  89:25   90:23   91:11   92:16   93:11   94:16   95:16
  96:8   97:16   98:18   99:14   100:18  101:16  102:11  103:16
  104:18 105:9   106:9   107:17  108:9   109:27  110:18  111:18
  112:18 113:18  114:13  115:13  116:11  117:18  118:15  119:22
  120:15 121:15  122:14  123:17  124:16  125:17  126:28  127:33


}W


{W10
FontSize:16 chFirst:32 chLast:127
  32:9   33:10   34:12   35:25   36:16   37:31   38:24   39:8
  40:13  41:13   42:16   43:28   44:8    45:11   46:8    47:17
  48:16  49:16   50:16   51:16   52:16   53:16   54:16   55:16
  56:16  57:16   58:9    59:9    60:28   61:28   62:28   63:15
  64:33  65:23   66:21   67:23   68:25   69:22   70:19   71:26
  72:25  73:11   74:13   75:22   76:22   77:28   78:25   79:25
  80:20  81:25   82:22   83:18   84:21   85:24   86:21   87:29
  88:22  89:20   90:22   91:14   92:17   93:14   94:16   95:16
  96:8   97:18   98:17   99:15   100:18  101:14  102:10  103:15
  104:17 105:9   106:9   107:16  108:9   109:27  110:18  111:17
  112:17 113:17  114:11  115:12  116:9   117:18  118:15  119:22
  120:14 121:13  122:13  123:17  124:16  125:17  126:28  127:33
```

continued...

...from previous page

```
}W

{W11
FontSize:16 chFirst:32 chLast:127
 32:9   33:11   34:12   35:25   36:16   37:26   38:26   39:8
 40:13   41:13   42:16   43:28   44:8   45:11   46:8   47:18
 48:16   49:16   50:16   51:16   52:16   53:16   54:16   55:16
 56:16   57:16   58:9   59:9   60:28   61:28   62:28   63:16
 64:33   65:21   66:22   67:23   68:24   69:22   70:20   71:25
 72:26   73:13   74:16   75:25   76:21   77:32   78:24   79:26
 80:20   81:26   82:23   83:19   84:21   85:24   86:21   87:30
 88:23   89:20   90:22   91:14   92:18   93:14   94:16   95:16
 96:8   97:17   98:18   99:14   100:18   101:15   102:11   103:16
 104:19   105:10   106:10   107:18   108:10   109:27   110:19   111:17
 112:18   113:18   114:14   115:14   116:11   117:18   118:15   119:21
 120:16   121:15   122:14   123:17   124:16   125:17   126:28   127:33
```

continued...

...from previous page

}W

{W12
FontSize:144 chFirst:32 chLast:255
 32:17   33:12   34:15   35:30   36:23   37:35   38:35   39:12
 40:15   41:16   42:22   43:23   44:14   45:23   46:12   47:21
 48:23   49:23   50:23   51:23   52:23   53:23   54:23   55:23
 56:23   57:23   58:10   59:12   60:24   61:25   62:24   63:22
 64:39   65:35   66:29   67:31   68:34   69:30   70:28   71:36
 72:35   73:16   74:20   75:38   76:30   77:42   78:35   79:33
 80:26   81:33   82:34   83:22   84:30   85:37   86:34   87:38
 88:36   89:33   90:31   91:13   92:21   93:14   94:24   95:35
 96:12   97:21   98:25   99:21 100:25 101:21 102:19 103:23
104:25 105:14 106:17 107:25 108:13 109:37 110:25 111:23
112:25 113:24 114:18 115:17 116:15 117:25 118:24 119:34
120:24 121:24 122:20 123:16 124:8   125:17 126:26 127:32
128:31 129:25 130:21 131:21 132:21 133:21 134:21 135:21
136:21 137:21 138:21 139:14 140:14 141:14 142:34 143:34
144:30 145:31 146:40 147:23 148:23 149:23 150:25 151:25
152:24 153:33 154:37 155:24 156:23 157:33 158:26 159:30
160:21 161:14 162:23 163:25 164:25 165:35 166:20 167:20
168:22 169:12 170:16 171:21 172:21 173:12 174:26 175:26
176:35 177:17 178:17 179:16 180:31 181:21 182:35 183:25
184:12 185:22 186:30 187:23 188:33 189:20 190:30 191:24
192:21 193:21 194:23 195:25 196:21 197:21 198:23 199:25
200:21 201:21 202:23 203:25 204:21 205:21 206:23 207:25
208:34 209:14 210:35 211:40 212:21 213:14 214:25 215:31
216:34 217:14 218:33 219:37 220:30 221:14 222:26 223:33
224:34 225:34 226:21 227:36 228:26 229:16 230:16 231:33
232:33 233:33 234:23 235:22 236:17 237:37 238:33 239:24
240:26 241:26 242:17 243:17 244:17 245:17 246:38 247:21
248:21 249:20 250:20 251:26 252:25 253:26 254:24 255:17

continued...

...from previous page

```
}W

{W13
FontSize:144 chFirst:32 chLast:255
 32:17   33:17   34:18   35:27   36:23   37:32   38:32   39:10
 40:20   41:20   42:21   43:23   44:11   45:23   46:12   47:31
 48:23   49:23   50:23   51:23   52:23   53:23   54:23   55:23
 56:23   57:23   58:18   59:17   60:31   61:26   62:31   63:21
 64:42   65:30   66:29   67:31   68:33   69:29   70:29   71:30
 72:35   73:19   74:24   75:31   76:30   77:40   78:33   79:33
 80:28   81:33   82:32   83:28   84:30   85:33   86:31   87:35
 88:34   89:29   90:33   91:24   92:13   93:24   94:23   95:33
 96:10   97:23   98:22   99:20  100:26  101:20  102:21  103:25
104:23  105:14  106:21  107:24  108:15  109:36  110:23  111:22
112:24  113:22  114:18  115:19  116:14  117:22  118:19  119:31
120:26  121:23  122:23  123:22  124:7   125:21  126:25  127:32
128:31  129:22  130:20  131:23  132:23  133:23  134:23  135:20
136:20  137:20  138:20  139:14  140:13  141:12  142:30  143:30
144:29  145:28  146:41  147:22  148:22  149:22  150:22  151:22
152:23  153:33  154:33  155:21  156:29  157:29  158:28  159:27
160:23  161:12  162:22  163:22  164:23  165:33  166:19  167:19
168:21  169:13  170:16  171:16  172:16  173:17  174:23  175:24
176:33  177:17  178:17  179:16  180:31  181:20  182:33  183:23
184:17  185:21  186:29  187:29  188:29  189:24  190:27  191:21
192:23  193:20  194:22  195:22  196:23  197:20  198:22  199:22
200:23  201:20  202:22  203:22  204:23  205:20  206:22  207:22
208:30  209:13  210:33  211:41  212:23  213:12  214:22  215:28
216:30  217:12  218:33  219:33  220:29  221:14  222:26  223:32
224:30  225:30  226:23  227:33  228:26  229:19  230:19  231:33
232:33  233:33  234:22  235:28  236:19  237:33  238:29  239:23
240:27  241:25  242:17  243:17  244:17  245:17  246:36  247:16
248:16  249:19  250:19  251:23  252:24  253:24  254:31  255:17
```

continued...

...from previous page

}W

{W14
FontSize:144 chFirst:32 chLast:255
```
 32:17    33:14    34:18    35:28    36:24    37:39    38:34    39:12
 40:18    41:19    42:18    43:24    44:14    45:24    46:14    47:22
 48:24    49:24    50:24    51:24    52:24    53:24    54:24    55:24
 56:24    57:24    58:12    59:12    60:25    61:26    62:25    63:22
 64:40    65:32    66:31    67:31    68:32    69:29    70:27    71:35
 72:37    73:18    74:24    75:33    76:29    77:39    78:33    79:34
 80:28    81:34    82:32    83:26    84:30    85:35    86:33    87:40
 88:32    89:31    90:32    91:13    92:22    93:14    94:26    95:33
 96:12    97:23    98:24    99:21   100:24   101:21   102:19   103:23
104:27   105:14   106:17   107:26   108:14   109:36   110:25   111:23
112:24   113:24   114:18   115:18   116:16   117:24   118:20   119:32
120:24   121:23   122:20   123:16   124:8    125:17   126:30   127:32
128:31   129:24   130:21   131:23   132:23   133:23   134:23   135:21
136:21   137:21   138:21   139:15   140:15   141:14   142:32   143:32
144:29   145:29   146:40   147:23   148:23   149:23   150:24   151:24
152:23   153:34   154:35   155:23   156:24   157:31   158:28   159:32
160:23   161:14   162:23   163:24   164:25   165:33   166:21   167:20
168:22   169:12   170:17   171:19   172:19   173:14   174:25   175:25
176:33   177:17   178:17   179:13   180:31   181:21   182:33   183:25
184:14   185:22   186:31   187:24   188:31   189:21   190:32   191:23
192:23   193:21   194:23   195:24   196:23   197:21   198:23   199:24
200:23   201:21   202:23   203:24   204:23   205:21   206:23   207:24
208:32   209:15   210:34   211:40   212:23   213:14   214:24   215:29
216:32   217:14   218:34   219:35   220:29   221:15   222:27   223:34
224:32   225:32   226:23   227:34   228:25   229:18   230:18   231:34
```

continued...

...from previous page

```
232:34   233:34   234:23   235:26   236:19   237:35   238:31   239:23
240:27   241:25   242:17   243:17   244:17   245:17   246:36   247:19
248:19   249:21   250:20   251:25   252:25   253:25   254:29   255:17
```

}W

{W15
FontSize:24 chFirst:32 chLast:127
```
 32:13   33:16   34:16   35:38   36:25   37:47   38:41   39:12
 40:19   41:19   42:25   43:42   44:12   45:16   46:12   47:25
 48:25   49:25   50:25   51:25   52:25   53:25   54:25   55:25
 56:25   57:25   58:14   59:14   60:42   61:42   62:42   63:25
 64:49   65:38   66:34   67:35   68:40   69:35   70:31   71:41
 72:41   73:18   74:22   75:37   76:32   77:47   78:38   79:40
 80:30   81:40   82:38   83:27   84:33   85:41   86:38   87:49
 88:38   89:38   90:36   91:16   92:25   93:16   94:25   95:25
 96:12   97:25   98:27   99:22  100:27  101:25  102:16  103:24
104:27  105:14  106:13  107:26  108:14  109:41  110:27  111:27
112:27  113:27  114:19  115:19  116:16  117:27  118:23  119:34
120:22  121:22  122:22  123:25  124:25  125:25  126:42  127:51
```

}W

continued...

...from previous page

```
{W16
FontSize:24 chFirst:32 chLast:127
  32:13   33:15   34:17   35:38   36:25   37:47   38:36   39:12
  40:19   41:19   42:25   43:42   44:12   45:17   46:12   47:25
  48:25   49:25   50:25   51:25   52:25   53:25   54:25   55:25
  56:25   57:25   58:14   59:14   60:42   61:42   62:42   63:23
  64:49   65:35   66:32   67:35   68:37   69:33   70:31   71:40
  72:39   73:19   74:19   75:33   76:34   77:44   78:37   79:38
  80:30   81:38   82:34   83:27   84:31   85:37   86:32   87:44
  88:34   89:31   90:34   91:21   92:25   93:21   94:25   95:25
  96:12   97:26   98:26   99:22  100:26  101:22  102:15  103:21
 104:27  105:13  106:14  107:25  108:13  109:41  110:27  111:26
 112:26  113:25  114:16  115:18  116:14  117:27  118:22  119:33
 120:21  121:20  122:20  123:25  124:25  125:25  126:42  127:51

  }W

{W17
FontSize:24 chFirst:32 chLast:127
  32:13   33:16   34:16   35:38   36:25   37:39   38:39   39:13
  40:19   41:19   42:25   43:42   44:12   45:16   46:12   47:25
  48:25   49:25   50:25   51:25   52:25   53:25   54:25   55:25
  56:25   57:25   58:14   59:14   60:42   61:42   62:42   63:24
  64:49   65:32   66:33   67:35   68:37   69:33   70:30   71:38
  72:39   73:20   74:25   75:38   76:32   77:47   78:37   79:39
  80:31   81:39   82:35   83:29   84:31   85:37   86:32   87:46
  88:35   89:32   90:33   91:21   92:25   93:21   94:25   95:25
  96:13   97:26   98:27   99:22  100:28  101:22  102:16  103:24
 104:28  105:15  106:16  107:27  108:15  109:41  110:28  111:25
 112:28  113:27  114:21  115:21  116:17  117:28  118:23  119:32
 120:24  121:22  122:22  123:25  124:25  125:25  126:42  127:51
```

continued...

...from previous page

}W

{TO
cCSD:1 chFirst:128 chLast:175
```
  128: "^0264 "    129: "^0317 "    130: "^0305 "    131: "^0300 "
  132: "^0314 "    133: "^0310 "    134: "^0324 "    135: "^0265 "
  136: "^0301 "    137: "^0315 "    138: "^0311 "    139: "^0335 "
  140: "^0321 "    141: "^0331 "    142: "^0330 "    143: "^0320 "
  144: "^0334 "    145: "^0327 "    146: "^0323 "    147: "^0302 "
  148: "^0316 "    149: "^0312 "    150: "^0303 "    151: "^0313 "
  152: "^0357 "    153: "^0332 "    154: "^0333 "    155: "^0277 "
  156: "^0273 "    157: "^0274 "    158: "P"    159: "^0276 "
  160: "^0304 "    161: "^0325 "    162: "^0306 "    163: "^0307 "
  164: "^0267 "    165: "^0266 "    166: "^0371 "    167: "^0372 "
  168: "^0271 "    169: "^0251 "    170: "^0252 "    171: "^0370 "
  172: "^0367 "    173: "^0270 "    174: "^0373 "    175: "^0375 "
```

}T

{P
byte:0 mod:0 "^[&lole6D^[(sB^[&k12H"
byte:4 mod:0 "^[&l1H"
byte:8 mod:1 magic:0 value:0
byte:14 mod:0
byte:18 mod:4 magic:0 value:0 "^[&1"
byte:24 mod:0 "C"
byte:28 mod:8 magic:0 value:126 "^[&a+"
byte:34 mod:0 "H"
byte:38 mod:0 "^[&l1H"
byte:42 mod:0
byte:46 mod:0 "^[&l4H"

continued...

...from previous page

```
byte:50 mod:0
byte:54 mod:0
byte:58 mod:0
byte:62 mod:0
byte:66 mod:0
byte:70 mod:0
byte:74 mod:0
byte:78 mod:0
byte:82 mod:0
byte:128 mod:0 "^[(s3B"
byte:132 mod:0 "^[(s0B"
byte:136 mod:0 "^[(s1S"
byte:140 mod:0 "^[(s0S"
byte:144 mod:0 magic:0 value:0 "^[&dD"
byte:150 mod:0 "^[&d@"
byte:154 mod:2 magic:0 value:0
byte:160 mod:0
byte:164 mod:2 magic:0 value:0 "^[&dD"
byte:170 mod:0 "^[&d@"
byte:174 mod:0 magic:0 value:0 "^[&a-45V"
byte:180 mod:0 "^[&a+45V"
byte:184 mod:0 magic:0 value:0 "^[&a+45V"
byte:190 mod:0 "^[&a-45V"

}P
E
```

APPENDIX C: VERSION 4 FUNCTION KEYS

F1	F2
CTRL - Zoom Current Window	CTRL - Format as Header
SHIFT - Undo	SHIFT - Outline View
ALT - Set Tabs	ALT - Format as Footer
NO MOD - Move to Next Window	NO MOD - Calculate

F3	F4
CTRL - Execute Macro Step by Step	CTRL - Update List
SHIFT - Record Macro	SHIFT - Repeat Last Search
ALT - Copy	ALT - Set Margins
NO MOD - Expand Glossary	NO MOD - Repeat Last Edit Command

F5	F6
CTRL - Line Draw Mode	CTRL - Thesaurus
SHIFT - Outline Organize	SHIFT - Column Select Mode
ALT - Jump to Page	ALT - Spell Check
NO MOD - Overtype ON/OFF	NO MOD - Extend Selection

F7	F8
CTRL - Transfer Load	CTRL - Print
SHIFT - Select Previous Sentence	SHIFT - Select Next Sentence
ALT - Printer Display ON/OFF	ALT - Change Fonts
NO MOD - Select Word Left	NO MOD - Select Word Right

F9	F10
CTRL - Repaginate	CTRL - Save
SHIFT - Select Current Line	SHIFT - Entire Document
ALT - Text/Graphics Mode	ALT - Record Style
NO MOD - Select Previous Paragraph	NO MOD - Select Next Paragraph

APPENDIX D: VERSION 3 FUNCTION KEYS

Word version 3 uses the function key commands much less than version 4 does. Following is a listing of what those keys do in verison 3.

F1 SHIFT - Move to Previous Window NO MOD - Move to Next Window	**F2** SHIFT - Outline View NO MOD - Calculate
F3 NO MOD - Expand Glossary	**F4** SHIFT - Repeat Last Search NO MOD - Repeat Last Edit Command
F5 SHIFT - Outline Edit (Organize) NO MOD - Overtype ON/OFF	**F6** CTRL - Thesaurus (3.1 only) SHIFT - Column Select Mode NO MOD - Extend Selection
F7 SHIFT - Select Previous Sentence NO MOD - Select Word Left	**F8** SHIFT - Select Next Sentence NO MOD - Select Word Right
F9 SHIFT - Select Current Line NO MOD - Select Current Sentence	**F10** SHIFT - Entire Document NO MOD - Select Next Paragraph

INDEX

in macros 335
Variants 208
Vertical tabs 72, 291
VGA 8
Video
  character mode 7
  graphics mode 7

W

WC program 181
WFBG.SYN 15
What You See is What
  You Get 7
Width tables. *See*
  Character width tables
Wilder, Billy 141
Window
  clearing 130
  closing
    with keyboard 128
    with mouse 124
  footnote window
    244-245
  maximum number 31
  moving
    with keyboard 128
    with mouse 124
  number 31
  opening
    with keyboard 127
    with mouse 123
  options 61, 129, 257
  switching 123
  zooming 129
Word count 86, 177, 181
WORD.COM 14
WORD.INI 55
Wordfind program 177,
  178

Wordfreq program 177,
  179
Working disks
  preparing 13
Writing process 92
  drafting. *See* Drafting
  invention. *See* Invention
  revision. *See* Revision
Writing with Power 95
Wtps 412
WYSIWGY 7

RELATED TITLES
FROM MIS:PRESS